America

credits and contributors

PRESIDENT AND CEO, RAND MCNALLY & COMPANY
Richard J. Davis

SENIOR VICE PRESIDENT, MARKETING
Margaret A. Stender

DIRECTOR, REFERENCE PUBLISHING
Kendra L. Ensor

EDITORS
Kathryn Martin O'Neil, Brett R. Gover, Ann T. Natunewicz

ART DIRECTION AND DESIGN
Kym Abrams Design, Inc.

CREATIVE DIRECTOR
Amy Hynous Tillotson

DESIGNERS
Michelina McCann, Kerry LaCoste

JACKET DESIGN
John C. Nelson, Peggy R. Hogan, John Fu

THEMATIC MAP ILLUSTRATOR
Susie Cooper

WRITERS
Katie Arnold, Donald Beaulieu, William Brown, Susan Clinton, Brett R. Gover, Stephanie Gregory, Sarah Horowitz, Michael Kessler, J. P. MacBean, Kathryn Martin O'Neil, Louise Miller, Ann T. Natunewicz, Jay Pridmore, Jerry Reedy, Gretchen Reynolds, John Sarvay, Sara Shapiro, Roger Slavens, Joanne Trestrail, Catherine Van Patten, Ryan Ver Berkmoes

CARTOGRAPHY DIRECTORS
Michael W. Dobson, Ph.D., Vice President and Chief Cartographer
David Lanter, Research Director
Jeffrey K. Harris, Digital Cartography Director

CARTOGRAPHY
Chris Adomshick, Hans A. Anderson, Robert K. Argersinger, Gregory P. Babiak, Barbara Benstead-Strassheim, David M. Bukala, Brian L. Cantwell, Kerry B. Chambers, Marzee L. Eckhoff, Winifred V. Farbman, Julie A. Geyer, Michael B. Healy, Susan Hudson, Gwynn L. Hurshman, Lynn N. Jasmer, William R. Karbler, Brian M. Lash, Felix Lopez, Nina Lusterman, Rebecca MacBain, Michelle Rusch, Jill M. Stift, Thomas F. Vitacco, Richard A. Wanzo, Steven R. Wiertz

EDITORIAL ADVISORY BOARD
- Dennis R. DeCock, Vice President and General Manager, Educational Publishing, Rand McNally
- Michael W. Dobson, Ph.D., Vice President and Chief Cartographer, Rand McNally
- Lawrence Gyenes, Senior Vice President and Chief Financial Officer, Rand McNally
- John C. Hudson, professor of geography, Northwestern University, Guggenheim Fellow, and former councilor of the Association of American Geographers
- Sharon E. Kohn, Assistant General Counsel, Rand McNally
- James F. Marran, author of *Geography for Life: National Geography Standards* and past president of the National Council for Geographic Education
- Jeffrey Osier, Managing Editor, Rand McNally
- Dan Santow, Managing Editor, Rand McNally

MARKETING
Amy C. Krouse, JoEllen A. Klein

MANUFACTURING
Terry D. Rieger

PHOTO RESEARCH
Feldman & Associates, Inc.

PHOTO CREDITS
(l=left, r=right, c=center, m=middle, b=bottom, t=top)

Animals Animals: © Zig Leszczynski, 135 (b r)

© Ken Archer Wildlife/Nature Photography, 164 (b l)

Archive Photos: 92 (m l); © Frank Driggs Collection, 92 (t l & b l)

Peter Arnold, Inc.: © Galen Rowell, 83 (t r)

Art Resource, New York. Cropsey, Jasper Francis. New England Landscape. Private Collection, 22

© Cheyenne Frontier Days, 148 (b l)

© ChromoSohm Media Inc., 4 (b l), 4-5 (t)

© Bob & Suzanne Clemenz, 139 (b r)

Bruce Coleman, Inc.: © Eric Horan, 63 (b r); © Raymond Tercafs, 134 (b l)

© Corbis/Bettmann, 84 (b l)

© Terry Donnelly, 113 (c r)

Envision: © Paul Poplis, 98 (b l); © Guy Powers, 47 (b r)

Ric Ergenbright Photography: © Ric Ergenbright, 18-19 (t), 48-49, 60-61, 110-111 (t), 122-123 (t), 138, 158 (t r), 168-169, 176-177 (t); © George Schwartz, 88

FPG International: 19 (c l), 40 (b l), 113 (t r); © Paul and Lindamarie Ambrose, 111 (c r); © Walter Bibikow, 17 (b r); © James Blank, 156; © Willard Clay, 145 (b r); © Dwight Ellefsen, 201 (t); © Peter Gridley, 17 (c l), 43 (t r); © Steve Kahn, 112 (c l); © Richard Laird, 32 (t); © Vladimir Pcholkin, 56 (c l); © Mark Reinstein, 43 (m r); © Arthur Tilley, 17 (c l); © John Terence Turner, 163 (t r); © J. Zimmerman, 147 (t)

First Image West: © Jim Arndt, jacket (cowboys), 1; © Jim P. Garrison, 103 (b r)

Jeff Gnass Photography: © Jeff Gnass, 79 (c l), 182

H. Armstrong Roberts: 13 (b r), 40 (c), 108 (c); © H. Abernathy, 89 (b r), 99, 112 (b r); © Camerique, 59 (b r); © Charles Phelps Cushing, 40 (c l); © Roger Miller, 44 (b l); © D. Petku, 183 (b r); © K. Scholz, jacket (New York skyline), 1; © A. C. Shelton, 54 (c r)

© David W. Harp, 36-37; 46 (t)

Grant Heilman: © Jim Strauser, 70 (c); © Larry Lefever, 86-87

© Holland (MI) Area Convention & Visitors Bureau, 97 (b r)

Gary Irving Photography: © Gary Irving, 10-11, 112 (t), 202 (t r)

Kelly/Mooney Photography: © Kelly/Mooney, 42 (t)

© Kerrick James, 136 (c l)

© Bob Krist, 200 (b l)

Lazelle Nature Photography: © Keith Lazelle, 166

Liaison Agency: © Hulton Getty, 83 (b l)

Joan Marcus Photography: © Joan Marcus, 31 (b r)

Robert & Linda Mitchell Photography: © Robert & Linda Mitchell, 125 (b l)

David Muench Photography: © David Muench, 57 (t & c l), 64 (b l), 68 (t l), 69, 75 (b r), 77 (t r), 79 (t), 82, 85 (t), 134 (t); © Mark Muench, 26, 38

Masterfile: © J.A. Kraulis, 129 (b r)

North Wind Picture Archives: 55 (t r), 93 (m l), 174 (c l)

Pacific Stock: © Joe Carini, 189 (c r)

Panoramic Images: 136-137 (t); © Skip Brown, 44-45 (t); © Charles Mauzy, 154-155; © Jim Millay, 100-101; © New Moon Productions, 96 (b); © James Schwabel, 58-59 (t), 70-71 (t); © Mark Segal, 160-161 (t); © Sitki Tarlan, 34 (m r); © Vladpans, 66 (t); © Laurence Parent, 93 (t), 102, 114-115, 121, 122 (c l), 126-127, 128, 132 (t), 135 (c r), 137 (b r)

Photo 20-20: © Richard Reynolds Photography, 116, 123 (c r)

© PhotoDisc, jacket (flag background), 3 (flag), 167 (b r)

PhotoEdit: © Jose Carillo, 178 (c l); © Gary Conner, 171 (b r); © Jonathon Nourok, 174 (b r)

Photonica: © Eric Rank, 34 (t)

Richardson Photography: © Jim Richardson, 72-73

© Sage Productions, 164 (c l)

Tom Stack: © Tom Algire, 14 (b l), 125 (t); © John Cancalosi, 117 (b r); © Terry Donnelly, 74, 94, 146 (b l), 151 (c l), 165 (b l); © Victoria Hurst, 51 (b r);© Mark Newman, 199 (c l); © Ed Robinson, 185 (b r); © Inga Spence, 178 (b l); © Greg Vaughn, 186 (b r), 188 (b r)

The Stock Market: © Tom Bean, 133 (b r); © Richard Berenholtz, 24-25, 30-31 (t); © William Manning, 193 (b r); © Clark Mischler, 194 (t l); © Alan Schein, 35 (t r); © Eleanor Thompson, 80 (t l)

Tony Stone Images: © Glen Allison, 81 (t); © Brian Bailey, 142; © James Balog, 152 (b l); © John Beatty, 132 (c l); © Ken Biggs, 177 (b r); © Warren Bolster, 184 (t l); © Michael Busselle, 110 (b l); © Rosemary Calvert, 120 (t r), 125 (c l); © Milan Chuckovich, 187 (t); © Jim Corwin, 161 (m r); © Cosmo Condina, 21, 35 (b r); © Richard A. Cooke III, 186 (t l), 189 (b r); © Daniel J. Cox, 68 (b l); © Cameron Davidson, 45 (b r); © Terry Donnelly, 54 (b); © Richard Elliott, 33 (t c); © Robert Frerck, 96 (m r); © Ken Graham, 188-189 (t), 198-199 (t); © Sylvain Grandadam, 29 (b l), 133 (c r); © Darrell Gulin, 200 (c); © Gregg Hadel, 179 (t); © Bob Handelman, 33 (b r); © Fred Hirschmann, 201 (b r); © Kevin Horan, 197 (t r); © Kim Heacox, 190-191, 196 (c r); © Gary Holscher, 180-181; © H. Richard Johns, 165 (t); © Johnny Johnson, 198 (b l); © Byron Jorjordian, 78 (t l); © Richard Kavlin, 174 (t); © Nikolas Konstantinou, 68 (c l); © Rich LaSalle, 27 (m r); © Siegfried Layda, 12; © G. Brad Lewis, 143 (b r), 187 (c l); © Renee Lynn, 153 (b r); © Matthew McVay, 105 (b r); © David Muench, 52 (t l), 131 (t r), 138 (b l), 192; © Marc Muench, 147 (b c); © David Myers, 200 (t l); © Joseph Nettis, 39 (b r); © Stan Osolinski, 149; © Vito Palmisano, 96 (t l); © Peter Pearson, 163 (m l); © Chuck Pefley, 157 (m r); © Jim Pickerell, 42 (b l); © Peter Poulides, 125 (c r); © R.G.K. Photography, 170; © Jake Rajs, 23 (t), 109 (c r); © James Randklev, 62 ; © Tom Raymond, 70 (b l); © Donovan Reese, 5 (b r); © G. Ryan and S. Beyer, 113 (b r); © Ron Sanford, 66 (b l), 150-151 (t), 176 (b l); © Kevin Schafer, 157 (b l), 200 (t r); © Dave Schiefelbein, jacket (farm), 1; © David Schultz, 153 (t); © Pete Seaward, 177 (c l); © Nancy Simmerman, 196 (b l); © Joseph Sohm, 40 (t); © Paul Souders, 46 (b l), 47 (m r), 163 (b); © Don Spiro, 32 (b l); © T Resource, 175 (t r); © Tom Till, 50; © Peter Timmermans, 134 (b r); © Larry Ulrich, jacket (San Juan Mountains), 1, 6 (t l), 106 (c), 135 (t r), 140-141; © Greg Vaughn, 165 (m r); © Gary Vestal, 124 (b l); © Terry Vine, 118 (b l); © Stuart Westmorland, 66 (c r); © Keith Wood, 120 (c l)

© SuperStock International, 23 (m l), 34 (b l), 58 (b l), 84 (t l), 164 (t l)

Transparencies, Inc.: © Billy E. Barnes, 71 (c)

Travel Stock: © Ric Ergenbright Photography, 90 (b l)

Unicorn Stock Photos: © Martha McBride, 85 (b r)

Valan Photos: © Fred Bruemmer, 199 (b r)

© Jack Vartoogian, 84 (c r)

© Randy Wells, 108 (t)

Woodfin Camp & Associates: © Roger Werth, 162 (t l)

JACKET AND INTRODUCTORY PHOTOS
Jacket and page 1, clockwise from top: Colorado's San Juan Mountains; cowboys riding at sunset; New York City skyline; colorful Native American totem pole; wheat field and old barn in Washington's Palouse Hills. **Pages 4-5:** Zion National Park, Utah (top); Statue of Liberty (bottom left); pumpkins on a New Hampshire farm (bottom right). **Page 6:** Pigeon Point Lighthouse in San Mateo County, California. **Page 202:** Windmill and shed in rural Illinois.

SOURCES FOR THEMATIC MAPS
Glaciation map, page 95: *Physical Geology*, Richard Foster Flint and Brian J. Skinner, Copyright © 1974. Reprinted by permission of John Wiley and Sons, Inc.

Texas Oil Fields map, page 120: *1997 International Petroleum Encyclopedia,* a publication of PennWell Publishing Company.

America
Copyright © 2000 by Rand McNally & Company

10 9 8 7 6 5 4 3 2

www.randmcnally.com

This product is protected under copyright law. It is illegal to reproduce or transmit it in whole or in part, in any form or by any means (including mechanical, photographic, or electronic methods), without the written permission of Rand McNally. Published and printed in the United States.

America: a celebration of the United States / Rand McNally.
p. cm.
Includes index.
ISBN 0-528-84174-2
1. United States--Description and travel.
2. United States--Geography. 3. Human geography--United States. 4. United States--Pictorial works. I. Rand McNally and Company.
   E169.04.A34 1999
   973--dc21   99-14258
                                                  CIP

For information on licensing and copyright permissions, please contact us at licensing@randmcnally.com.

America

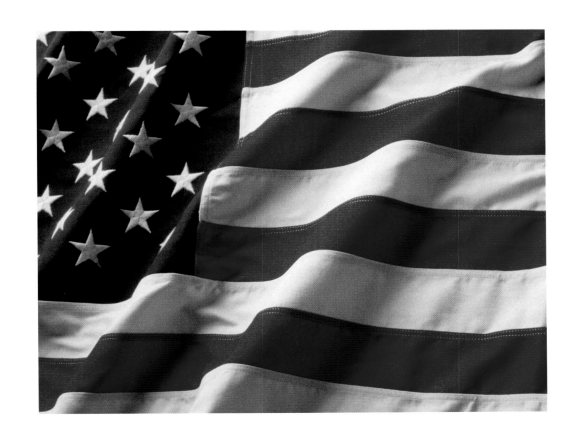

A Celebration of the United States

table of **contents**

letter to the reader

In my role as Rand McNally's Chief Cartographer, and as an avid traveler, I spend a lot of time exploring the byways of the United States and the world. During business discussions abroad I am often introduced as being from "America's Rand McNally." On the streets of foreign cities and towns, casual conversations with strangers almost always include the words "You're American." It is clear that the world has distinct views and opinions of America. Yet I always find the concept of a homogeneous America too narrow to convey the wonder and diversity of the place that is home to Americans. To discover the true America beyond our increasingly indistinguishable highways and cities is to discover regions that look, feel, and are vastly different. Rand McNally's *America* is truly a celebration of geography, landscapes, cultures, lifestyles, and history.

In developing *America* we have worked hard to show one view of America's regions by highlighting them according to shared landscape, culture, and history. Thus, our regions are often carved along geographic features that comprise physical regions, or according to history and shared culture that contribute to each region's specific lifestyle and creates its sense of place. People may disagree with these regionalizations, especially when a state is divided among several regions. For example, we think that much of Colorado is part of the Mountain West region, but its southwestern corner has the identity of the Southwest, and its eastern corridor has the sense of the Plains.

Clearly, regions are easiest to describe at their cores and much harder to describe at their edges, where landscapes and history overlap, creating a sense of place that often reminds us of somewhere else. Ultimately, the task of defining the regions fell to Rand McNally's talented editorial staff and a special advisory board that included the leading geographers at Rand McNally as well as renowned geographers from America's educational institutions.

In the end, however, the manner in which we have regionalized America serves only as a geographical format that allows us to present a compendium of uniquely American stories through large, dramatic photographs; brand-new, beautifully illustrated maps; featurettes and sidebars highlighting culture and lifestyle; and essays that weave the tale of each region's origins, identity, and sense of place. These images and impressions portray the country from a wonderfully descriptive and fresh point of view.

We hope that you will enjoy reading *America* as much as we enjoyed developing it. Sometimes it takes a closer look to realize the wisdom in that simple saying, "There's no place like home."

Michael W. Dobson

Michael W. Dobson, Ph.D.
Vice President and Chief Cartographer
Rand McNally and Company

index map and legend

HYDROGRAPHIC FEATURES

	Perennial river
	Seasonal river
Hoover Dam	Dam
	Falls
Los Angeles Aqueduct	Aqueduct
	Lake, reservoir
	Seasonal lake
	Salt lake
	Seasonal salt lake
	Dry lake
395	Lake surface elevation
	Swamp, marsh
	Reef
	Ice sheet

TOPOGRAPHIC FEATURES

All elevations and depths are given in meters.

▲ 2278	Elevation above sea level
▼ 1700	Elevation below sea level
⋈	Mountain pass

TRANSPORTATION FEATURES

	Major road
	Other road
	Navigable canal
	Tunnel
	Ferry
⋈	Bridge
✈	International airport
✈	Other airport

BOUNDARIES

	International
	State/province

CITIES AND TOWNS

The size of symbol and type indicates the relative importance of the locality.

■	**NEW YORK**
▣	**CHICAGO**
◉	**Milwaukee**
◉	Chattanooga
◉	Daytona Beach
○	Sheridan
∘	Placerville
	Urban area

CAPITALS

WASHINGTON	National
Santa Fe	State

CULTURAL

▭ or ·	National park
▭	Other park
·	Point of interest
	Indian reservation
∴	Ruins
	Military installation

THE UNITED STATES

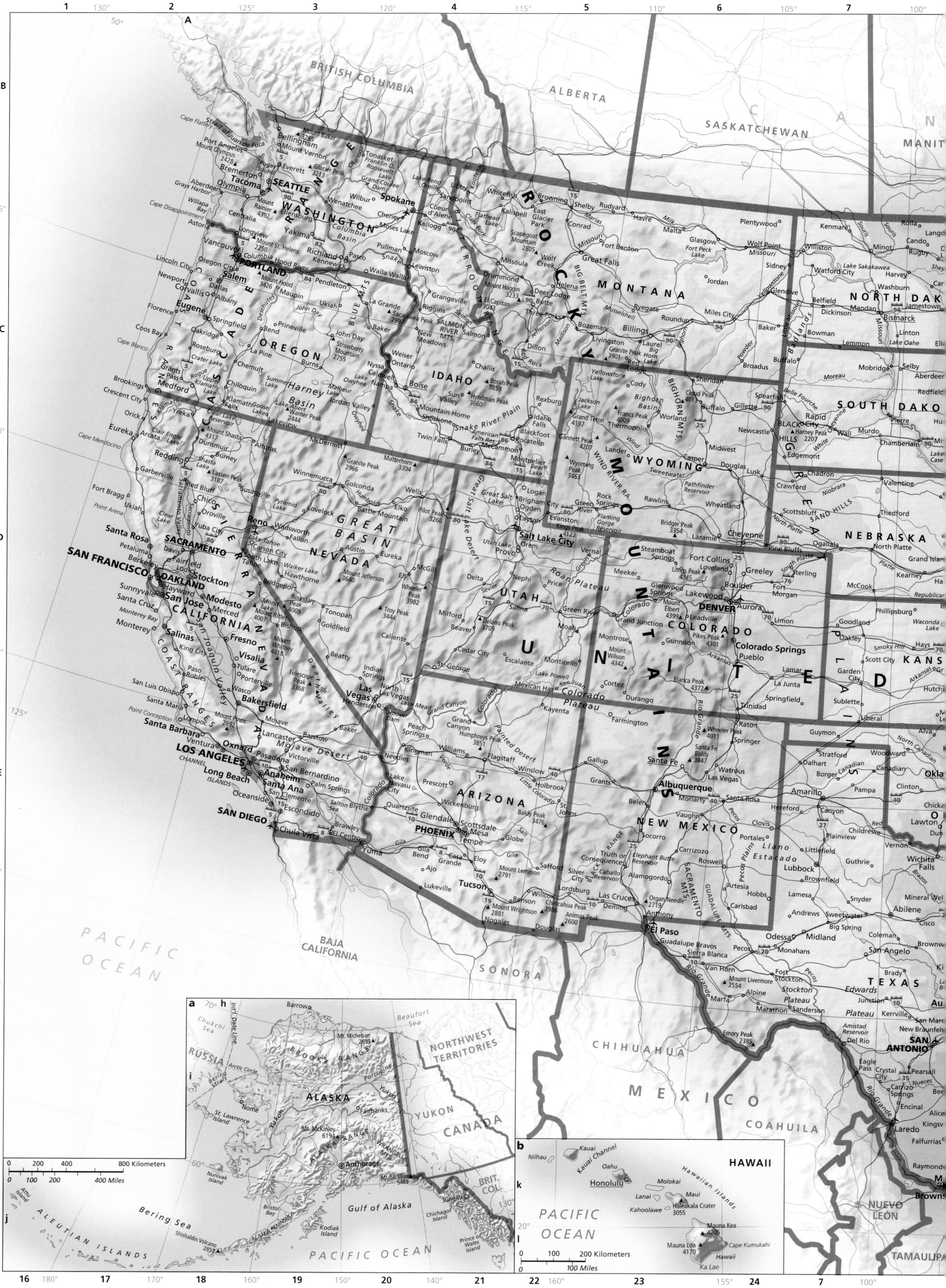

New England
and the Adirondacks

Celebrating the Old New World

 A few years back, an **outspoken** governor of Connecticut proposed that the states of New England be united into one. It would make the region more powerful politically, he said, and make economic planning more efficient. Predictably, the proposal and the governor who advanced it were treated with all the respect accorded to traitors and blasphemers.

The lesson was that this old and historic region—Connecticut, Massachusetts, Rhode Island, Vermont, New Hampshire, Maine, and the neighboring Adirondack Mountains of New York—absolutely thrives on its diversity, despite its shared geography and history. It's as if the contrariness of the Vermonter, the conservatism of the New Hampshirite, the provincialism of the Mainer, and the solitariness of the Adirondacker are among this region's major natural resources, indelible parts of its culture.

From a distance, the region represents a rich and varied panorama of many of the country's most familiar and fabled places. Within just a few hundred miles, the terrain changes from the vast sand spit of Cape Cod to the fertile Connecticut River Valley, on to the wild forests of upstate New York, and back to the granite coast of Maine. The landscapes are splendid, not just to the natives but to anyone who loves the ancient rhythms of panoramic mountains, cool mists shrouding quiet fishing villages,

Lighthouse and rocky shore near Portland, Maine (left); bull moose (right). Preceding pages: East Corinth, Vermont, one of New England's many charming hill towns

the simple perfection of venerable towns like Connecticut's Litchfield, the fiery brilliance of fall foliage.

A brief Baedeker of the region might begin by describing the White Mountains of New Hampshire—with their magisterial "Presidential Range"—which were created as molten granite exploded from the earth. This resort region was once a high-society retreat, but today reasonably priced resorts, campgrounds, and other family-friendly lodgings have replaced the grand hotels. While their foothills are welcoming, the White Mountains are known mostly for their extremes. Mount Washington has attracted tourists since the 1800s, but it can challenge survival with bitter cold and winds that often blow with hurricane force. In fact, the world's highest surface wind gust was recorded on Washington in 1934: 231 miles (372 km) per hour.

To the west, the Green Mountains of Vermont are gentler and more inviting. Time has caressed them; they've been sculpted by glaciers, embroidered by forests, and settled with pleasant towns and lovely white churches. In the winter, skiers flock to Vermont's resorts, notably Stowe and Killington, for the best downhill runs east of the Rockies. In the summer, mountain bikers coast the hillsides and back roads.

The Berkshire Hills of western Massachusetts and the nearby Connecticut River Valley have made peace with time in their own way, too. Old industries like silversmithing, tobacco farming, and even maple syrup production still connect this civilized part of the world directly to its past. Tucked away among the forests, parkland, and quaint villages with old churches lies Tanglewood, the summer home of the Boston Symphony Orchestra.

On the western edge of the region are the Adirondacks, sometimes called the "Black

Albany Covered Bridge (right), built in 1858, still carries vehicles and pedestrians over the Swift River in New Hampshire.

Mountains" for their dark, wild aspect. Their cliffs, canyons, and abrupt changes of terrain bear the rough look of battle between the upward thrust of the ancient Earth and the horizontal havoc wreaked by Pleistocene glaciers. And

Sailing and windsurfing on Boston's Charles River (top right), lobster traps on Maine fishing docks (middle right), Connecticut's Mystic Seaport (bottom right)

today they remain an incongruous wilderness, not too different from the settings of James Fenimore Cooper's stories, but also within a few hours of New York and Boston. The Adirondacks still attract artists in some places, serious outdoorsmen in others, and fortunate romantics at the splendid lodges and resorts like Saratoga Springs, built by and for wealthy Eastern families.

The region's greatest river, the Hudson, originates high on the flanks of New York's Mount Marcy, the tallest Adirondack peak. After spilling out of the mountains, it is joined by the Mohawk River, its major tributary, and flows southward through a deep, glacier-carved gorge. The breathtaking highland vistas along the river inspired America's first recognized group of landscape painters, the Hudson River School. Because of its striking scenery and its vital role as a transportation artery, the Hudson is often compared to Germany's Rhine. During the 19th century, many of the East Coast's wealthiest people—perhaps inspired by the castles along the Rhine—built spectacular mansions overlooking the Hudson. The overstated architectural style associated with these Italian villas, French chateaus, and Greek temples became known as Hudson River Gothic.

At the northeast edge of the region lies Maine, largest of the New England states and the most sparsely populated state east of the Mississippi River. Dense forests of pine, spruce, and fir cover more than four-fifths of Maine's land. Loons call from the countless lakes and bogs that are legacies of the last Ice Age. Along the convoluted, fog-shrouded coast are high cliffs of granite, endless beaches of bleached-white cobbles, and traditional fishing villages that seem to have changed little in the past 200 years.

boston's reclaimed land

As New England's preeminent city, Boston experienced the country's first urban crowding. Its original site, 783 acres (317 ha) on a tiny peninsula connected to the mainland by a neck of land less than a mile (1.6 km) wide, left little room to expand. By the mid-19th century the town was severely overcrowded: Between 1790 and 1825 its population tripled to nearly 60,000, and by 1860 the population had more than doubled again.

During the 1800s, the city undertook a series of projects to expand its land area by filling in surrounding marshes and tidal flats. The largest and best-known of these projects, the Back Bay landfill, began in 1857 and transformed more than 450 acres (182 ha) of stagnant, polluted mud flats into usable land over the next 40 years. Dirt was transported from neighboring Needham because earlier projects had already depleted sources closer to the site, such as Beacon Hill and Copps Hill.

Marshy areas around Charlestown, the South End, and East Boston were reclaimed during the same era, and the city continued to fill areas adjacent to annexed land until 1970. Boston is now more than 40 times its colonial size, with a land area of 50 square miles (130 sq km).

The Back Bay landfill project resulted in the flat tract of land that is now the fashionable Back Bay residential district. Its centerpiece, Commonwealth Avenue, a wide boulevard with a grassy mall, was modeled after the Champs Élysées in Paris. Stately brownstones now line the grand-scale street.

Boston's early site restrictions are still noticeable: The city is built more densely than any other in America, even New York. Its compact scale allows visitors to enjoy much of the city on foot, walking across reclaimed land that has been called Boston's greatest contribution to urban design.

BOSTON THEN AND NOW

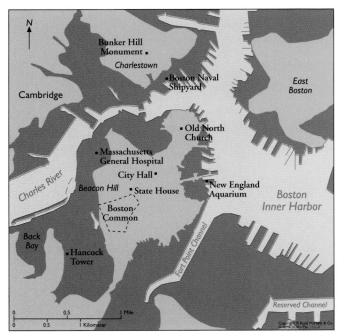

☐ Original land area
■ Reclaimed land

new england's maritime legacy

New England's colonists discovered very early that farming their new land was a struggle. The coastal soil was too rocky, the growing season too short. So they turned to the region's greatest natural resource: the sea. Farmers became skilled fishermen, and carpenters learned the art of shipbuilding. Ever since, New England's coastal communities have been intricately linked with the sea.

The colonists made a wise choice. The Atlantic waters teemed with fish. Cod, halibut, mackerel, flounder, clams, and lobster were part of the bounty.

Cod became such an integral part of Massachusetts' early economy that a carved wooden "Sacred Cod" was hung in the State House in 1784. It still hangs there today.

Fishing, both for domestic consumption and export, became big business, as did whale hunting, since people depended on whale oil as their chief lamp fuel. Trading quickly grew in importance, too. Colonial shipbuilders, working with native woods, soon produced ships that were in great demand in England, where forests were already depleted.

Life on the sea was difficult and dangerous, but it could bring great wealth. Large, expensive homes built by successful sea captains, whalers, and traders still line the coast from Connecticut to Maine.

Today, New England's economy is far less dependent on the sea than it was in colonial days. But its ports and fishing villages still hum with

activity and remind visitors and natives alike of the region's rich maritime legacy.

The cobblestone streets of Mystic Seaport in Mystic, Connecticut, hark back to the days of whalers and clippers. Cruises on clipper ships and schooners are a popular pastime in this re-creation of a mid-19th-century fishing village. Newport, Rhode Island, another maritime town, is the birthplace of the U.S. Navy, longtime home of the America's Cup race, and still a world sailing capital. The town features the vacation mansions of some of the country's wealthiest 18th- and 19th-century families.

Maritime history is also ubiquitous in Boston, one of the world's major seaports. Tourists can take trips aboard topsail schooners, explore the New England Aquarium, or visit Boston Harbor, site of the Boston Tea Party.

To the northeast, Portland, Maine, was called "the beautiful town that is seated by the sea" by Henry Wadsworth Longfellow. Whale-watching expeditions are popular here, as are restaurants serving Maine's native lobsters. The Old Port Exchange, a renovated waterfront area, is the heart of Portland's maritime culture.

The most popular destination along the coast of Maine is Acadia National Park, an unspoiled preserve of spruce forests, rocky shores, and placid bays punctuated by tiny islands. Among the park's highlights are Sand Beach, formed from the broken fragments of mollusk shells, and Thunder Hole, a chasm that thunders with the echoes of crashing waves. Visitors seeking more solitude ride the twice-daily mail boat to Isle au Haut to explore its 2,800 acres (1,120 ha) of pristine beauty. In a sense, the country's day begins in Acadia: The peak of Cadillac Mountain receives the first rays of sunlight to strike the United States each morning.

The southern end of the region also possesses splendid coastal recreation spots. Reaching seaward from mainland Massachusetts is Cape Cod, a long, hook-shaped peninsula lined with seemingly endless stretches of beach, shops, and seafood restaurants. Cottages, weathered by the ocean air, teem with salt-spray roses tumbling over trellises and gates, and 18th-century towns showcase classic village greens. In the fall, the Cape bursts with fiery foliage and serves as a migratory stop for hundreds of thousands of birds.

A short ferry trip from Cape Cod is Martha's Vineyard, perhaps the region's most popular resort area. Both dignitaries and tourists zip along on mopeds among the island's seven Victorian communities searching for antiques, good wine, and restful spots. Lighthouses abound on the coastline, among the cliffs, dunes, and soft beaches. The Vineyard's population jumps from

Race Point at the northwestern tip of Cape Cod (above), John Trumbull's 1775 painting *Battle of Bunker Hill* (right)

the cradle of the revolutionary war

The Revolutionary War was fought across all 13 of the American colonies, but most of the pivotal events leading up to the war, as well as the critical first battles, occurred in Massachusetts.

By the time the first shots were fired—early in the morning of April 19, 1775, in the villages of Lexington and Concord—momentum toward revolution had been building for more than a decade. British Parliament, anxious to tighten its reins on the colonies and raise money for its expanding empire, enforced a series of strict new taxes. Angered over "taxation without representation," Massachusetts colonists began demonstrating their resistance to British rule.

Their first significant protest came in December of 1773, when 60 patriots dumped hundreds of chests of East India Company tea into Boston Harbor. The so-called Boston Tea Party was just the first of many localized revolts that would escalate into a bloody eight-year fight for independence.

Today, the Boston area is dotted with historic sites and battlefields memorializing this momentous era in American history. The Boston National Historical Park comprises several prominent sites from the Revolutionary era, linked by a 2.5-mile (4-km) footpath called the Freedom Trail. The Boston Massacre memorial is a simple ring of cobblestones next to the Old State House in downtown Boston; it marks the place where, on March 5, 1770, British soldiers killed five colonists in an attempt to quell mounting unrest. The incident outraged many Boston patriots, who used it as a rallying point to demand the removal of British troops from the city.

The Paul Revere House is a restored 17th-century home commemorating its most famous resident. Revere, a local silversmith and army colonel, is best known for his "midnight ride." On the night of April 18, 1775, he road on horseback from Boston to Lexington to warn patriot leaders that British soldiers were marching there to seize the patriots' stockpile of weapons. Accompanied by William Dawes and Samuel Prescott, Revere continued on toward Concord but was captured by a British patrol.

The Bunker Hill Monument marks the site of the first significant engagement between the newly unified colonial army and the Redcoats on June 17, 1775. Though it is popularly called the Battle of Bunker Hill, most of the fighting took place on nearby Breed's Hill, which is today the site of a 221-foot (67.4-m) granite obelisk that pays tribute to the Revolution's first major battle.

Twenty-two miles (35 km) west of Boston, Minute Man National Historical Park encompasses the Lexington and Concord battlefields and preserves original sections of the Battle Road, the route by which British troops arrived for the first skirmish of the War. The Minute Man statue honors the militia units that formed in towns throughout Massachusetts in the 1770s, ready to bear arms and defend their communities at a minute's notice.

Today, these and other notable sites offer visitors a chance to reflect on the ideals—freedom of speech, religion, government, and self-determination—for which the Revolutionary War was fought.

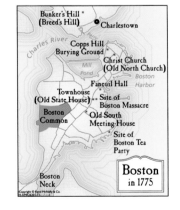

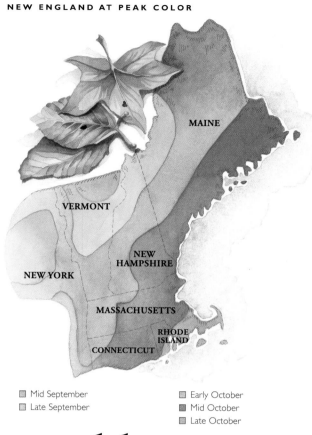

Mid September
Late September

Early October
Mid October
Late October

hills ablaze with color

It begins in northern Vermont, along the Canadian border, usually in the middle of September. First, isolated patches of reds and yellows and oranges appear on the green forested hillsides. Cautiously, these upstart hues spread to neighboring trees; before long, whole valleys and ridges are aflame. Gathering confidence, the colors of fall sweep southward across the region, transforming counties overnight, entire states in a matter of days, and chasing away the greens of summer.

Most regions of the United States experience the spectacle of autumn foliage, but nowhere does Mother Nature put on a show like she does in New England and the Adirondacks. For this the region can thank its favorable fall weather—warm, sunny days and chilly nights—and its abundance and variety of broad-leaved deciduous trees.

Beeches, white birches, butternuts, and elms burst into radiant yellows and oranges, as do several varieties of ash. Maples dazzle the eye with intense reds: cranberry, scarlet,

and violet. Yellow birches and aspens shimmer in gold, while witch hazels, white ashes, and red oaks wear rich cloaks of purple and burgundy.

Autumn's shorter days and waning sunlight are the impetus for fall color changes. As daylight decreases, the leaves produce less and less green chlorophyll; when green is no longer the dominant color, yellow and orange pigments such as carotene and xanthophyll begin to show through. Additional chemical changes yield other colors: Anthocyanin, a pigment formed from sugars trapped in the leaves, produces fiery reds and deep purples. Tannin, a waste product, tints leaves gold and brown.

Natives and visitors alike celebrate the New England leaf season with ritualistic intensity. Weathercasters predict the arrival of "peak colors," and foliage hot lines are jammed with calls. Zealous "leaf peepers" clog scenic routes from Maine to Massachusetts, including New Hampshire's Kancamagus Highway and U.S. 7 between Burlington and Bennington, Vermont.

10,000 in the off-season to more than 80,000 during the summer, and elbowroom comes at a hefty premium. Nearby is the island of Nantucket, once the largest whaling port in the world. Today, this little outpost attracts those looking for quieter activities and greater seclusion. Island-circling bike tours present the opportunity to inhale the crisp Atlantic air, and more adventurous pastimes such as sea kayaking and surf fishing give this charming spot a modern appeal.

The great urban agglomeration of America's eastern seaboard, nicknamed the "Bos-Wash Corridor" and "Megalopolis," angles across the southern third of the region. But even in this nearly unbroken stretch of urbanization, New England's cities and towns retain strong individual identities. Boston, the region's largest city, is a worldly enclave of universities, scientists, philosophers, and technological innovation. With its long history of private learning (Harvard is the country's oldest university) and its superabundance of colleges and universities, Eastern Massachusetts is sometimes referred to as "one big college town." But education also represents a strong economic asset that generates competition, creativity, and farsightedness—keeping Boston forever young despite its centuries of experience. A short distance to the southwest is Providence, founded by religious dissenters fleeing Puritan intolerance in Massachusetts; today large old jewelry factories prosper in the shadow of high technology. Hartford, situated in the heart of the Connecticut River Valley, boasts a flourishing financial industry with roots deep in the past: In the 1700s, the city became America's insurance center, serving the nation's fragile young industries. Along the coast, the old whaling city of New Bedford, the Gilded Age splendor of Newport, the submarine-building center of Groton, and the green suburbs of Fairfield County represent layers of history and ways of life that seem worlds, not miles, apart from one another.

Alongside the inveterate differences, there are certain elements common to all parts of New England and the Adirondacks. Two of these common elements

Brilliant fall yellows, oranges, and reds creep up the slopes above Heart Lake in New York's Adirondack State Park (right).

are human resourcefulness and a strong work ethic, which turned scant natural resources into prosperous economies. The rocky land, with its

New England Landscape by Cropsey (left); Hudson Valley near Garrison, New York (top right); clam chowder (lower right)

hudson river
school of painters

shallow, poor soil, always was "more exciting to the eye than susceptible to the plow," as the geographer Neal Peirce wrote. But natural water power, combined with technical ingenuity, brought about thousands of enterprising textile mills on the banks of the region's many rivers. In 1790, the development of the power loom by Samuel Slater in Pawtucket, Rhode Island, led to the growth of mill cities on rivers throughout New England and the upper Hudson—Lowell, Lawrence, Watertown, Troy, and many other places where America evolved from agrarian communities into an industrialized society.

Another shared element is the region's rich legacy of philosophical and political thought. The towns of New England and the Adirondacks served as the flash points for one of history's greatest experiments: American independence. Nationhood can be traced back to the Pilgrims, a small band of religious dissenters who were headed to a more temperate shore than the one they found. But when they arrived at Plymouth they applied faith and steadfastness, and they made peace with the Indians, the winter, and themselves. In their respect for self-reliance and simplicity the Pilgrims represented the beginnings of an American ideal.

The New England spirit, then as now, combined reason, a sense of faith, and intense freedom of thought. It was manifest in the character of the Minutemen, a militia built on pure patriotism and bravery and commemorated poignantly at the narrow battlefields of Lexington and Concord. Later came the Transcendentalists, most notably Henry David Thoreau, who concluded that nonconformity was the road to true peace, and that an individual's first duty was "to live life as his principles demand." Then there were the abolitionists, centered in Boston, who became a kind of conscience for the nation through their unflagging fight against slavery.

The intensely creative and staunchly independent spirit of New England and the Adirondacks survives and flourishes today. Call it pride

In the summer of 1825, artist Thomas Cole ventured north from his New York City home to sketch in the Catskill Mountains. Though seemingly insignificant, Cole's excursion in fact marked the birth of this country's first native genre of painting. A loosely knit group of artists who specialized in reverential paintings of the American landscape, the Hudson River School grew out of a desire to create a national artistic style—one that was wholly independent from that of European master painters and focused on a subject that was wild, evocative, and distinctly American: untamed nature.

For founder Cole and fellow artists Asher B. Durand, Frederick Church, Jaspar Cropsey, and Albert Bierstadt, the most accessible wilderness was to be found in the cliffs, crags, waterfalls, and highlands of the lower Hudson River and the Catskills. Though the styles and techniques of the artists varied, their paintings were imbued with a shared reverence for the romantic grandeur and unpredictability of nature in the vast American interior. They sought to accurately portray light effects and spatial relationships, but also to exalt the landscapes they painted, to capture a feeling of sublimity.

Cole's 1826 oil painting *The Falls of Kaaterskill* depicts a series of waterfalls (today, a well-known landmark near the Catskill village of Palenville), with dark and ominous clouds overshadowing the otherwise tranquil scene. For his 1838 *View of Schroon Mountain*, Cole traveled farther north to paint a dramatic portrait of this iconic Adirondack peak after a violent thunderstorm. Following Cole's death in 1848, Durand paid tribute to him and to the Catskill region with his archetypical Hudson River School painting *Kindred Spirits*, which depicts the late artist with poet William Cullen Bryant on a rocky ledge overlooking the Kaaterskill cascades and the surrounding landscape.

By mid-century, the Hudson River School had expanded its focus and was attracting new painters who carried Cole's view of American wilderness with them to regions beyond the Hudson Valley. In 1857 Church captured the monumental forces of Niagara Falls in the celebrated painting *Niagara*. And six years later Bierstadt completed his dramatic portrait of the Mountain West: *The Rocky Mountain, Landers's Peak*. By the late 1860s, the school's legacy was assured: Two generations of painters had created an artistic style that was as internationally acclaimed as it was uniquely American.

clam chowder

The darling of New England cuisine, clam chowder is also one of America's most distinctive regional dishes. In one version or another, it is ladled out to thousands of locals and visitors every year and can stir the passions of even the most taciturn Down-Easter.

Chowder appeared in the region in the 18th century. It is thought to have migrated from Newfoundland and Nova Scotia, where French fishermen brought it from their native Breton shores. The word "chowder" probably comes from the French word *chaudière*, a large pot into which fishermen in Brittany threw leftovers from the day's catch and stewed it up on the beach.

The earliest written chowder recipe was recorded in the *Boston Evening Post* on September 3, 1751. Its ingredients included salt pork, onions, potatoes, flour, biscuits, herbs, fish, and red wine. It wasn't until the late 19th century that milk or cream became common. These days, traditional clam chowder consists of fresh quahog (pronounced co-hog) clams and their juice, called liquor; salt pork or bacon; potatoes; onions; and salt and pepper. It is often served with a dollop of butter and always includes a generous supply of crackers on the side.

This regional dish has thrived because the raw materials—clams, salt pork, potatoes—have always been easily available. So has the *chaudière*: Since fireplaces acted as stoves, most colonial meals were simmered in one cast-iron pot.

Today at fairs and restaurants, chowder is often made with non-traditional ingredients: Mexican spices, corn, carrots, or celery. But at regional festivals like Boston's Chowderfest, New Englanders consistently vote for the ageless traditional recipe.

or call it provincialism: There's a lot of it when someone from Down East Maine or Western Massachusetts talks about the powerful landmarks or historic hardships that connect people to the place and to each other.

So don't talk about New England as a single state. There is and always will be Vermont, with its history of dissent (it has threatened secession from the Union) and liberal, sometimes even collectivist, politics. Don't ever confuse it with New Hampshire, the anti-tax and anti-planning curmudgeon whose major newspaper, the *Manchester Union-Leader*, still oozes the truculent conservatism of its late publisher, William Loeb. And if Vermonters and New Hampshirites agree on anything, it's that they're glad they aren't in "Taxachusetts"—big, sophisticated, and politically complicated. Whether these traits (and others belonging to residents of Connecticut, Rhode Island, Maine, and the Adirondacks) represent subtle distinctions or brickbat prejudices, they are deep-seated enough to make the thought of "one-state-ism" anathema to anyone with a smidgen of the Yankee in his or her bones.

Metro New York

America's Urban Core

 One of the **contradictions** of geography, Metro New York is small on the map, hardly a region of its own—rather a corner of the Mid-Atlantic Coast, or perhaps a southern extension of New England. Yet its importance is immense, entirely disproportionate to its physical size.

The urbanized heart of the region radiates a mere 30 or 40 miles (48 or 64 km) from Grand Central Terminal, yet some 20 million people live here. Which begs the question: How did New York become the cultural and financial capital, the all-around power center, of the civilized world?

Indeed, New York City has always been a magnet, drawing everything around it toward the center. Outside the city, the component parts of the region—Long Island, the southern tip of mainland New York State, northeastern New Jersey, and Connecticut's southwestern corner— all have distinct identities, but each is defined

Quiet beach on New Jersey's Sandy Hook peninsula (left), colorful street scene in Chinatown (above). Preceding pages: Manhattan at dusk

strongly by its relationship to New York. The outer boroughs of the city— Queens, Brooklyn, Staten Island, and the Bronx—are themselves diverse and independent, but likewise revolve around the gravitational pull of Manhattan.

History suggests that the ambitious, if not always the wealthy, have been drawn to New York since at least 1604 when Henry Hudson, seeking an elusive route to China, passed through the harbor and up the

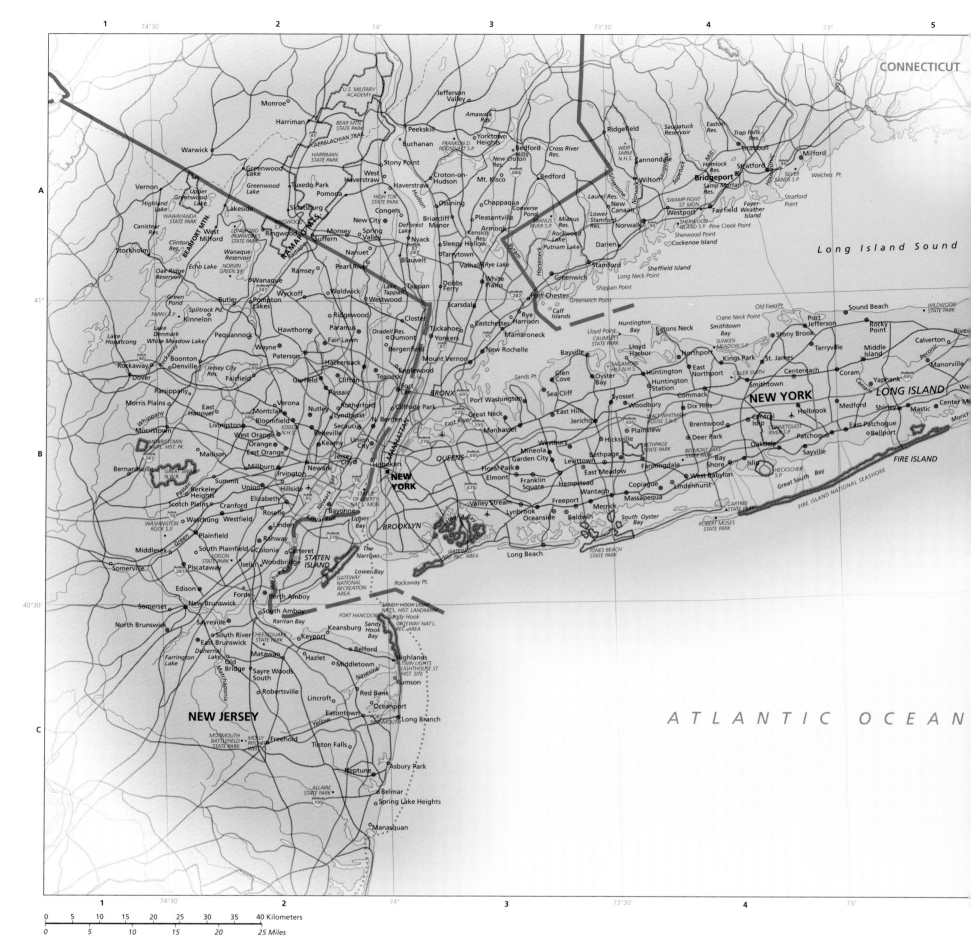

river that would bear his name. Hudson was off target for the Orient, but his enterprise was contagious. A steady stream of Europeans followed.

What impressed the earliest visitors most was that the New York area was lush and full of fur-bearing animals, particularly beavers. In 1625, Dutch business interests established a trading post, and the following year they purchased Manhattan Island from the Algonquins for $24 worth of azure-colored beads. The trading center of New Amsterdam, as it was called, led to a shipping center in what is unquestionably one of the world's most perfect natural harbors— ice-free throughout the year and deep enough to allow large oceangoing ships to reach its piers even at low tide. Shipping led naturally to banking; the Dutch minted money here in the 1600s.

In 1664, the English seized control of New Amsterdam and renamed it in honor of the Duke of York. No blood was shed in the political transition, mainly because the Dutch disliked their ironhanded governor, Peter Stuyvesant. At the time of the English takeover, New York held some 1,500 people and was confined to the extreme southern tip of Manhattan. As promising as the city's setting was, its residents could not have predicted the spectacular growth—in population, area, and stature—that the next three centuries would bring.

By 1790 its population had climbed to 33,000, and New York surpassed Philadelphia as the largest city in the fledgling United States. Early in the following century, manufacturing began to spread across the region, with textile mills both large and small making use of the many swift-moving streams cascading down the banks of the Hudson River. This industry brought new job opportunities and a new growth spurt, as did the opening of the Erie Canal in 1825. The canal, which connected the Hudson to the Great Lakes and thus to growing markets of the Midwest, significantly increased New York's role as a center of shipping and commerce. By 1830, the city's population had reached 200,000. Then, toward the middle of the century, great waves of European immigrants began to wash onto America's shores; the majority entered the country through New York Harbor. Recognizing the opportunities available to them, many of the new arrivals chose to stay in New York. In 1870 the city held close to a million people, of whom nearly 400,000 were foreign-born.

Throughout the century, New York grew northward but was still confined to the island of Manhattan. The city acquired its present-day

New York Marathon runners cross the graceful Verrazano Narrows Bridge (left), which connects Staten Island and Brooklyn.

Signs of the times at Times Square (above), the popular Broadway musical "Les Misèrables" (bottom right)

boundaries in 1898 when it merged with Brooklyn, Queens, The Bronx, and Richmond (Staten Island). The five boroughs of newly created Greater New York spread over an area 11 times the size of Manhattan alone.

The rise of the United States as a world power in the 20th century was paralleled by New York's rise to international preeminence. In 1925 it became the most populous city in the world, overtaking London. Although it lost that title to Japan's Tokyo-Yokohama agglomeration in 1965, New York City nevertheless is generally held to be the world's greatest metropolis—the modern equivalent of ancient Rome.

New York has always been open to new arrivals, tolerant of outsiders, and this characteristic has made it perhaps the most international place on Earth. The Statue of Liberty and nearby Ellis Island, point of entry for some 12 million immigrants between 1895 and 1924, commemorate the importance of New York as a destination for people seeking a better life. Today, Manhattan is home of the United Nations. Wall Street drives the world's economic engines. And New York's people, its neighborhoods, its restaurants, and its stores make up a place of kaleidoscopic multicultural diversity.

But in the midst of such worldly trappings, New York is also a city of distinctive local culture. There's Greenwich Village, for example, with its narrow streets, brick town houses, small churches, Washington Square (a park where socialists mingle with socialites), and McSorley's Ale House, an

broadway theaters

Broadway theater and its namesake avenue have shared a history since New York was founded in the early 17th century.

The city's first theaters were located in Lower Manhattan on and off Broadway, which was once an Indian path stretching the length of Manhattan. As the city progressed steadily northward, so did the theater district: first to the area now known as SoHo, then to Union Square, next to the areas now called Chelsea and the Garment District, and finally, at the end of the 19th century, to Times Square. Today almost 40 Broadway theaters and hundreds of small Off-Broadway houses throughout the city constitute the venerable institution called New York theater.

Just as the establishment of the present-day Broadway/Times Square theater district was a turning point in New York theater history, so is the current renaissance of Broadway and Times Square. Sparking this

rebirth was the restoration of Broadway's oldest existing playhouse, the Theater Republic (which first opened its doors in 1900), now the New Victory, on 42nd Street. Then came, in quick succession, the restoration and refurbishing of 42nd Street between Seventh and Eighth Avenues, a building boom on Broadway itself (new office buildings, hotels, and mega-stores), and a blaze of spectacular new neon advertising signs that returned Broadway to its glory days as The Great White Way.

The vitality of New York theater today—including music and dance—is palpable. Broadway is booming, vibrating with blockbuster hits such as "Chicago" and "Rent," which join long runs like "Cats" and "Les Misèrables." Even dramatic plays, especially pre-tested imports from London and regional U.S. theater, are once again packing in the crowds. For the first time in years, there is actually a theater shortage, with several incoming shows banging on the doors.

If Broadway has become the museum of New York theater,

staging only plays that are "sure things," Off-Broadway, with more than 300 houses (ranging from a few seats to a few hundred) is New York theater's experimental caldron. Here is where avant-garde ideas can be tried out at lower costs. And if a show clicks, Broadway calls: "A Chorus Line," "Rent," "On Golden Pond," "Sunday in the Park With George," and "Ain't Misbehavin'" all began Off-Broadway.

Why did New York develop into the nation's—and now the world's—leading theater city? The most important factor is

New York's cultural, ethnic, and racial diversity—a yeasty mix essential for dynamic growth in the arts. Also vital is the city's enormous pool of talent: writers, actors, singers, dancers, directors, musicians, designers, technicians, and stagehands. Finally, New York is one of the world's foremost training grounds for careers in the theater, with classes and workshops at renowned schools like Lincoln Center's Juilliard, The Tisch School of the Arts at New York University, The Actors Studio, and The New School.

commuter culture

"Commuters give the city its tidal restlessness," wrote E. B. White in his book *Here Is New York*. And what a vast tide it is!

A detailed map of the metropolitan area reveals an incredibly complex tangle of thruways, expressways, railroads, and bus, subway, and ferry routes. So vital are these transportation lines that catastrophes such as blizzards, blackouts, and strikes bring the metropolis almost to its knees.

The commuter load borne by New York's transportation facilities is staggering. Daily, the Long Island Rail Road into Penn Station carries some 60,000 commuters. About 100,000 Metro-North riders pour into Grand Central Terminal, and more than 6,000,000 ride the city's subways and buses. Almost a million vehicles use the bridges and tunnels leading into and out

of Manhattan; of these, more than 250,000 cross the George Washington Bridge.

For the millions of commuters who live in New York City's outer boroughs of Brooklyn, Queens, Staten Island, and The Bronx, the average commute is well under an hour. The suburban commuters of outer Long Island, Westchester and vicinity in New York State, southwest Connecticut, and northeast New Jersey take the train or drive, and an average commute is about an hour.

Why do commuters commute? Income, rents and real estate prices, a growing family, schools, a love of close-knit communities, a yearning for trees and grass—all are factors. Sizeable co-op or condo apartments and town houses in Manhattan's upscale neighborhoods now cost in the millions, and monthly rents for studio apartments in once-reasonable Greenwich Village have soared out of sight. In contrast, houses are relatively affordable—at least by New York standards—in many parts of the outer boroughs and the suburban areas.

unreconstructed New York bar that excluded women until recently and whose motto is: "Be good or be gone."

There's Harlem. The superficial view is that it's a ghetto, but the deeper reality is that it has been an undeniable focal point of African-American culture and history since the days of W. E. B. Du Bois, Duke Ellington, Langston Hughes, and many other icons of the 20th century.

There's Brooklyn, which has the diversity of a bona fide city (which it was until the 1898 merger): a botanical garden, a world-class museum, Prospect Park, and a history that involves notable figures from poet Walt Whitman to comedian and filmmaker Mel Brooks. And there's Queens, a seemingly unwieldy conglomeration of communities from Astoria to Forest Hills, with world's fairgrounds, two major airports (La Guardia and John F. Kennedy), and a baseball team, the Metropolitans or "Mets."

Each corner of Metro New York possesses distinctions and unique charms, but the region shares a common quality—call it dynamism, or incipient change, or simply the unmistakable feel of New York. Westchester County, for example, was once "classic suburbia" with fine brick houses and neatly trimmed hedges. In recent decades, however,

Subway train and skyline of lower Manhattan (top), rush hour crowd at Penn Station (left), overview of Central Park from the south (top right), boating fun at Bethesda Terrace (bottom right)

central park

The most remarkable thing you can say about New York's Central Park is that it removes you from the asphalt jungle very quickly indeed. Just steps from the Plaza Hotel, you can be skating on the Wollman Memorial Rink. A stone's throw from Fifth Avenue, there's the Central Park Wildlife Conservation Center (formerly the Zoo), which includes an equatorial "climate zone" that is home to swinging monkeys and free-flying birds.

The pleasures of nature were certainly what the great newspaperman William Cullen Bryant had in mind in 1844 when he promoted the idea of a major park for New York. If Bryant returned today, he would carry on approvingly about the ponds and promenades that embroider Central Park's leafy groves and expansive pastures. A rain forest, on the other hand, would surprise him. But there always was something other-worldly about the plan that landscape architects Frederick Law Olmsted and Calvert Vaux designed in 1858 for the dead center of Manhattan Island.

The park was created when American landscape design— of which Central Park became (and still is) a prime example— was understood as something naturalistic, to echo in miniature the splendors of the American countryside. Olmsted and Vaux spared no effort, creating a place that outlived them and will out-live all of us. On a rectangular, 843-acre (341-ha) expanse that stretches 50 blocks north to south, they discarded New York's strict urban grid and wove their trails around natural escarpments, man-made water features, and what are now 26,000 trees. Among the notable features are an urban forest called the Ramble, scented with sassafras and filled with birds; Belvedere Castle, where the view from the turret surveys the park as its designers imagined it; the Mall, a broad walkway whose southern end is shaded by ancient American elms and lined with statues of literary notables such as Shakespeare and Robert Burns; and the Delacorte Shakespeare Theater, a more recent addition to the park's cultural terrain.

Over the years, several "improvements" have been added to Central Park. An early one came with the now-sprawling Metropolitan Museum of Art, despite the fact that Olmsted preferred open space for his park and felt that great art should be housed elsewhere. Another addition is Bethesda Terrace, an extravagant baroque folly with fountain and double staircase leading to the edge of a naturalistic lake. Harlem Meer now has a narrow stretch of yellow sand beach and a Discovery Center with exhibits about natural life in the park and beyond.

At its best, Central Park blends the gifts of nature with the presence of humankind.

On the broad expanse of the Sheep Meadow, for instance, New Yorkers crowd fearlessly together for free concerts. Around the Reservoir, the young, middle-aged, and old jog en masse seemingly endlessly. Around the bronze sculptures of Alice in Wonderland and Hans Christian Andersen at Conservatory Water, children gravitate for storytelling, some-times curling up in Andersen's bronze lap. In Strawberry Fields, individuals and couples wander through gardens restored as a memorial to the Beatles' John Lennon, who lived in the nearby Dakota building.

Uninspired things can happen in Central Park, too, and its after-dark reputation is not sterling. But such factors are far outweighed by the dazzling paintings, intriguing tales (such as *Catcher in the Rye*), unforgettable songs (like Simon and Garfunkel's "At the Zoo"), and popular movies that have made Central Park not just a beautiful piece of real estate but one of the country's most evocative, meaningful, and cherished public parks.

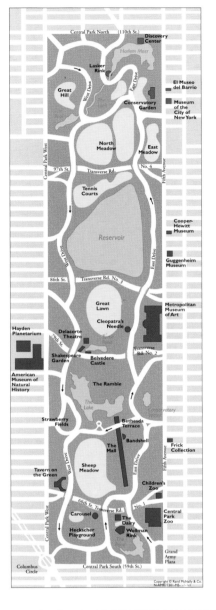

the faces of long island

Long Island, in its 125-mile (200-km) east-west thrust into the Atlantic Ocean, is a narrow strip of land with a broad range of personalities. Anchoring its western end are the urban New York City boroughs of Brooklyn and Queens, while its eastern end holds the rural, pastoral areas of Montauk, the Hamptons, and the North Fork. In between lie thriving business and commuter communities with names like Mineola, Deer Park, Babylon, Amityville, Valley Stream, Levittown (the pioneer postwar housing development), Port Jefferson, and Patchogue.

Sandy, flat, and low-lying, Long Island served as hunting and fishing grounds for Native Americans in pre-colonial days. The past three centuries have

transformed much of the island. Brooklyn and Queens are heavily populated and completely urbanized. Nassau, the island's middle county, is composed of one bedroom community after another, connected to the city by the Long Island Rail Road and several island-long parkways. Suffolk, the easternmost county, is where Long Island regains its green and rural look, with numerous state parks and nature preserves, long and sweeping beaches along the pounding Atlantic shore and the calmer waters of Long Island Sound, and the internationally renowned resorts of Sag Harbor (the former whaling port), the Hamptons, and Shelter Island.

Brooklyn and Queens, which were independent entities until New York was consolidated in 1898, still maintain their individuality but are nevertheless firmly geared to the pace of the big city. Originally settled by waves of immigrants—Germans, Irish, and Italians—the boroughs in recent years have been invigorated by new immigrant groups that have created

populous ethnic communities representing such origins as the Dominican Republic, Jamaica, China, Guyana, and Haiti. These communities exist alongside more established places such as Forest Hills, Flushing, Astoria, Kew Gardens, Jackson Heights, and Woodside.

The business and commuter centers of middle Long Island occupy lands once farmed by European settlers. Farming still exists (as roadside fruit and vegetable stands attest), but it has been greatly reduced and pushed eastward. Today, banking, publishing, and investment and insurance firms, as well as huge shopping malls, have moved into towns like Garden City and Rockville Centre.

Although there are year-round residents in the gilded Hamptons, these fabled shores—which boast some of the world's most spectacular unspoiled beaches—exist primarily as summer playgrounds for the rich, the well-connected, the successful, and the celebrated (plus, of course, their guests). Southampton, the stately grande

dame of the Hamptons, is the oldest and most conservative resort. West Hampton is the liveliest, Bridgehampton the most unassuming, and East Hampton the trendiest. All are governed by strict rules of zoning and behavior, and commercialism is kept under decorous control.

Naturally, all this wealth requires maintenance and service. Nearby towns such as Center Moriches, a delightful community of modest houses and charming small churches, are home to the builders, bus drivers, plumbers, electricians, and boatmen who serve their ritzier near-neighbors.

Lighthouse and beach at Montauk (top left), waterfront at Greenport (bottom left), Brooklyn Heights (middle left), Grand Central Terminal (top right), Chrysler Building (bottom right)

corporate headquarters have moved up from the city—IBM to Armonk and Pepsi to Purchase—bringing with them diversity and displacement. New Rochelle once seemed like a self-contained town (it was the prosaic fictional home of "The Dick Van Dyke Show"). But change overtook it, and its business district experienced a long period of urban-like decay.

In Connecticut, Fairfield County still has the ambience of New England, but feels increasingly like New York's modern Gilded Age, with huge homes, expensive yachts, and inextricable exclusiveness. Nearby in New Jersey, Hudson and Essex Counties are still home to heavy industry, but they also boast distinguished gentrified districts for the upper-middle-class. High-rise apartment buildings that line the Palisades across the Hudson from Manhattan offer an appealingly short commute as well as spectacular views of the city.

Despite the fast pace and constant change that characterize life in Metro New York, some things have stayed the same. There is still Coney Island, for example, whose amusement park, sideshows, and boardwalk offer a kind of nostalgic trip down memory lane, and Fire Island, which still seems remote despite its proximity to the city. What also hasn't changed is the vitality and spirit of New Yorkers, something that F. Scott Fitzgerald captured in a passage from *The Great Gatsby*. The scene was Long Island. The backdrop was old mansions.

Gay young women were surrounded by men in tuxedos, and there were eddies of conversation and splashes of laughter, and corks popped and liquor flowed, and you knew that it was a time that would never come again.

Fitzgerald wrote in the Jazz Age, of which New York was the center. We are past debutante parties and the like, but New York is still the center. And the people who dwell in and around the nation's largest city still live life as they lived it then—as if every moment is important and meaningful, but ultimately a passing fancy to be replaced by something new.

manhattan architecture

For architectural eclecticism, New York is unmatched. It has Georgian manses, Beaux Arts palaces, brownstone town houses, and, somewhere in Manhattan, probably every other kind of architecture known to civilization.

The city has been building and rebuilding for more than 200 years, and frightfully little is left of historic Manhattan. A few examples of Georgian or Federal style remain—mostly in the southernmost (and oldest) reaches of the island—looking small, out of scale, and charming. Best-known among these are City Hall, St. Paul's Chapel, and the Fraunces Tavern block. By the time New York outgrew these old quarters, well into the 1800s, the French-inspired Beaux Arts style was in full flower. The result is that midtown Manhattan's most palatial houses (such as the Frick mansion), museums (the Metropolitan Museum of Art), hotels (the Plaza), and train stations (Grand Central Terminal) have little to do with American architecture but everything to do with New York's grandeur.

Grandeur was still the keynote when the 792-foot (242-m) Woolworth building became the tallest edifice in the world in 1913. Architect Cass Gilbert embellished it with a blanket of Gothic decoration, and its admirers nicknamed it the "Cathedral of Commerce." Still, it does nothing to overshadow an earlier Gothic Revival masterpiece, proud and soaring St.

Patrick's Cathedral (1879–88). More "American" in conception is the Flatiron Building (1903), whose audacious "prow" cuts across the oblique intersection of Fifth Avenue and Broadway.

But if there's a universal image of Manhattan, it is streamlined towers soaring into the sky. The most famous skyscrapers—many of which were built in the 1920s when New York found itself, quite suddenly, at the world's center stage—are nothing if not theatrical. The Chrysler Building looks less like an office tower than a monument, or perhaps the grille of a fancy car. Rockefeller Center was inspired, it seems, by a surging bolt of lightning. And the Empire State Building never looks so good as when it has an airship docked by its side or Godzilla climbing its walls.

The skyscraper tradition continued in post-war New York with the Seagrams Building, by Mies van der Rohe, which might be the world's most elegant international-style glass tower. Lever House, seemingly suspended on stilts over its lot, shows that you can enjoy commercial buildings not just from a distance but from the street below, too. And the Citicorp Center makes its distinct horizontal slice in the sky for no architectural reason except corporate identity, which in New York is a very good reason indeed.

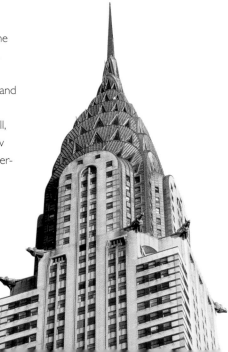

The Mid-Atlantic Coast

Where North Meets South

 **Matinee idols** have never sung romantic ballads about congressmen on the Potomac. The life of a Tilghman Island crabber has never been chronicled in a foot-stomping musical. The Mid-Atlantic Coast does not lend itself to easy characterization. This isn't that kind of region.

Stretching from the foothills of the Appalachians to the Atlantic Ocean, and from northern New Jersey to the southern tip of the Delmarva Peninsula, the Mid-Atlantic Coast is, in a sense, the meeting ground of the North and the South. Its personality incorporates traits of both, sometimes to unusual effect. President John Kennedy once quipped that Washington, D.C., was blessed with Northern charm and Southern efficiency. Maybe so, but the undeniable influence of both North and South has endowed this diminutive region with an importance out of proportion to its size.

The heart of the region, and its greatest resource, is Chesapeake Bay. This broad tidewater basin, which Spanish explorers dubbed "Bay of the Mother of God," attracted many of America's earliest settlers, and the plantations that soon lined its shores represented the New World's earliest commerce. With its countless estuaries and its webs of rivers, the bay served as nothing less than North America's first highway system,

Farm in Sussex County, New Jersey (left); Liberty Bell (below). Preceding pages: Waterfront of St. Michaels, Maryland

philadelphia's
sons and daughters

From its earliest days, Philadelphia has been home to a disproportionate number of the country's greatest and most influential people. In fact, the city's founder, William Penn, was himself a remarkable and visionary man. His ideal of peaceful inclusiveness, strengthened by his own experience of religious persecution and imprisonment as a Quaker, made the "City of Brotherly Love" an oasis of religious toleration that attracted a varied and generally civic-minded group of citizens.

Printer Ben Franklin settled in Philadelphia and helped found the city's first volunteer fire company, library, hospital, college, and learned society. The American Philosophical Society included John Bartram, a self-taught botanist who studied native plants; physician and founder of American psychiatry Benjamin Rush; and clockmaker-turned-astronomer David Rittenhouse, who built the country's first planetarium.

Merchant Robert Morris founded the nation's first bank to help finance the Revolution, and lawyer and diplomat Nicholas Biddle waged war with Andrew Jackson as president of the Second Bank of the United States. John Wanamaker started one of the country's largest department stores, and nickel and steel magnate Joseph Wharton endowed the Wharton School of Business at the University of Pennsylvania.

Portrait painter Charles Willson Peale founded the Pennsylvania Academy of Fine Arts and taught many of his own 17 children there. Feminist Lucretia Mott and her husband, James, made their home an Underground Railroad stop. Paleontologist Edward Drinker Cope made spectacular finds of dinosaur bones in the West.

Wilt Chamberlain was one of the greatest players in the history of professional basketball. For 42 years, Eugene Ormandy conducted the Philadelphia Orchestra.

Thomas Gallaudet, noted educator of the deaf, was born in Philadelphia, as were screen personality W. C. Fields, abstract sculptor Alexander Calder, anthropologist Margaret Mead, linguist Noam Chomsky, entertainer Bill Cosby, and dancer and choreographer Judith Jamison.

allowing the region to play the lucrative role of middleman between the agriculture of the South and the traders of the North. More importantly, the waters of the bay were—and still are—an amazingly rich source of fish, oysters, clams, and crabs.

West of the Tidewater the land rises to the Piedmont Plateau. Here, in the forested foothills of the Appalachians, settlers found the abundant resources—especially lumber and waterpower—that guaranteed successful enterprise. If the Tidewater was a place of landowners and large plantations, the Piedmont became a place of ingenuity and creativity; by the time of the Civil War, Richmond, Virginia, was the Confederacy's most industrialized city.

Distinctions between the Tidewater and the Piedmont are less important now than they were a century ago. Today, a more relevant delineation is that of the region's rural countryside and its urban, densely settled core. Much of the Mid-Atlantic Coast consists of farmland, forests, and wetlands, where the bustle of civilization really does seem to be worlds away. Southern New Jersey, for example, bears little resemblance to the crowded, industrialized northeastern part of the state. First-time visitors are pleasantly surprised to find verdant farms, delightful old coastal towns such as Cape May, and the vast, mysterious realm of swampy forest known as the Pine Barrens, whose reclusive residents shun development and earn their livings by harvesting blueberries and cranberries. Also relatively undeveloped is Maryland's Eastern Shore, which shares the Delmarva Peninsula with Delaware and part of Virginia.

Philadelphia skyline (above); three famous Philadelphians: Ben Franklin, Lucretia Mott, and W. C. Fields (top to bottom left)

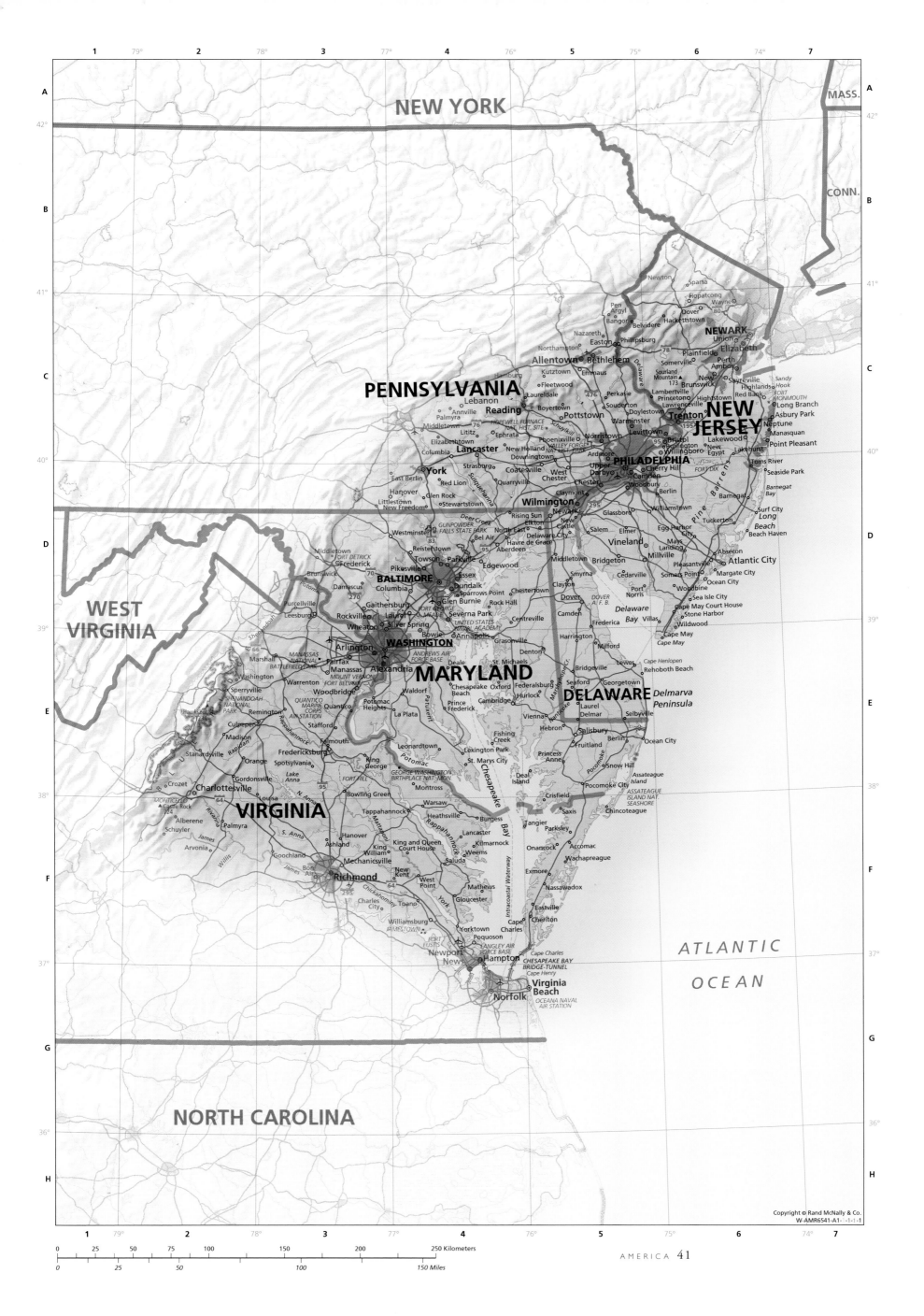

atlantic beach resorts

Less glamorous than the French Riviera and less dramatic than Hawaii's Waikiki, the resort towns of the Mid-Atlantic Coast nevertheless have a charm all their own. With their white sand beaches, cooling ocean breezes, bustling boardwalks, and endless variety of recreational activities, the resorts lure millions of fun-and-sun seekers every summer.

The best-known destination, Atlantic City, is doubly favored by geography: The curve of New Jersey's coast protects it from many of the violent storms that roar down from the northeast, and the warm waters of the Gulf Stream flow close to its shore, keeping air temperatures pleasant through much of the year. Incorporated in 1854, the city thrived for nearly a century before sliding into a slow decline. Its rebirth began in 1977 when New Jersey legalized casino games; today more than a dozen glitzy hotel-casinos line the six-mile (9.5-km) boardwalk, and the city draws 37 million visitors annually.

Some 40 miles (65 km) to the south lies Cape May, the oldest seaside resort in the United States. As early as the 1760s it was a fashionable retreat for wealthy Philadelphians and New Yorkers. Today's visitors are drawn by the town's beautifully restored Victorian homes and buildings, its quaint brick sidewalks, and its four miles (6.5 km) of sparkling beaches.

When the summer heat of Baltimore and Washington becomes unbearable, many residents escape to the Delaware coast. In fact, Rehoboth Beach attracts so many of Washington's legislators and diplomats that it has earned the nickname "the nation's summer capital." The lively nightlife, along with activities such as swimming, sailing, and walking along cherry-tree-lined Rehoboth Avenue, offer a powerful antidote to the pressures of running the country.

Maryland's only seaside resort, Ocean City, stretches for ten miles (16 km) along a narrow barrier peninsula. Its year-round residents number 7,500, but on summer weekends the population often swells to more than 250,000. Among its attractions are excellent deep-sea fishing, two amusement parks, and shops selling the traditional Ocean City souvenir: saltwater taffy.

Despite its proximity to large urban centers, the Shore is still a place of truck and poultry farms, of "watermen" who speak in accents that hark back 300 years to early settlers from England, and of the sublime Blackwater National Wildlife Refuge, proof that this area is serious about preserving what is important.

Legacies of the past do reside in the region's largest cities—Philadelphia, Washington, Baltimore—but they can also be found in many of its smaller cities and towns, in its historic homes, and on its battlefields. A good example is Annapolis, capital of Maryland and site of the renowned U.S. Naval Academy. Founded as Provincetown by Virginia Puritans in 1649, the city has carefully preserved its colonial legacy; it has more pre-Revolutionary brick structures than any other city in the country. To walk through the narrow, twisting streets of the city center is to be transported back in time 200 years.

History comes to life in Williamsburg, Virginia, a restored colonial village of undeniable charm. It may be that the Williamsburg taverns were less savory and museum-like in the old days when the merits of independence were discussed over grog and gruel. And perhaps not all Williamsburg residents were political philosophers at that time. But the symbolism of Williamsburg is strong, especially with the fine brick

Atlantic City (above); Rehoboth Beach (bottom left); Washington, D.C. (top right); Arlington National Cemetery (middle right)

washington, d.c.

In 1783, as the Revolutionary War drew to a close, the fledgling U.S. Congress became embroiled in a prolonged and fractious debate: where to permanently site the country's new capital. Both southern and northern legislators recognized the symbolic prestige associated with the federal city and they undermined efforts to establish it outside their own territories. In June 1790, a deal was struck between Secretary of State Thomas Jefferson from Virginia and Secretary of the Treasury Alexander Hamilton from New York: The federal government would assume the states' war debts (which fell heavily on the north) in exchange for a southern location of the new capital, along the banks of the Potomac.

George Washington, a surveyor by trade, was asked to choose the exact site. In 1791 he settled on a location where the Anacostia River meets the Potomac, incorporating the existing port towns of Alexandria, Virginia, and George-town, Maryland—a central and easily defensible location that he felt held great commercial potential, especially if a canal were built to link the Potomac to the Ohio River.

That year Washington appointed engineer Pierre L'Enfant as the city's designer. L'Enfant's plans envisioned a grid pattern of streets intersected by broad diagonal avenues, bordered by open green spaces and grandiose edifices. For "Congress House," the U.S. Capitol, L'Enfant chose Jenkins Hill, which he called a "pedestal waiting for a monument." George Washington himself chose the site for the "President's House," the White House. L'Enfant's ambitious public scheme rubbed private landowners the wrong way, and he was relieved of his duties after only a year. Happily, much of his scheme was executed in his absence.

Though it grew slowly, Washington, D.C., found prosperity in the economic booms after the Civil War and World War I. Today the city's economy is dominated by the business of governing the nation—fully one-third of its inhabitants are employed by, or work in service to, the federal government.

Washington receives about 21 million visitors a year. Most make pilgrimages to the Smithsonian Institution's museums that flank the Mall—the immense national town square between the Washington Monument and the U.S. Capitol. From the Mall visitors have easy access to the White House and the triad of presidential memorials, beginning with the Washington Monument, at 555 feet (169 m) the tallest masonry structure in the world. Overlooking the Tidal Basin is the Jefferson Memorial, modeled after the Roman Pantheon, and further west stands the Lincoln Memorial, whose massive white colonnade shimmers in the reflecting pool.

Look closely at Washington and you will see a city of contra-dictions—a city built by slave labor that became a bastion of abolitionism, and a city where today homelessness and poverty abut power and privilege. "It is

our national center. It belongs to us," wrote abolitionist Frederick Douglas, "and whether it is mean or majestic, whether arranged in glory or covered with shame, we cannot but share its character and destiny."

CENTRAL WASHINGTON, D.C.

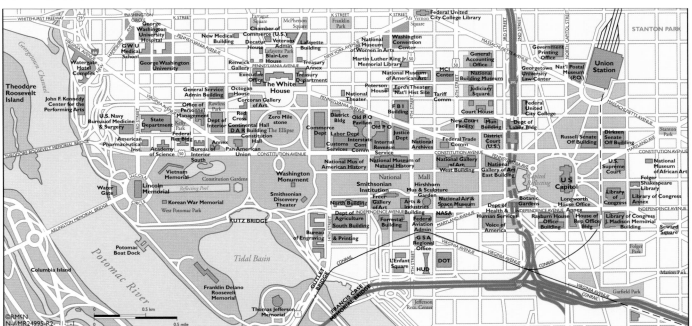

wild ponies
of assateague island

Believed to be the only wild herd of horses east of the Rocky Mountains, hundreds of Chincoteague ponies graze amidst the dunes and salt marshes of Assateague Island, off the Maryland and Virginia coasts.

There are several conflicting theories as to how these domesticated animals ended up on Assateague and reverted to the wild. One asserts that the ponies escaped from the cargo hold of a shipwrecked 16th-

century Spanish galleon and swam ashore. More likely they were turned out on Assateague in the 17th century by mainland owners who wanted to avoid new fencing laws and livestock taxation. Standing approximately 12 to 13 hands high, they are hardy, good-natured, and intelligent animals, with large, soft eyes and tapered muzzles. Their characteristic

bloated look is caused by the high concentration of salt in their diet, which causes them to drink twice as much fresh water as domestic horses.

The "Chincoteague" ponies are named for their annual swim across the channel that separates Assateague from Chincoteague Island. The Chincoteague Volunteer Fire Company rounds up the ponies on Pony Penning Day, the last Wednesday of each July. After their swim, most of the foals are auctioned off on Thursday, and the remaining horses swim back to Assateague on Friday. The auction was designed to preserve local ecology by maintaining the size of each herd at approximately 150 animals.

Popular with local residents and tourists, the ponies didn't gain national attention until Marguerite Henry published her 1947 book, *Misty of Chincoteague*. The heartwarming story catapulted the ponies into the hearts of children everywhere, many of whom raided their piggy banks in 1962 to help relief efforts after a bad storm damaged the island.

House of Burgesses, the colonial legislature where Patrick Henry cried, "Give me liberty or give me death."

Many pivotal figures from the country's early history resided in the Mid-Atlantic Coast region, and their homes are among its most precious treasures. George Washington's home at Mount Vernon still exemplifies the simple and stately values that the first President came to represent. Another shrine, Thomas Jefferson's unique home at Monticello, reflects that President's constant impulse to experiment, as an architect, a gardener, an inventor, and an original thinker.

Numerous Civil War battlefields are scattered across the region, as well. When historical divisions between North and South exploded, it was perhaps inevitable that the Mid-Atlantic Coast, the meeting ground of the two sides, would bear the brunt of the fighting. Fully two-thirds of the battles of the war were fought in Virginia. One of the first serious clashes was at Manassas, close enough to Washington for dignitaries of the city to come out to witness what they thought would be an easy victory for the Union. The first Battle of Bull Run, as it was called, proved otherwise, and the war continued in the Piedmont and the Shenandoah Valley for four long, bloody years. It was also fought on the region's rivers, significantly at Hampton Roads where the *Monitor* and the *Merrimac* battled for control of the critical waterways. And the war

reached a crescendo just outside the region, in Pennsylvania, where the Rebels met the Union army at the little town of Gettysburg.

Like the rest of the country, the Mid-Atlantic Coast has experienced a pronounced rural-to-urban migration in the 20th century, and its population and economic strength have become heavily concentrated in a densely populated corridor that extends from Philadelphia to Washington, encompassing Wilmington, Baltimore, and hundreds of other cities, towns, and suburbs along the way. This 150-mile (240-km) expanse is characterized by nearly unbroken urbanization and development, yet its largest component cities have each managed to retain their unique identities.

Chincoteague Island marsh (top); pony on Assateague Island (far left); Annapolis, Maryland, and its 1772 state capitol (below)

Despite President Kennedy's remark implying that it lacked both charm and efficiency, Washington remains the true center of our nation's patrimony. It is home to great cultural institutions: the Smithsonian, the National Gallery, and the Library of Congress, among others. It is also a lovely place—a city of high vistas and broad avenues, of grand monuments and imposing neoclassical buildings, of cherry blossoms and forested parks—thanks in large part to a careful plan conceived by the engineer Pierre L'Enfant in the early 1800s.

Philadelphia, which was already more than a hundred years old when Washington was founded, is imbued with a rich history that few American cities can rival. It was the home of Benjamin Franklin, printer, inventor, and free spirit of colonial America. At the time of the

chesapeake bay

In 1608, Captain John Smith sailed from the newly settled colony of Jamestown into what he called a "very goodly bay." The Algonquin Indians who inhabited its shores had already named it "Chesepiook," or "great shellfish bay." Now Smith, the first European to completely explore the Chesapeake Bay, encountered an astonishingly abundant habitat writhing with so much life he claimed he could catch fish by merely dipping a skillet in the water. "Heaven and earth," he later wrote, "never agreed better to frame a place for men's habitation."

Four centuries later the Chesapeake's shores and tributaries are home to 13 million people, and this vast and varied ecosystem supports a seafood industry worth over $100 million a year, supplying more than half the blue crabs (100 million pounds or 45 million kg) and clams caught in the United States. Only the Pacific and Atlantic Oceans yield a larger marine harvest.

This "immense protein factory," as author H. L. Mencken once called the Chesapeake, is an estuary, where salty ocean water collides and intermingles with fresh river water, forming an undulating broth of varying salinity that nurtures 2,700 plant and animal species.

For the animals, birds, and marine life that live or visit here, the bay is itself a year-round smorgasbord. In the fall, migrating red-winged blackbirds feast on wild rice in the upper tidal marshes. In winter, extra-low tides expose clam flats to hungry raccoons, and otters harvest killi-fish minnows stranded in shallow water. In spring, copepods, tiny shrimp-like crustaceans, provide a staple diet for larval perch and rockfish as they mature. In summer, sandbar sharks move into the bay to feast on blue crabs. Then in late summer, monarch butterflies en route to the Florida panhandle descend on Chesapeake marshes to feed on milkweed nectar (which renders them poisonous to birds).

During the last Ice Age the Chesapeake Bay was a river valley carved by the Susquehanna River and its tributaries. The valley flooded 20,000 years ago when temperatures and sea level rose, and the advancing Atlantic created a bay 195 miles (315 km) long north to south, and more than 25 miles (40 km) wide at its broadest. The bay's irregular shoreline, comprising a matrix of marshes and coves perforated by 48 tributaries, would stretch 4,000 miles (6,400 km) if straightened out—longer than the U.S. Pacific coast.

The thriving seafood industry drives the local economy, along with shipbuilding and repair, the military, and tourism. Sport-fishing boats ferry into the bay every year some 900,000 anglers who catch ten million pounds (4.5 million kg) of fish. Sailing enthusiasts revere the bay for its benign climate (bay breezes temper the region's steamy summers) and steady winds. Bird-watching is also popular, thanks to the one million waterfowl that alight here.

Over the years, the health of this shallow bay (averaging only 21 feet or 6.5 m deep) has been threatened by excess nutrients (such as phosphates), toxins, and sediment that run off from the tributaries. Due to overharvesting and pollution, the oyster population is now only 1 percent of what it was 100 years ago, and the once-abundant rockfish nearly disappeared before a fishing ban was enacted in 1986. Conservation efforts are just beginning to halt the damage and, potentially, restore the bay to the teeming richness that Captain John Smith observed.

Chesapeake fisherman (top left), Chesapeake Bay Bridge (bottom left), steaming crabs (right), blue crab (bottom right)

Revolutionary War, it was the largest city in the 13 colonies. As the seat of the Continental Congress, it functioned as the capital of the colonies during the war. It was here that the country's two most important documents—the Declaration of Independence and the Constitution—were debated, drafted, and signed. Today, the City of Brotherly Love holds firmly to the past; beneath its modern surface lies a deep resistance to change. Its suburbs are famously insulated, and its "Philadelphia lawyers" still constitute a ruling elite.

Baltimore also boasts a long and proud history. Situated around an excellent natural harbor near the head of Chesapeake Bay, it became an important and prosperous seaport soon after its founding in 1729. While Philadelphia was under British siege during the Revolutionary War, Baltimore served as temporary seat of the Continental Congress. Half a century later, it became the point of origin for the first railroad in the United States, the Baltimore and Ohio. After a devastating fire in 1904, the city was quickly rebuilt, but soon went into a long, slow decline. A dramatic rebirth began to take shape in the 1970s; today, in formerly run-down parts of the city, redevelopment projects represent a triumph of public and private investment. The city's politics are progressive and popular. Its museums and nightlife districts represent a true urban renaissance. The Inner Harbor and Camden Yards baseball stadium—a splendid throwback to the sport's glory days—have revitalized the old city and brought new confidence to the state and the region.

Today, the Mid-Atlantic Coast draws millions of visitors each year. They come to see its battlefields and countless other historical sites. They come to tour its great cities, to fish and sail on its bays, to relax on its beaches. They come to taste its marvelous seafood—especially its famous crab cakes—and to breathe its salty sea air. But in a more general sense, they come to experience the region's unique and charming blend of North and South, city and country, past and present.

crab cakes

To fully appreciate the Maryland crab cake, it is important to appreciate the Maryland crab. The blue crabs that inhabit Chesapeake Bay are properly known as *Callinectus sapidus*, or "beautiful swimmer," for the oddly adept way they propel their tapered bodies forward or backward through the water with their rear legs, or hover in mid-water, legs spinning like rotor blades. The muscles that control these posterior limbs yield the treasured lumps of backfin meat that collectively form the crab cake. And only in the crab cake, according to many Chesapeake Bay natives, do these impeccable morsels of seafood—sweeter and more delicate than lobster, more savory than sole—reach their full culinary potential.

The history of the crab cake dates back to the Native Americans inhabiting the Chesapeake shores, who combined crab meat with corn meal, vegetables, and herbs, and fried them in bear fat. The essential preparation has changed little over the centuries, but the precise recipe for crab cakes varies from region to region and family to family, and can be a source of local pride and even bitter dispute (mustard or red pepper? mayonnaise or egg?).

Besides the crab meat itself, a crab cake contains some combination of breading or sauce or mayonnaise or egg that binds the meat together, along with seasoning (Worcestershire sauce and Old Bay seasoning are common). The patties are traditionally deep fried but can be sautéed or broiled for the health-conscious, and served by themselves or on a bun or, as Baltimoreans prefer, between two saltine crackers.

Maybe Baysiders are so passionate about this delicacy because the tedious effort of excavating the lumps of meat from these small crustacean fortresses, forming the delicate patties, and searing in the moisture and flavor is a labor that only accentuates the reward of a perfect crab cake. And what is the perfect crab cake? An objective Marylander (if you can find one on this subject) will admit that the perfect crab cake is simply the one that leaves you hungry for another.

The Appalachian Mountains

Ancient Mountains, Strong Traditions

The **serene blue** ridgelines and gentle valleys of the 6,000-foot-high (1,800-km) Appalachian Mountains ebb like waves into the hazy distance. In the first days of pioneer settlement, the mystical, ethereal Appalachian ranges, from the Catskills to the Cumberlands, deterred many early explorers from moving westward. Then as now, they sheltered and isolated hardy souls who homesteaded their hollows, helping to preserve strong traditions and create a provincial culture. Their timber, minerals, and arable valleys also fueled the young nation's economy, but did little to alleviate the poverty of people living in the backwoods and highlands, where mining interests extracted—but did not return—prodigious mineral wealth. Though coal production has waned today, the once-isolated communities of the Appalachians have opened themselves to the rest of the United States to meet the challenges of a changing economy without sacrificing the natural beauty of their mountains and valleys.

Raccoons (above); Cades Cove, Tennessee (left). Preceding pages: Clingmans Dome, Great Smoky Mountains National Park

Worn down by weather and by wind, the rolling peaks and valleys belie the rugged nature of the Appalachian Mountains, which stretch 1,600 miles (2,560 km) from Quebec's Gaspé Peninsula south through central New York, Pennsylvania, West Virginia, western Maryland and Virginia, eastern Kentucky, Tennessee, western North and South Carolina, Georgia, and northern Alabama. These are

A waterfall cascades down a lush hillside in Virginia's Shenandoah National Park (above).

ancient mountains, once rivaling the height of the Himalayas but now eroded into relatively low, even ridgelines. The easternmost ranges, including the Blue Ridge, contain the oldest rocks and the highest relief—North Carolina's Mount Mitchell, at 6,681 feet (2,037 m), is the loftiest peak east of the Mississippi River. Farther west lie the Appalachian Plateau and the Alleghenies, carved by the elements into rugged peaks and deep valleys. This terrain defines Appalachia: craggy topography that hides highland communities and rich seams of coal.

The Cherokee were among the first to settle in the hidden nooks and valleys in what are today the states of North Carolina, Tennessee, and Georgia, at least 500 years before Hernando de Soto's Spanish expedition of 1539–40 found them living in log cabins and cultivating maize, beans, and squash. They hunted in the highlands but did not live there, on what they considered sacred ground—mysterious and dangerous. Three centuries later, most were forced from their homes to trudge westward to Oklahoma on the Trail of Tears.

Until the American Revolution, the Appalachians were the American Frontier. Beginning in 1775, however, thousands of settlers—many of them European immigrants—passed through the Cumberland Gap along the Wilderness Road, which would become the most-traveled route of pioneers heading west. German refugees from Europe's Thirty Years' War found homesteads scarce around their coastal ports of entry, and first settled Pennsylvania's fertile Appalachian valleys early in the 1800s. To the north, Dutch settlers put down stakes in the eastern Catskills. They were followed by the Scotch-Irish, who came to America to escape religious and economic persecution and settled in the hollows of the Appalachian Plateau to become what many people derisively

appalachian coal country

Coal has contributed to the Appalachian economy since the mid-18th century, but it wasn't until the Industrial Revolution that mining interests began to exploit the region in earnest. Burgeoning factories and power plants required a resource that burned hotter and more dependably than wood: coal.

Heat and pressure created Appalachian coal from successive layers of lush swamp foliage that decayed between 286 and 360 million years ago. The hard, lustrous-black anthracite of east-central Pennsylvania and southern Virginia is the highest quality coal. It burns with a steady blue flame and is virtually dust- and smoke-free, but it accounts for only two percent of U.S. coal. The intense heat produced by the softer, more plentiful bituminous coal makes it more suitable for producing the coke necessary for steel.

When coal companies set out to acquire Appalachian mineral rights in the late 1800s, they found that the isolated highlanders were fiercely self-sufficient but desperately poor. Their hillside farms were barely productive and they were easily convinced to sell their land at ten to 50 cents an acre (four to 20 cents a hectare).

The people of Appalachia then worked to mine the coal, which was shipped by rail to heat homes and power factories in Midwestern and Eastern cities. For their efforts, mining families were housed in company towns. Scrip—redeemable only at the company store or for company services—was advanced to miners as loans against their wages. Miners endured grueling conditions and lived in constant fear of mine collapses, fires, and the dreaded "black lung" disease. During the late 1930s, the United Mine Workers' successful but bloody campaign to organize the miners improved wages and benefits, but the good times didn't last.

After World War II, union mismanagement, the oil and natural gas boom, and increased strip-mining gutted the deep-mining industry. Mines closed, leaving residents behind in abandoned company towns. Those who didn't migrate to larger cities faced abject poverty on a land poisoned by environmental abuse.

After John F. Kennedy made an issue of their plight in 1960, Appalachian highlanders received relief and benefits. Volunteers came to teach, rebuild towns, and help locals establish businesses.

Today, although parts of the region still suffer poverty and high unemployment, entrepreneurial programs support small businesses and cottage industries. Even the scarred peaks, strip-mined down to bedrock, are being reclaimed. Clean air and water regulations are also beginning to positively impact the highland environment.

COAL DEPOSITS AND PRODUCTION

Current production in million short tons ■ Anthracite □ Bituminous

called "hillbillies." Isolated by geography, they retained much of the music, folkways, and lore of their European forebears, including the string-band music that would evolve into "bluegrass" and the storytelling tradition of "Jack Tales."

The remoteness and isolation of these early communities forced people to rely on raw materials and their own ingenuity to carve necessities—furniture, farm implements, and weapons—from the land around them. This fine crafting tradition of wooden furniture, toys, copper goods, textiles, blown glass, and pottery has become one of the mainstays of the southern Appalachian cottage-industry economy. Today, craft coalitions such as HandMade in America and the Southern Highland Handicraft Guild's Folk Art Center, both in Asheville, North Carolina, support cottage industries and craftspeople.

Corn whiskey, or "moonshine," was also born of economic necessity. The difficulties of transporting whole corn from isolated hardscrabble farms made distillation the most efficient way to bring it to market. So important was moonshine to the regional economy that, when Alexander Hamilton imposed an excise tax on the drink in 1794, highland farmers in Pennsylvania took up arms. President George Washington had to send in troops to put down the Whiskey Rebellion.

Despite mountain poverty, the timber and mineral wealth of the Appalachians gave an early hint of the colonies' economic promise. Farmers cleared vast forests and used the wood to build towns and to fuel the many iron furnaces that dotted the mountains. Iron deposits were discovered and exploited early, but the mountains are also rich in copper, lead, gemstones, salt, granite, marble, and, most notably, coal.

The discovery of coal was both a boon and a bane to the Appalachian highlanders. The mining of vast reserves brought rail and surface roads that connected isolated mining towns to larger cities. The mines employed whole communities, easing their rural poverty. But the coal companies rarely returned any profits to the miners, many of whom worked their whole lives and never received

Coal-filled railcars (top left), the Tennessee Smokies (bottom left), frontiersman Daniel Boone (top right)

an actual paycheck. After World War II, the popularity of oil and gas energy, along with increasing labor and environmental disputes, caused

cumberland gap

Before the late 1700s, the Appalachians seemed an unassailable barrier to westward expansion. Yet deer and bison had been migrating for thousands of years through an 800-foot-deep (242-m) natural pass in the Cumberland Mountains near the point where the boundaries of present-day Virginia, Kentucky, and Tennessee meet. So important was this track to Native Americans, who called it the Warriors Path, that legends tell of numerous tribes battling for its control.

Although others had traversed the gap—named for King George II's son, the duke of Cumberland—Daniel Boone blazed its first official trail. He first crossed it in 1767, and he and a few hunting companions made several trips between 1769 and 1771. Boone's 1773 effort ended after a Cherokee attack killed two in his party, including his son. In 1775, a group of wealthy North Carolina landowners, the Transylvania Company, bought 20 million acres (8.1 million ha)—nearly all of present-day Kentucky and Tennessee—and hired Boone to blaze an official trail through the gap. After a year, Boone and 28 mountaineers had built a road that linked Virginia's Shenandoah Valley to Kentucky, and established a fort, Boonesborough. By 1810 some 200,000 to 300,000 people had traveled west on Boone's Wilderness Road, a moniker adopted in 1796 after the route was widened to accommodate Conestoga wagons. New canal and rail routes across the mountains lessened traffic in the early 1800s, but the gap was still considered a strategic corridor by both sides during the Civil War.

In 1996 the Cumberland Gap Tunnel replaced the treacherous highway, once dubbed "Massacre Mountain," that wound through the gap.

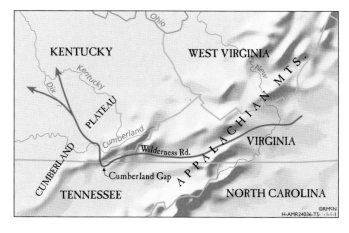

many mines to fold and left behind a shocking economic devastation. The petroleum crisis of the 1970s forced the country to reconsider the benefits Pittsburgh skyline (left), lookout on Virginia's Catawba Mountain (top right), hiker on the Appalachian Trail (center right) of coal energy, and technological advances since then have made coal easier to mine and cleaner to burn. Today, the American coal industry is booming again, although with fewer, more efficient

rebirth of pittsburgh

Founded at the confluence of the Allegheny and Monongahela Rivers, and nestled among hills rich with coal, Pittsburgh was destined to become the heart of America's burgeoning iron and steel industries. As manufacturing grew in the 1800s, workers flocked to western Pennsylvania to stoke furnaces, and the city evolved into an industrial colossus.

Pittsburgh's economy peaked around 1900 as the Industrial Age moved forward, and again during the world wars with the military's voracious demand for steel. Andrew Carnegie and Andrew Mellon made their fortunes in the city, profiting greatly from the labors of the working class. Yet smoke and soot darkened the city during its most productive days, and after World War II rising costs and new domestic and foreign competition crippled the Steel City. Mills shut down, throwing thousands of people out of work as big industry slowly ground to a halt.

City planners worked to attract diversified businesses, revitalize the downtown, and clean up environmental damage from decades of factory waste. Steel production has relocated, but much of the industry's administration still takes place here. The Golden Triangle—as the downtown area is known— is thriving with shops, attractions, and new high-tech and financial services buildings. The legacies of Carnegie and Mellon have helped: Their philanthropic gifts gave this blue-collar town a bounty of metropolitan culture, including the acclaimed Frick, Carnegie, and Andy Warhol Museums, and an abundance of performance halls and parks.

Balancing a small-town heart with big-city amenities, Pittsburgh ranks as one of the most livable U.S. cities. Big business seems to agree: With more than 100 firms based there, Pittsburgh ranks with New York, Chicago, and Los Angeles as a top location for corporate headquarters.

mines in operation. Kentucky and West Virginia follow only Wyoming in coal production, and a concerted effort to replace topsoil and trees lost to strip-mining operations has restored much of the devastated landscape.

Other efforts are being made to balance the region's commercial and ecological interests. Little of the virgin Appalachian forest remains intact, but there are many healthy second- and third-growth forests protected by the National Park and National Forest Services. Each autumn, the ridge forests take on glorious reds, golds, and purples, attracting droves of tourists. Within the forested parklands live black bears, white-tailed deer, raccoons, flying squirrels, bobcats, red-tailed hawks, turkey vultures, and cougars, rejoined recently by river otters, beavers, and red wolves that have been successfully reintroduced.

Although vast tracts of the Appalachian Mountains remain wilderness areas, the region has its share of bustling cities. Native coal and iron made Pittsburgh the steel capital of the world, thanks to Andrew Carnegie, whose mills by 1900 produced more steel than all the mills in Britain combined. Roanoke, Virginia, and Asheville, North Carolina, began as trading and transportation centers, while Wheeling, West Virginia, and Knoxville, Tennessee, served as river ports, later as railroad hubs. As heavy manufacturing and dependence on coal waned, and as the country's economic focus shifted westward, the region's cities declined. But recently, concerted community efforts to attract diversified industries have revitalized cities throughout the Appalachians. Smaller cities, a reasonable cost of living, scenic surroundings, and a relatively mild climate have made the region a popular destination for both retirees and families. Many retirees are jokingly referred to as "half

the appalachian trail

In 1921, conservationist Benton MacKaye had an idea. Why not build a series of community camps throughout the Appalachians, connected by a hiking trail that traversed the entire range? For urban dwellers, it would be a sylvan sanctuary from the concrete jungle, within a day's drive of half the country's population. MacKaye called it a "barbarian utopia."

The camps never materialized, but a few dozen Civilian Conservation Corps volunteers began clearing a trail the following year near Spaulding Mountain in Maine. By 1937, they had connected a 2,155-mile (3,450-km) path from Springer Mountain in Georgia to Mount Katahdin in Maine, known as the Appalachian Trail.

Though MacKaye had designed the trail long enough to seem endless, hiker Earl Schaffer navigated the entire route with road maps and a compass in 1948, becoming the first to trek it end-to-end. More hikers followed, including Emma "Grandma" Gatewood, who completed her first of three through-hikes in 1956 at age 67, wearing high-top sneakers. The invasion had begun.

Until the 1960s most of the Appalachian Trail still passed through private property, and housing developments were encroaching on its boundaries. The trail that was in America's backyard began to look more like a tour of America's backyards. Then, in 1968 the National Trail Systems Act surrounded it with publicly owned land. Today all but 35 miles (56 km) in Maine is on protected land.

The trail attracts between three and four million weekend nature-seekers and long-distance soul-searchers annually. Of the 1,500 adventurers who attempt the entire cross-country pilgrimage every year, only 300 end up completing it. White blazes painted on rocks and trees mark the way, and overnight shelters appear every ten to 12 miles.

Most through-hikers start in Georgia around April 1 to ensure their arrival in Maine by the end of September, before the first snowfall. They begin at the base of Amicalola Falls, which descends in seven cascades to make up the tallest waterfall east of the Rockies. By mid-April they are in the Great Smoky Mountains summitting Clingmans Dome, the highest point on the trail at 6,643 feet (2,025 m). May and June bring hikers through the gaps and peaks of the Nantahala section and several crossings of Virginia's famed Skyline Drive and the Blue Ridge Parkway.

One especially torturous stretch is the Pennsylvania Poconos, where the trail follows a glacial terminus known for its jagged rocks that shake hikers to their treaded soles. Those who persist are treated to a spectacular view at Rausch Gap Shelter, dubbed the "Halfway Hilton." In August hikers pass through the Massachusetts Berkshires in the shadow of Mount Greylock, and by September they reach Maine's 100-Mile Wilderness amidst the multi-hued leaves of fall. At the end they can admire the reflection of Katahdin, the "Great Mountain," in Daicey Pond.

So why do it? For some it's a rite of passage, akin to a Native American spirit quest. For many it's a challenge in which everyday worries are reduced to the primitive essentials, and life is sustained by the contents of a 45-pound (20-kg) pack.

mountain music

Like the landscape that gave it shape and soul, the root music of the southern Appalachians is spare, haunting, and spirited. Shaped by the inward focus of isolated communities and the influence of traditional African American musicians, it is alternately called Appalachian, hillbilly, mountain, or old-time music. Instruments like the fiddle, banjo, mandolin, and dulcimer blend with pitched, harmonized vocals to make its characteristic "high lonesome sound."

The Appalachian sound established its foothold in American musical culture in 1925, when Nashville's Grand Ole Opry radio program began broadcasting nationwide. Its first acts included flamboyant Appalachian fiddler Uncle Jimmy Thompson, Dr. Humphrey Bate and his hell-for-leather string band, and minstrel-influenced banjoist Uncle Dave Macon.

In 1927, a western Virginia mountain family, the Carters, made the first country music recordings at the now-famous Bristol Sessions in Virginia. Their traditional Appalachian material, framed by a guitar and autoharp, typifies music still played in country stores and on porch stoops. Old-time musicians and enthusiasts also pick, pluck, and play throughout the region at festivals such as the Blue Ridge Old-Time Music Week in Mars Hill, NC; Old-Time Week in Asheville, NC; the Appalachian Heritage Festival in Shepardstown, WV; and the Appalachian String Band Festival in Clifftop, WV.

backs": Having originally retired to Florida from northeastern states, they found that they missed the change in seasons and moved "halfway back" to their pre-retirement homes.

The Appalachians provide a scenic backdrop for a wide range of recreational activities. Every year the winding 2,155-mile (3,450-km) Appalachian Trail seduces diehard and novice hikers alike with the promise of pastoral vistas in 13 states—all in direct proportion to the amount of physical exertion expended. For rafters and kayakers, West Virginia's Gauley and New Rivers are popular whitewater streams, attracting paddlers from all over the United States. Virginia's Shenandoah National Park offers one of the country's most spectacular mountain road trips, along Skyline Drive, 105 miles (169 km) of hardwood forests that crest the Blue Ridge Mountains with panoramic views of the Shenandoah Valley.

Another famous road, the Blue Ridge Parkway, winds southwest from Shenandoah along the mountain spine for 469 miles (755 km), flanked by the torrents of waterfalls, masses of woodlands, and hunched foothills rolling ever eastward. The road provides access to more hiking,

camping, and sightseeing opportunities between Waynesboro, Virginia, and Cherokee, North Carolina, one of the gateways to Great Smoky Mountains National Park. The most-visited national park in the United States, Great Smoky Mountains hosts more than nine million visitors each year. Established to protect the region from logging interests, the park preserves more than 500,000 acres (200,000 ha) of cool, wooded mountains cloaked in thick, rain-induced mist. Although light mist falls on most other Appalachian ranges, precipitation in the Smokies is heavier, due to increased rainfall and the fact that cold air from the Atlantic mingles with warmer, damper air over these mountains. The air condenses into a characteristic mist or "smoke" that shrouds the peaks and treetops.

Newfound Gap Road, Great Smoky Mountains (above); claw-hammer banjo (left); mill at Babcock State Park, Virginia (below)

A region of ancient landforms and long-lived historical traditions, the Appalachians are being redefined through the efforts of hardy people who live in their valleys and amidst their peaks, proud of their mountain heritage, economic resources, and even the isolation that gives the Appalachian Mountains their mystique.

The Coastal Southeast

Endless Sunshine, Gracious Living

 **Sun-drenched** skies reign in the Coastal Southeast, over beaches gently massaged by the soft rhythmic *swoosh* of waves wielding the power to soothe. Trickles of light filter through dense forest canopies, heating soggy swamps and glades while nourishing miles of citrus groves down the road. Through the winter, sunshine endures, warming the hearts and homes of retirees who have escaped cold weather in the north, and enticing thousands of families to vacation at Disney World, Epcot Center, Busch Gardens, Sea World, and in coastal beach communities. The Coastal Southeast issues a call to relax. Everywhere you look here, there's someone or something reminding you to slow down, kick back, look around.

Buoyed by the mild climate, residents have developed a warm laid-back charm, bred by hundreds of years of gracious, easygoing living. They revel in the genteel traditions of the southern United States, even while they tolerate the annual invasion of vacationing college students and families. Having successfully rebuilt their devastated towns after the Civil War, Coastal Southeasterners now turn to the stewardship of the land that boasts many of America's most popular vacation and retirement destinations.

Beginning in southeastern Virginia, the Coastal Southeast sweeps southward to take in eastern North Carolina, all of South Carolina except the far northwest corner, central and

The Florida Keys (left), Hilton Head Island (below). Preceding pages: cypress gardens in Charleston, South Carolina

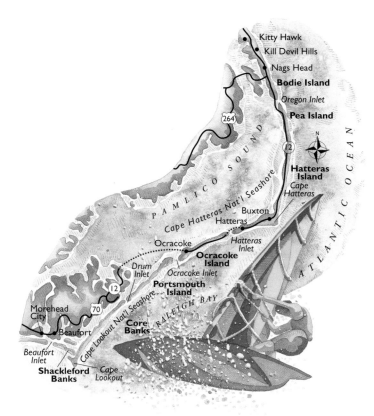

the outer banks

The pirate Blackbeard had little luck concealing his tall ship among these North Carolina barrier islands where he was captured and killed. Flat except for sand dunes, the Outer Banks comprise 150 miles (240 km) of low islands and sandspits barely a mile (1.6 km) wide, along with beaches, mud flats, salt marshes, and ponds populated by great blue herons.

A product of the Ice Ages, the tidal sounds separating the Outer Banks from the mainland were carved and filled as glacial meltwater penetrated the coastal lowlands. Today most of the barrier islands lie 20 to 30 miles (32 to 48 km) out in the Atlantic Ocean and are protected as part of two national seashores: Cape Hatteras (which covers Hatteras, Ocracoke, and the southern tip of Bodie Island) and Cape Lookout (which includes the islands of Portsmouth, Core Banks, and Shackleford Banks).

A prime recreation spot for the sun-and-surf set, the Outer Banks are a popular venue for beach camping, bird-watching, and windsurfing Pamlico Sound or oceanside breaks. Fishing is a major pastime—either surf-casting the island inlets for red drum and bluefish, or deep-sea fishing for marlin and mackerel. Colorful hang gliders dot the sand dunes outside Nags Head. Hikers and walkers scale Jockey's Ridge, at 138 feet (41 m) the highest coastal sand dune on the Atlantic coast, or climb 268 steps up the country's tallest lighthouse at Cape Hatteras. The view from the top surveys the Graveyard of the Atlantic, where warm Gulf Stream waters from the south meet the North Atlantic Current in waves powerful enough to sink nearly a thousand ships, including the Union warship *Monitor* and a Nazi U-85 submarine.

Tourist towns include Nags Head, full of old hotels with wraparound porches; Kitty Hawk, home of the Wright Brothers; and Kill Devil Hills, where Wilbur and Orville successfully landed their airplane in 1903.

eastern Georgia, and Florida except for its panhandle. Bounded on the east by the Atlantic Ocean, it extends west to Florida's Gulf Coast and to where the foothills of the Piedmont Plateau give way to the Appalachians. A narrow carpet of white sand runs the length of the coast, blending into the fertile soil of the Atlantic Coastal Plain, which stretches inland for approximately 100 miles (160 km). The rugged Piedmont rises west of the plain, beginning at the fall line. Here, rushing streams from the plateau slice deeply into the plain's soft soil, transporting crystalline rock particles over lines of rapids. Because rough water prevented further navigation upstream and provided a source of power, fall line locations were destined to attract colonists in the early 17th and 18th centuries. Many of the region's great cities, including Richmond, Virginia; Raleigh, North Carolina; and Columbia, South Carolina, were sited to capitalize on these natural advantages.

The landscapes along water's edge are difficult to generalize. Off the Virginia and North Carolina coasts, the Outer Banks barrier islands defend the mainland against unruly ocean swells and squalls. Visitors flock to explore their deep inlets and secluded coves, and to admire the stalwart network of lighthouses that has guided many a ship to safety; the wrecks of less fortunate vessels rest beneath the swirling confluence of currents. South Carolina's coast contrasts glitzy seaside attractions on Myrtle Beach and the rest of the "Grand Strand" with more sedate, tree-lined beaches on Hilton Head Island. All of Georgia's beaches are in the public domain, a holdover from an old Native American tradition to preserve the land for future generations. And in Florida, beaches are the state's hallmark. In many places the constant lapping of tides has overlaid the sand with a glistening rim of white scallop and conch shells. Hotels and resorts tower over palm-fringed beaches, hosting more and more people who come here to while away their summers—and winters.

Swamps and marshes are also very prominent features of the coastal landscape. The best known swamp is the Florida Everglades, a 50-mile-

The Cape Lookout lighthouse (bottom left) on North Carolina's Outer Banks rises 163 feet (49 m) above the sandy dunes.

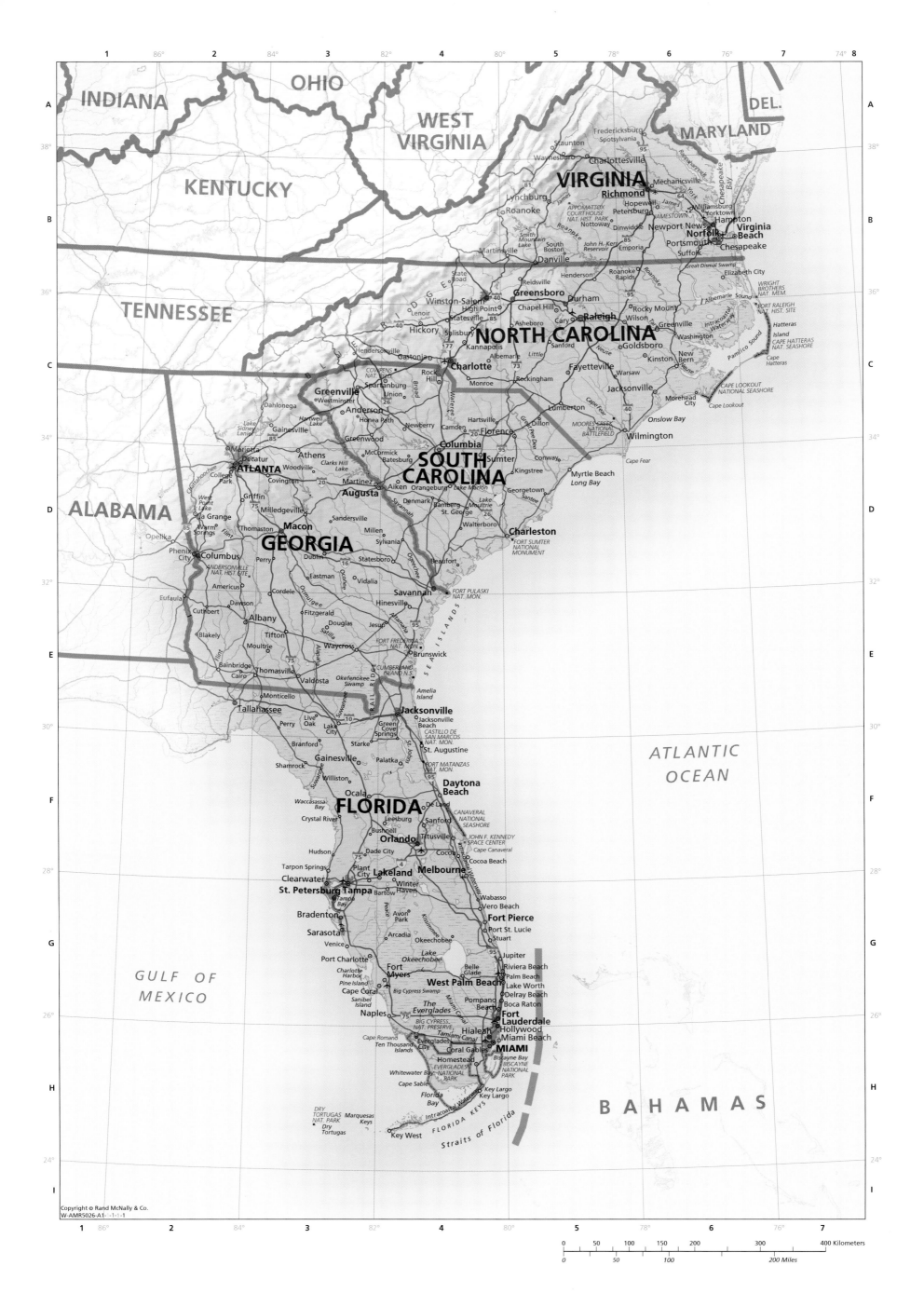

miami, fountain of youth

Miami, Florida, is a dynamic, lively city that continually reinvents itself with youthful vigor, aided by its everchanging multinational array of residents. It sizzles with heat, with activity, and with sophistication.

Along its newly cemented streets, melon, mint, lavender, and pink buildings dazzle the eye. The aromas of expensive perfume and Cuban coffee fill the air. Whimsical skyscrapers and swaying palm trees alternate on the horizon. Mambo and merengue rhythms blend with hip-hop music, reggae beats, and police sirens. Late night club-hoppers crowd the streets. Daytime sun worshippers fill the beaches. With an ethnically and economically diverse

population of more than three million people, Miami pulsates with energy.

This energy defies its languid setting. Sprawled along the southeastern tip of the Florida peninsula, Miami is bounded by Biscayne Bay and the Atlantic Ocean to the east, Everglades National Park to the west, the Florida Keys to the south, and Broward County to the north. It began as a swamp, but railroad access in 1896 transformed it into a tropical haven for tourists, transplanted Northerners, and the very rich. Miami and Miami Beach, its oceanside neighbor, roared into the 1920s—until a devastating 1926 hurricane killed 100 people and flattened hundreds of housing developments. The Great Depression followed fast on the heels of the rebuilding effort, disrupting the economy until World War II.

After the war, retirees, servicemen, and vacationing families, anxious to revel in sun and relaxation, flocked to south Florida, and Miami's fortunes improved. Fidel Castro's 1959 rise to power in Cuba spurred another massive human influx: Cuban refugees who escaped to Miami by the boatload. Immigrants from Latin America

and the Caribbean followed, straining the city's municipal and economic resources. Ethnic tensions flared as immigrants and Anglos competed for the same jobs, and the economy took a nosedive.

Again Miami rallied. Buoyed by an increasing number of Cuban professionals who immigrated during the late 1960s, and by the establishment of the Miami Dolphins professional football team, the local economy improved. By the 1970s, Miami's harbor had become the largest cruise ship port in the world, and in the 1980s a $3-billion building boom transformed the downtown area with glass skyscrapers and other striking examples of modern architecture. Miami Beach's transformation from a crumbling art deco district into South Beach, America's ultra-hip Riviera, lured the rich and famous from all over the world.

More now than ever, Miami is the U.S. gateway to Latin America. The Port of Miami handles more than one-third of all U.S. trade with Central and South America, and 42 percent of all trade with the Caribbean. The city's tourism and high fashion industries, thriving manufacturing operations, and position as an international financial corporate center have helped Miami deal with overcoming an illegal drug trade.

More than half its vibrant population is of Hispanic descent, and Latinos from Cuba, Mexico, Nicaragua, El Salvador, Honduras, Colombia, and Peru— as well as Caribbean natives— distinguish themselves as business and community leaders. Today, Miami is one of the country's most international cities, with a plethora of ethnic restaurants and cultural festivals.

Hotel facades (left) along the famed sands of Miami's South Beach (center), preening flamingo (bottom left)

wide (80-km) "river of grass" that flows from Lake Okeechobee south to the Gulf of Mexico. Everglades National Park contains one million acres (400,000 ha) of land and more than 500,000 acres (200,000 ha) of coastal water and low islands. Travelers who venture into the Everglades encounter an environment so remote that this place is considered by some to be the last real American frontier. Those who penetrate the interior, armed with insect repellent and waterproof boots, observe a heady blend of subtropical and temperate life forms. Much of the Everglades' flora and fauna is native to continental North America, but nonnative species, carried north from the Caribbean, also wriggle and wade in tangled roots and murky water. Farther north, Georgia's delicate Okefenokee National Wildlife Refuge and Wilderness Area is a maze of burnished waterways, cypress roots anchoring floating islands, and trees draped with lacy Spanish moss.

Native Americans from northern North America came to the Coastal Southeast in pursuit of big game, joining Caribbean migrants who were already settled in the region. The Seminole, Timucua, Yamasee, Creek, Catawba, and Tuscarora tribes hunted, fished, and farmed here for several thousand years prior to the arrival of the first European, Spanish adventurer Juan Ponce de León. His 1513 landing in Florida piqued European interest in exploration and settlement. Although Ponce de León found neither the gold nor the famed Fountain of Youth that he had expected, the Spanish wasted no time in founding St. Augustine—now the country's oldest continually inhabited European settlement—in 1565. Abundant sunshine and water, dry autumns, and a long growing season proved to be ideal conditions for citrus fruit and sugarcane. Cotton, tobacco, and rice followed. As the Spanish pushed northward, English plantation owners bore down from the Virginia Tidewater region, anxious to profit from the land.

Centuries later, the Civil War brought ruin to the Confederacy, but it set the stage for an economic rebirth. The Coastal Southeast couldn't compete head-on with a highly industrialized North, but it capitalized

MOST INTENSE COASTAL SOUTHEAST HURRICANES SINCE 1900

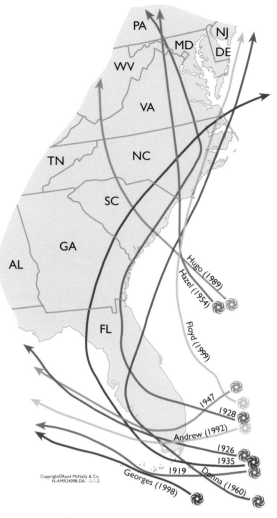

the hurricane coast

There is old mariner's poem about the Atlantic hurricane season: *June too soon/July stand by/August look out you must/September remember/October all over.* These are words to live by in the Coastal Southeast, where hurricanes wreak more havoc than in any other region. Florida is most often hit, with nearly 60 hurricanes this century, but a typical hurricane originating in the Caribbean often wallops other southeastern states, too.

A hurricane's destructive force comes from strong winds that swirl around a calm low pressure center known as the "eye." The "eye" develops when warm, humid air in equatorial latitudes is lifted by denser, colder air, creating an updraft. When wind speeds reach 74 miles (118 km) per hour, tropical storms become hurricanes.

Hurricanes fall into one of five categories. A Category 5, with winds of more than 156 miles (250 km) per hour and an 18-foot (5.5-m) surge, is more than enough to destroy homes, flip cars, flatten trees, and kill people. Even a Category 1, with

winds half that velocity, can cause extensive damage. Hurricane Andrew, which hit south Florida in 1992 and became the costliest disaster in U.S. history ($26.5 billion), was a Category 4.

Sophisticated tracking systems monitor approaching hurricanes, and usually provide ample time for safeguarding and evacuation. Residents in the path of the storm shut off electricity, gas, and water; board up windows, or at the very least crisscross them with duct tape; stock up on bottled water, flashlights, and portable radios; and, if necessary, retreat inland to shelter. At a hurricane's landfall, wind-driven rainstorms batter buildings, rip off roofs, and heap boats like driftwood. A surge of water often floods low-lying areas.

Coastal residents stay on high alert throughout hurricane season, which runs from June 1 through November 1. The U.S. Weather Service identifies hurricanes by proper names, alternating by gender and progressing alphabetically through a predetermined list.

handsomely on its natural advantage: sunshine. Ironically, it was a northern developer named Henry Morrison Flagler who recognized this opportunity.

Alligators, manatee, and great white egret (top to bottom left), one of the drier sections of the Florida Everglades (right)

Flagler built the first Palm Beach hotels in the late 1880s and stimulated the growth of Miami by building streets and developing water and power systems; he also extended rail lines to Key West by 1912. Beginning in the 1920s, Florida and the Southeast boomed, and the population soared over the next several decades. Since then, the region has become a retirement capital: Almost 20 percent of Floridians are over age 65, and retirees congregate in communities such as Palm Beach, Miami Beach, Naples, and Venice.

New arrivals to the Coastal Southeast contribute to a kaleidoscope of ages, ethnic backgrounds, and lifestyles. The region's traditional mix of Anglos and African Americans—descendants from the thousands brought from Africa to toil on plantations—has been supplemented by a large infusion of Hispanics, beginning with the mass Cuban exodus in the late 1950s. Miami has emerged as the gateway city to Latin America, vitally important considering that Hispanics make up more than 12 percent of the U.S. population. Miami's bilingual business community has forged strong ties to Central and South America, and throughout Florida Spanish can be heard in many places with the same, if not a higher, frequency than English.

The benevolent climate benefits industry and trade in the Coastal Southeast. NASA's space shuttles blast off from Florida's Cape Canaveral because the mild weather maximizes windows of opportunity for rocket launches. Professionals from around the country have flocked to high-level finance, management, and research jobs in North Carolina's Triad (Greensboro/Winston-Salem/High Point) and Research Triangle (Raleigh/Durham/Chapel Hill), transforming quiet "down-home" towns into bedroom communities. And the influx of sunseeking retirees provides new clientele for the real estate, banking, and insurance industries, as well as hospitals and assisted-living communities. Agriculture also thrives, as the subtropical climate pampers scores of finicky and fragile plants. Hurricanes and subsequent flooding are the only weather downsides.

swamp and glade life

The Coastal Southeastern wetlands harbor an amazing abundance of animal life. A single Everglades species, the Florida tree snail, occurs in more than 50 varieties, each with its own distinctive bands of color spiralling around its two-inch (five-cm) shell. Twenty-two kinds of frogs share the Okefenokee with 37 snake species, including several poisonous ones: cottonmouths, coral snakes, and three kinds of rattlers. Many swamp-dwellers—white-tailed deer, red-winged blackbirds, alligator snapping turtles, and mosquitoes, to name a few—are also at home in other habitats. But the American alligator and the white ibis are found nowhere else in the United States, and the endangered American crocodile, Florida panther, and Eastern indigo snake exist nowhere else in the world.

These warm wetlands, with islands of trees for nesting, reedy shallows teeming with fish, and heavy air swarming with insects, attract spectacular wading birds: glossy ibis, roseate spoonbills, limpkins, egrets, all kinds of herons—great blue, little blue, green, and black- and yellow-

crowned night herons. Wood storks dredge the watery prairies with their curved bluish beaks, feeding by touch. Their fish-snapping speed: 1/25,000 of a second. Anhinga dive and swim with all but their snaky necks and heads submerged. Some birds such as the snowy egret, once hunted for its feathers, are rebounding from near-extinction. Others, like the wood stork and the crested caracara, still have dangerously small populations.

Tidal mangrove forests provide nesting grounds for brown pelicans, cormorants, crocodiles, and leatherback turtles. Huge tarpon and seagoing green turtles feed offshore; throngs of fiddler crabs sidestep the water's edge. Rotund West Indian manatees, weighing up to 1,500 pounds (675 kg), their backs often scarred by pro-pellers, calve in the mangrove bays and winter in the warm springs of Florida's Crystal River. Legend has it that these gentle sea cows, despite their wrinkled, whiskered faces, were mistaken for New World mermaids by sea-weary sailors.

agriculture of the southeast

Freshly squeezed orange juice and grapefruit slices. Pecan or sweet potato pie. Chicken or ham salad. Peanut soup. These are a few examples of the traditional culinary delights made from raw materials grown in the Southeast, all from the bounty of a flourishing regional agribusiness. No longer dependent solely on tobacco and cotton, the Southeast has diversified its agriculture to lead the country in production of many cash crops.

Surprisingly, some are more often associated with central California and the Midwest.

Because citrus fruits are easily damaged by frost, Florida's mild winters have propelled it to the epicenter of the U.S. citrus industry. Orange trees were first planted in the late 1500s, but production really took off in the 1950s, in response to demand from northern cities for winter fruit. Today, the state produces approximately three-fourths of U.S.-grown oranges and grapefruits. Its other products include sugarcane, tomatoes, potatoes, bell peppers, cucumbers, and walnuts, as well as catfish, hogs, honey, sheep, broilers (chickens), milk, eggs, and cabbage.

Agriculture is Georgia's largest industry, generating more than $46 billion annually. Central and southern Georgia yields the three Ps—peanuts, pecans, and

peaches—the latter of which has earned Georgia the nickname "The Peach State." In addition to these, Georgia produces grapes, blueberries, apples, onions, and watermelons. Tobacco, sorghum, hay, and small grains also figure prominently into the state's agricultural output.

South Carolina rivals Georgia with its own peach production, claiming that it grows the sweetest, juiciest peaches in the Southeast. Pecans, soybeans, corn, wheat, cotton, oats, and apples are also grown here, but tobacco is the number one cash crop. Broilers, cattle, turkeys, and hogs are important, too.

Agriculture is also a primary economic activity in North Carolina, which leads the country in the production of tobacco, turkeys, and sweet potatoes, and ranks just second in hogs, trout, and Christmas trees.

On the coastal plains of North Carolina and Virginia, tobacco has ruled since the colonial era: Virginia harvests two-thirds of the U.S. crop of flue-cured tobacco, and in North Carolina the city of Winston-Salem—the center of the country's tobacco processing operations—is home to long-time growers such as R.J. Reynolds. Along with other traditional crops of cotton and peanuts, Virginia also produces a wide variety of vegetables and dairy products; poultry production is the state's top agricultural enterprise.

Antebellum homes in Charleston, South Carolina (above); tobacco field and cotton plant (bottom left); Drayton Hall (right)

In southern Florida, where the lion's share of traveling vacationers go, the average January temperature is 72 degrees Fahrenheit (22 degrees C), some 40 degrees warmer than New York City. Visitors coated with sunscreen laze away their days sprawled across brightly colored beach towels. To escape oppressive heat, they often retreat to shaded verandas and wraparound porches—a tradition inherited from antebellum times.

For residents and vacationers alike, outdoor activities and amenities are abundant. Anglers can head to the Outer Banks in search of bluefish or blue marlin, or to the Florida Keys, where they can cast a line in either the Atlantic Ocean or the Gulf of Mexico. Other popular sports include stock-car racing, tennis, swimming, and windsurfing. And then there's golf. Prime venues include the PGA National Golf Club in Florida, North Carolina's Pinehurst Resort and Tanglewood Park, South Carolina's Kiawah Island Resort and Sandpiper Bay (where alligators add to the excitement of the game), and Georgia's famed Augusta National Golf Club—home of the annual Masters' Tournament. Even these storied greens embody the Coastal Southeast's relaxed pace: Tough Bermuda grass slows the speed of a putt.

antebellum architecture

Wealthy planters who came to the Coastal Southeast sought to create a world of unmatched civility and splendor. In architecture, they largely succeeded.

Antebellum—or pre-Civil War—architecture arrived from England, where the Georgian style was popular. One classic structure is South Carolina's Drayton Hall (1738): Square, symmetrical, and stately, it resembles neoclassical buildings from the Italian Palladio.

Although antebellum architecture retained a European character, it also incorporated local touches. South Carolinians flocked from steamy plantations to breezy Charleston, where they built Georgian-style homes. To conserve space near the harbor, the typical Charleston town house was turned 45 degrees, with its narrow side facing the street and the long side facing a narrow garden. A long porch, or "piazza," often faced the garden, positioned for shade and breeze.

Architecture in the late 1700s turned to the Federal style, strongly influenced by the archaeological discoveries of Pompeii and Herculaneum. Oval rooms and curving staircases became the rage, along with dramatic vaults, plaster niches, and ornate decorations. Architecture also adopted a new delicacy and grace. In Georgia, it flowered on the leafy squares that punctuate old Savannah's grid-like city plan.

Antebellum architecture evolved courtesy of migrating architects from New England (the restrained Puritans were less-than-ideal clients). After the War of 1812, U.S. tastes for the monumental and "democratic" spawned the Greek Revival. This style produced the pillars and porticoes of Southern courthouses and mansions. Thus grew the use of Corinthian and Doric orders, stately pediments, and, with an inspired draftsman, the proportions of a fine Greek temple—the most enduring representation of the antebellum house.

The South

Something Old, Something New

Since the **tumultuous days** of Reconstruction, journalists have been writing about the "New South." But for 100 years, efforts to modernize the region were agonizing and slow. It wasn't until the second half of the 20th century that promises of change were accompanied by real progress. And as if the time had simply come, the region developed with encouraging speed, spawning high-tech industries and a black middle class, among other evidence of the modern world—even a major "capital," Atlanta.

The New South joined the American mainstream. The Old South was dead and buried, or so it was thought. But it turns out that the Old South did not die, and today it rises up with increasing frequency to inform the rest of the world that it's surviving quite nicely, thank you. It survives in down-home cooking, in genteel manners and traditions, and in the doleful music of Cajun Louisiana, now well-known and fashionable almost to a fault. Old-time religion, Bible-thumping and God-fearing, has made a comeback. All signs point to an unmistakable message: The Old South provides a powerful antidote to the stresses of modern life.

In terms of geography, the South is roughly square in shape. It encompasses Louisiana, Arkansas, Mississippi, and Alabama, as well as the western two-thirds of Kentucky and Tennessee, the southern third of Missouri, the western edge of Georgia, and the panhandle of Florida. Despite common perceptions, the region exhibits

Sandstone cliff in Arkansas' Petit Jean State Park (left), magnolia blossoms (right). Preceding pages: Mississippi Delta in Louisiana

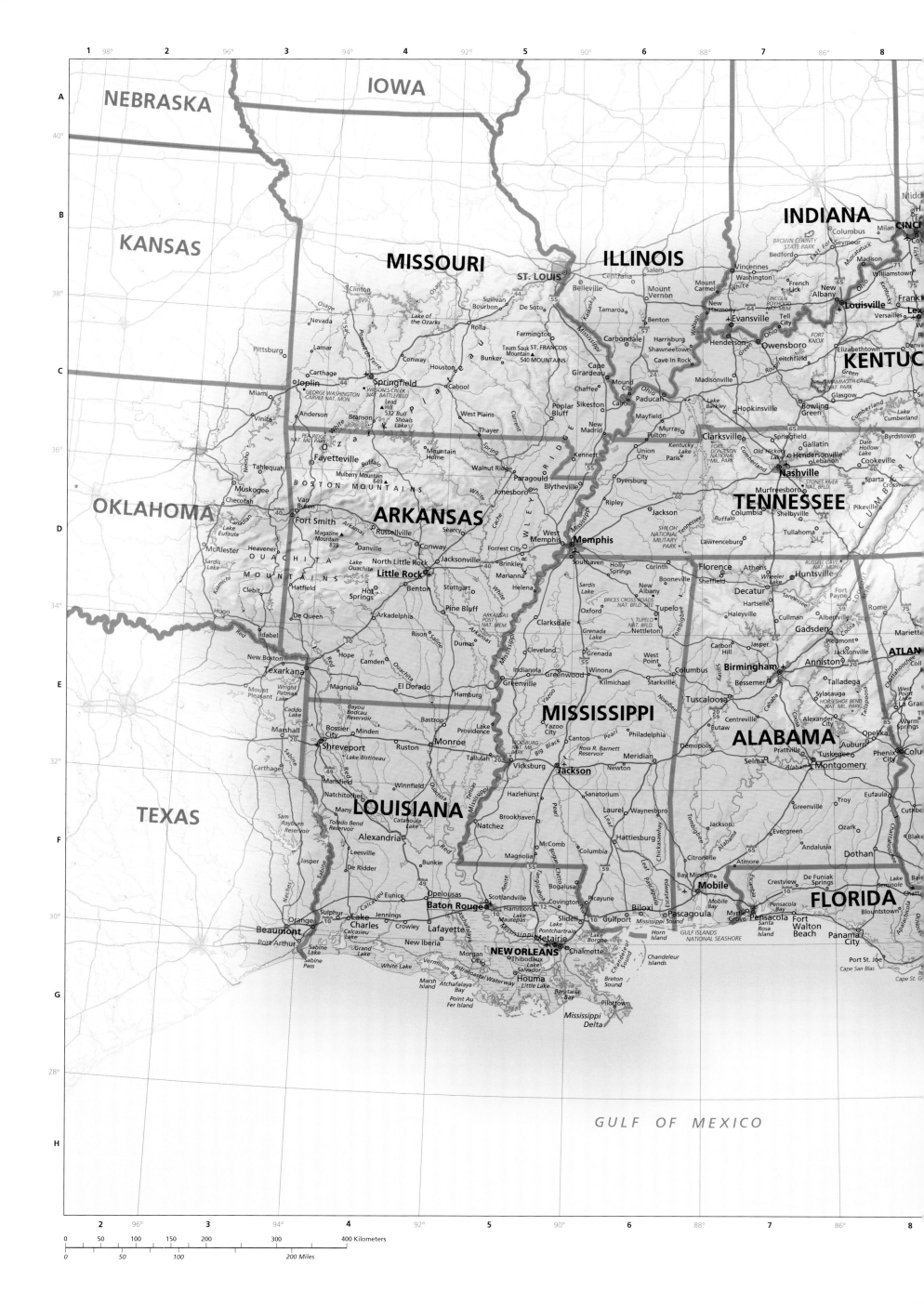

striking beauty and contrast. Its terrain varies from the extreme flatness of the Mississippi Delta to the

Charming old French buildings with elegant wrought iron railings grace a quiet corner of New Orleans' French Quarter (above).

gentle undulations of the Gulf Coastal Plain to the highlands and mountains of the Ozark Plateau and the southern end of the Appalachian range. Forests of pine and mixed hardwoods cover much of the region, but fertile lowlands have long since been cleared for farming; the Delta and the "Black Belt," an east-west swath of Alabama and Mississippi known for its rich dark soil, are among the most intensively cultivated areas in the world.

The South encompasses such divergent subregions as the haunting bayou country of Louisiana, the pastoral bluegrass region of Kentucky, and the sometimes tawdry "Redneck Riviera" of the Florida panhandle. It has quiet antebellum towns like Port Gibson, Mississippi—which escaped destruction during the Civil War when General Ulysses S. Grant declared it "too beautiful to burn"—and thriving modern cities like Atlanta, Memphis, Nashville, New Orleans, Birmingham, and Little Rock. In contrast to its plantation-dominated economy of the 19th century, the region today boasts diverse service industries, manufacturing (including chemicals, automobiles, and petroleum products), forest products, mixed agriculture (soybeans, rice, cotton, peanuts, hogs, and chickens), tourism, and commercial fishing.

Travel deep into the fabric of this Southern heartland, though, Great Blue Heron among cypresses in a Tennessee wetland (left), Mississippi River at Natchez (top right) and Vicksburg (center right) and vivid reminders of the past are everywhere: hope-filled rhythms of gospel choirs, stately white houses surrounded by ancient live oaks dripping Spanish moss, the deliberate articulation of incalculably clever politicians. Northern writers, and even Southern ones, once preferred to write about the South as a foreign country, which perhaps it once seemed to be. But

what enchanted them and continues to enchant visitors are these endless links to a stable and unchanging world.

Tradition is what sets the South apart and what attracts the rest of the world to a place that seems gentle in its ambition and its pace. The music, the manners, the "moonlight and magnolias," to use a well-worn phrase, are natural resources of the South. They survive for many reasons, but most of all for their immutable power to soothe, a strength on which the South has needed to draw at various points in its history. Indeed, the region has borne more than its share of blights, tragedies, feuds, and battles. Its history has seen the vagaries of nature (the economy was once largely agricultural and thus vulnerable to weather's caprices) and the hardships of memory (the Civil War remains deep in the psyche). The comforts of tradition don't erase wounds or insecurities, but they help make the aches tolerable and life, perhaps, more meaningful.

This sense of tradition is frequently accompanied by an abiding belief in the importance of small rituals—long evenings on the front porch, courtly manners even at the supermarket— which represent a powerful contribution to American life. These traditions are simple gifts which reflect the culture of small town life, still the dominant influence in the South. In this environment, family is the defining institution. "Who's your daddy?" is often the first thing a "good ol' boy" asks a new acquaintance. In many places, the formalities of "Mr." and "Mrs." and "Miss," of "ma'am" and "sir," are observed well beyond what is customary in other parts of the country. In fact, the state of Louisiana has codified this tradition: A newly passed law requires students to use these titles when addressing their teachers.

Other rituals of the South are more public and often more raucous, but no less embedded in the traditionalism of the Southern heartland. Mardi Gras, for instance, is conducted each spring in New Orleans and other places throughout the region. It's a time for excessive behavior, masks

old man river

The Mississippi River has long been the economic lifeline of the South. But it is a capricious and tempestuous natural resource, regularly confounding and visiting destruction upon those who live near its banks.

The Mississippi changes markedly in character as it flows into the South, as if recognizing that it is entering a new region. After following a generally straight course from its Minnesota headwaters, the river suddenly begins to loop and meander and generally give the impression that it is in no hurry at all to reach the Gulf of Mexico.

The point at which this change occurs—below the confluence of the Ohio River at Cairo, Illinois—marks the beginning of the Mississippi Delta. This broad alluvial plain,

as much as 80 miles (130 km) wide at some points, stretches southward 1,000 miles (1,600 km) to the Gulf.

Floods are a natural and common occurrence in the Delta. But in the last 200 years, as farms and cities and industry have sprung up along the river, the consequences of flooding have become increasingly disastrous, and efforts to control the river increasingly elaborate. Today, from Cape Girardeau, Missouri, just north of Cairo, down through New Orleans, the powerful stream is walled in by a complex system of levees. (The levees are not, of course, fail-safe: Severe floods in 1993 broke through at numerous points along the river's course.) In many places, articulated concrete mats have been laid in the river bed to keep surging water from further scouring its bed; strategically placed jetties redirect the current into midstream where necessary.

The Mississippi also has a tendency to change its course altogether: As silt accumulation raises its bed, the

river constantly seeks a steeper route to the sea. Prior to settling into its current course approximately 700 years ago, the lower Mississippi shifted its channel three times within the past 4,000 years, reaching the Gulf through outlets that geologists identify as the Teche, Lafourche, and St. Bernard.

Toward the middle of the 20th century, it became clear that the Mississippi was planning to change course again. From a point near Simmesport, Louisiana, the Atchafalaya River began to "capture" more and more of the Mississippi's flow. Experts predicted that within a few decades New Orleans and Baton Rouge would be left high and dry—river cities with no river. To prevent the unthinkable, the Army Corps of Engineers built massive control structures across the outlets to the Atchafalaya. Still, many experts predict that sooner or later the Mighty Mississippi will find a way to go where it wants to go.

THE LOWER MISSISSIPPI

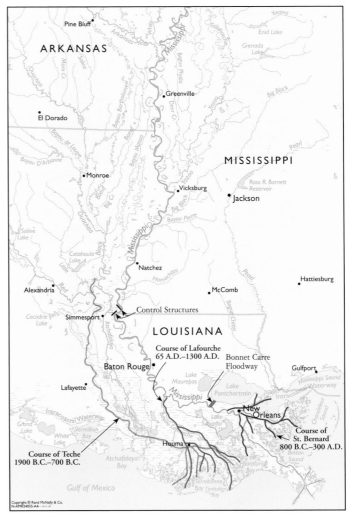

that conceal identity, and ritualistic merrymaking. However, the deeper impulse behind Mardi Gras is not its licentiousness, but the important

Southern fried chicken (left), horses grazing in the peaceful pastures of Kentucky's Calumet Farms (top right)

fact that the balls, parades, and drinking represent an opportunity to break rules in the last days before the strict observance of Lent.

Many Southern traditions have long histories, but nowhere is the sense of the past quite as pervasive as it is in Natchez, Mississippi. Natchez was once the riverfront home of wealthy growers. Today, splendid houses have been preserved not only as museums, but also as homes where real families still live and dine and socialize in ways that recall the antebellum era. Tourists flock to Natchez year-round to absorb the history and ambience, but especially in the spring when the trees are flowering and the mansions have been turned out for a new season.

Another glimpse of history can be seen not far from Natchez, at the great Civil War battlefield of Vicksburg. Today, the site of this long siege is a sweeping national park. But amidst quiet roads and solemn monuments, the place evokes vividly the sounds and the even smells of cannon bursts and awful melees of battle. It draws tourists by the thousands, of course, so many that it is easy to overlook a simple question: Why should the South, and the country at large, maintain such an elaborate interest in so distant a war? The answer lies in the nature and intensity of the emotions released at Vicksburg and at other battlefields, such as nearby Port Hudson, for example, and Pea Ridge in northern Arkansas. The Civil War was a such a unique tragedy—a war on our own soil, pitting brother against brother, and involving questions of race that remain in some measure unresolved.

The South, perhaps more than any other region, recognizes the importance of the past. Here, history is more than an entertainment. It addresses the contradictions of life. Only the rituals of history can explain a region that produced America's most violent rebels and also its staunchest patriots.

And only history can explain another apparent contradiction—the region's dismal racial history and its progress in civil rights. In states once

down-home
southern cooking

Down-home cooking lacks the formality of fancier fare, but what the South misses in culinary elegance it makes up for in a sense of tradition that makes the work of cooking and the pleasures of eating very serious indeed. In places like New Orleans and Mobile, as well as in small towns that are immune to fashion, dinners being turned out tonight are not too different from what was served a century ago.

Southern cooking goes back some 200 years. Historians relate that a period of intense creativity took place in the early 19th century, when the kitchens of wealthy plantations were run by slaves who made creative use of the modest greens, roots, rice, beans, and peppers that were familiar in Africa. Indigenous game birds—wild turkey, for example—were also an important part of the mix.

Southern cooking is not a single style. There's low-country cooking along the coast, which is different from Louisiana's Cajun-Creole. Dishes are as varied as red beans and rice, fried fresh trout with ground corn meal, and jambalaya. Influences are as broad as early American history

itself, including the cooking traditions of the French, Spanish, and Native Americans (who used ground sassafras leaves, or filé, to season and thicken stews).

Nor is down-home cooking always the "health food" that it may appear to be. True, they like vegetables in the South; eggplant grows wonderfully in the hot, humid summers, and okra is basic to many Southern dishes. But real biscuits are made with lard, and some say that pork is to the South what olive oil is to Italy.

Southern cooking is also characterized by a certain attitude or feeling. Many cooks call it "comfort food" and promise that what you get at their table is just like the home-made dishes that Mom serves. Even in upscale restaurants with down-home cooking, the menus aren't too different from the fare you'd find at roadside diners: collard greens, hoppin' John (rice and black-eyed peas), corn cakes, and of course fried chicken. There's even ketchup on the table, though you might not see any bottles because real Southern cooks make the condiments themselves.

bluegrass horse country

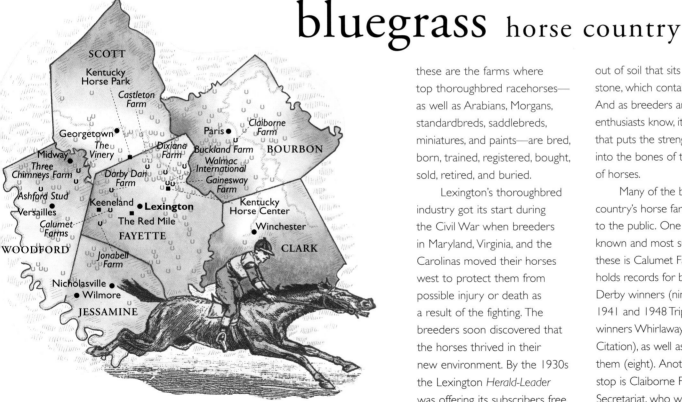

u u Horse farms
■   Equine points of interest
●   Cities and towns

When the winning horse crosses the finish line at the Kentucky Derby in Louisville, chances are good that the steed owes part of its success to one of the 431 thoroughbred horse farms of Kentucky's bluegrass country. Centered around Lexington, 68 miles (109 km) to the east, and in the surrounding counties of Bourbon, Scott, Jessamine, and Woodford,

these are the farms where top thoroughbred racehorses— as well as Arabians, Morgans, standardbreds, saddlebreds, miniatures, and paints—are bred, born, trained, registered, bought, sold, retired, and buried.

Lexington's thoroughbred industry got its start during the Civil War when breeders in Maryland, Virginia, and the Carolinas moved their horses west to protect them from possible injury or death as a result of the fighting. The breeders soon discovered that the horses thrived in their new environment. By the 1930s the Lexington *Herald-Leader* was offering its subscribers free papers on any day that at least one horse bred within 50 miles (80 km) of Lexington didn't win a race at a major track.

A lot of horse knowledge goes into the breeding and training of thoroughbreds. So does a lot of Kentucky bluegrass. The grass, which takes its name from its silver-blue color, grows

out of soil that sits atop limestone, which contains calcium. And as breeders and racing enthusiasts know, it's the calcium that puts the strength and speed into the bones of these fleetest of horses.

Many of the bluegrass country's horse farms are open to the public. One of the best known and most successful of these is Calumet Farms, which holds records for breeding Derby winners (nine, including 1941 and 1948 Triple Crown winners Whirlaway and Citation), as well as owning them (eight). Another popular stop is Claiborne Farm, where Secretariat, who won the Triple Crown in 1973 and is considered one of the greatest race horses in history, is buried. Claiborne is also the home of Derby winners Unbridled (1990) and Go for Gin (1994). Three Chimneys Farm offers visitors a chance to see 1977 Triple Crown winner Seattle Slew.

Other thoroughbred farms open to visitors include Jonabell Farm, The Vinery, Gainsway Farm,

Normandy Farm, Ashford Stud, Dixiana Farm, Darby Dan Farm, and Castleton Farm.

At Kentucky Horse Center and Keeneland Race Course visitors can see thoroughbreds in training. Keeneland also sponsors a simulcast of the Kentucky Derby; fans can watch the race from the infield while enjoying a picnic lunch.

The Kentucky Horse Park features a wealth of equine attractions, including the International Museum of the Horse, which traces the history of this remarkable animal. Visitors can also tour a working thoroughbred farm, complete with farrier and harness shops, and stroll through the Hall of Champions, whose famous residents include 1976 Derby winner Bold Forbes. Adjacent to the park is the American Saddle Horse Museum, which offers exhibits and multimedia presentations devoted to Kentucky's own breed.

synonymous with segregation, and in locales like Selma, Alabama, whose names represent crucibles of a kind, racial tensions have been genuinely assuaged. Here again, the answer lies in the small-town culture of the South. Common values and a fundamental sense of right and wrong have, over time, helped to steer communities away from the harsh past and toward a more harmonious future. While places like Selma are known in the rest of the country as flash points in the civil rights struggle, in the South there are known as places of real progress toward racial equality.

Sociologists explain the way things work in the South by writing about the region's "localism," and other writers also stress this tendency of communities to behave like families. Such idiosyncrasies are behind fictional Yokonapatawpah County, where William Faulkner set his novels, complex stories filled with contradictions—of impoverished gentry and a powerful black presence—but which ring absolutely true.

The enduring complexities of Southern life, perhaps, are what make Southerners such storytellers. "They are born reciters, great memory retainers, diary keepers, letter exchangers and letter savers, history tracers and debaters, and—outstaying all the rest—great talkers," said writer Eudora Welty. The list of distinguished Southern writers includes names like Walker Percy, Tennessee Williams, Truman Capote, Richard Wright, and Carson McCullers. Anne Rice uses the decayed mansions and families of New Orleans as a backdrop for gothic tales that have attracted a cult following of readers everywhere. And a different kind of storytelling, the

Gulf Islands National Seashore on Florida's panhandle (left), Atlanta skyline (right), civil rights leader Martin Luther King, Jr. (below)

lyrics of Nashville-style country music, somehow penetrate the soul not just of the region but of the human condition in general.

To Northern eyes, the South will always look peculiar. There are places like Elvis Presley's Graceland in Memphis, where the sacred, the profane, the splendid, and the honky-tonk all contribute to an icon that is one of America's most popular attractions.

atlanta

Atlanta is a fast-track modern city with an air of gracious Southern hospitality. It is hailed as the heart—and the hope—of the New South.

Georgia's capital and largest city, with 3.2 million people in its metropolitan area, Atlanta is a major transportation, financial, and commercial center. It was the site of the 1996 Summer Olympics, and is the home of Ted Turner's communications empire, the birthplace of Coca-Cola, and the corporate headquarters of Delta Air Lines. The city led the nation in the creation of jobs during the 1990s.

Atlanta's location has always been one of its most important assets. Its elevation of 1,050 feet (320 m) above sea level on the Piedmont Plateau ensures a moderate climate. Its position midway between the Mississippi River and the Atlantic Ocean makes it an ideal transportation center—which is how it began.

Built as a railroad hub in 1837 when cotton was hauled by rail, the city was initially called Terminus. In 1845, its name was changed to Atlanta, referring to its goal to be the connector with the Atlantic Ocean.

During the Civil War, the Union Army recognized Atlanta's importance as a Confederate shipping and supply center, and

in 1864 burned much of the city to the ground. Rebuilding quickly after the war, Atlanta became a Reconstruction center. It was declared the state capital in 1868, and by the turn of the century 100 trains a day converged on the city. Atlanta emerged as the leader of the New South— a term signifying the Southland's modernization and re-entrance into the country's economic and cultural mainstream.

Today, more than half of Metro Atlanta's residents come from someplace else, giving the city a cosmopolitan atmosphere. People are drawn to its climate, business opportunities, and Southern civility. Still, the hometown of Martin Luther King, Jr., remains largely segregated, with predominantly white suburbs surrounding a predominantly black city.

Visitors expect Atlanta to be filled with romantic plantations. After all, this was the home of Margaret Mitchell, author of *Gone With the Wind*. Instead of Tara, they find office parks, mini malls, and housing developments. Nearly every vestige of the Old South disappeared when the city was burned in 1864. But like the mythical phoenix, Atlanta has been reborn from its own ashes.

music of the south

From Jelly Roll Morton's Red Hot Peppers to the soulful blues, the regional music of the American South represents one of the country's richest and most varied musical traditions.

The blues are a good starting point for unraveling the fiber that threads various Southern musicians and genres into a common whole. The blues evolved from the work and spiritual songs, communal and plaintive, of black slaves. "In the most boisterous outbursts of rapturous sentiment, there was ever a tinge of deep melancholy," said escaped slave and abolitionist Frederick Douglas in describing these early songs.

The "Father of the Blues," Alabama-born black composer W. C. Handy, began his career in the traveling performances known as minstrel shows before heading for Memphis, where he led a black orchestra that popularized the blues style for black and white audiences. In 1914 his "St. Louis Blues" was

recorded, soon followed by popular blues recordings by Bessie Smith (the "Empress of the Blues"), Louis Armstrong, and others.

Robert Lockwood, a protégé of the legendary blues singer and guitarist Robert Johnson, helped give continuity to the strong country roots of Mississippi Delta Blues. Lockwood and Sonny Boy Williamson would later launch the King Biscuit Show in Helena, Arkansas, exposing thousands to the distinctive Delta style.

By the 1940s, blues singer and guitarist B. B. King was helping to develop the Memphis style of blues, while fellow Mississippian Muddy Waters' sound evolved from country blues to the electric, amplified sound that connected the Delta tradition to the Chicago style of blues.

Ragtime, another musical genre born in the South, also originated on the minstrel stage. This offbeat music was performed along the Missouri, Mississippi, and Ohio Rivers at the turn of the century. While Texarkana's Scott Joplin revolutionized music with his ragtime compositions, the genre's true impact was as a melodic element of instrumental jazz.

In the early 1900s, jazz was a new musical style, but it was firmly rooted in the past.

MUSIC CAPITALS AND BIRTHPLACES
OF SOUTHERN MUSIC LEGENDS

Dry Ridge *(Skeeter Davis)*

Rosine *(Bill Monroe)*

Brownie *(Don Everly)*

Overton Co. *(Lester Flatt)*

BRANSON
Popular Music Mecca

NASHVILLE
Home of Grand Ole Opry,
Country Music Hall of Fame &
Museum; birthplace of Kitty Wells

Tiptonville *(Carl Perkins)*

MEMPHIS
Site of Elvis Presley's Graceland, Sun
Records Studio, Beale Street Music Festival

Jackson *(Sonny Boy Williamson #2)*

Henderson *(Eddy Arnold)*

Pulaski *(James Brown)*

Colt *(Charlie Rich)*

Florence *(W. C. Handy)*

Marvell *(Robert Lockwood, Jr.)*

Friars Point *(Conway Twitty)*

Itawamba Co. *(Tammy Wynette)*

Villa Rica *(Thomas Dorsey)*

Clarksdale *(John Lee Hooker)*

Glendora *(Sonny Boy Williamson #1)*

Tupelo *(Elvis Presley)*

West Point *(Howlin' Wolf)*

Birmingham *(Emmylou Harris)*

Newnan *(Alan Jackson)*

Kingsland *(Johnny Cash)*

Itta Bena *(B. B. King)*

Texarkana *(Scott Joplin)*

Rolling Fork *(Muddy Waters)*

Meridian *(Jimmie Rodgers)*

Mooringsport *(Leadbelly)*

Richland *(Elmore James)*

Mt. Olive *(Hank Williams)*

Hazelhurst *(Robert Johnson)*

Ferriday *(Jerry Lee Lewis)*

Evangeline Parish *(Amédé Ardoin, Canray Fontenot, Dennis McGee)*

Opelousas *(Clifton Chenier)*

Scott *(Michael Doucet)*

NEW ORLEANS
Home of New Orleans Jazz and Heritage
Festival, Preservation Hall; birthplace of
Louis Armstrong, Fats Domino, Al Hirt,
Mahalia Jackson, and Jelly Roll Morton

This fusion of ragtime and blues came together in New Orleans' French Quarter and Preservation Hall with an essential component: instrumental bands with horns. While the first recordings of the Dixieland style of jazz were made in 1917 by the white, New Orleans-based Original Dixieland Jazz Band, it was the likes of Jelly Roll Morton's Red Hot Peppers and King Oliver's Creole Jazz Band that solidified the sound of New Orleans jazz. Their hot improvs quickly won audiences in Chicago and New York and on the west coast.

As jazz began to percolate, the small towns and cities of the South gave rise to a new sound: gospel. Nashville's Fisk Jubilee Singers sang spirituals on a successful tour of Europe as early as 1871, while the Holiness, or Pentecostal, Church introduced instrumental ensembles and dancing into small-town churches in the early 1900s. The "Father of Black Gospel," Thomas Dorsey, started as a blues piano player in the 1920s and founded the National Convention of Gospel Choirs and Choruses in 1932.

No musical genre was free of black influence, not even country roots music, whose kingpins included the "Father of Country Music" Jimmie Rodgers,

the "Father of Bluegrass" Bill Monroe, and the legendary Hank Williams. Rodgers, the first singer inducted into Nashville's Country Music Hall of Fame, blended black blues into his unique hillbilly yodeling, while Monroe learned his bluegrass stylings at the feet of a black Kentucky coal miner. Williams was mentored in his hometown of Georgiana, Alabama, by an old black blues singer named Rufus "Tee-Tot" Payne.

These three men helped launch yet another "new" Southern sound: country. In 1925, National Life and Accident Insurance sponsored a radio show based on one man's memories of an Ozarks mountaineer hoedown. That show exploded in popularity, and moved to Nashville's Ryman Auditorium in 1943. Ryman remained home to the Grand Ole Opry, "The Mother Church of Country Music," until the opening of Opryland USA in 1974.

The music coming out of Nashville, coupled with new fusions of black blues and white bluegrass, contributed significantly to the birth of rockabilly and rock and roll, new sounds that found early fame in the throats and fingertips of Carl Perkins, Elvis Presley, and Jerry Lee Lewis. These white up-and-comers joined black artists like Howlin'

Wolf and B. B. King in the now-legendary studios of Memphis' Sun Records in the 1950s to make some of the most distinctive and memorable recordings of the rock and roll era.

Two other musical genres native to the South evolved in southern Louisiana's rich cultural gumbo. Cajun music is rooted in the traditional songs of the French Acadians who settled in this area in the mid-1700s, but it incorporates strong Creole, Spanish, German, and Native American influences. Zydeco emerged from the area's black Creole culture, but shares many elements and influences with its Cajun cousin.

Why is it that the South is such a wellspring of musical creativity and innovation? No one can say for sure, but what is certain is that without the contributions of Southern musicians, American music today would be greatly diminished.

Music legends Elvis Presley, B. B. King, and Louis Armstrong (top to bottom left), bald cypresses in Louisiana's Atchafalaya basin (above), entrance to Mammoth Cave in Kentucky (bottom right)

Other peculiar blends also exist, such as Biloxi, Mississippi. A place of substantial notes of history, Biloxi is the site of Beauvoir, the post-Civil War estate of Jefferson Davis, the President of the Confederacy. Here, on property overlooking the Gulf of Mexico, Davis wrote his memoirs and lived out his life; his family later made it a home and cemetery for Confederate veterans. In recent years, Biloxi has become a gambling paradise with a casino-lined waterfront; the biggest and newest hotel-casino, Beau Rivage, sits within sight of Beauvoir. Glitzy casinos could not be further in spirit from Beauvoir, but Biloxi makes room for both.

Such culture clashes—the Old South and the New—can be found in nearly every corner of the region. In fact, the coexistence of Beauvoir and Beau Rivage serves as an appropriate metaphor for a region that has always cherished its past but is determined to embrace the present.

caves of the south

Deep within the Ozarks of northern Arkansas and southern Missouri lies a wonderland of spires and columns, delicate flowers of gypsum and massive waterfalls of stone, and strange fish and amphibians that are both blind and colorless. Similar marvels are concealed beneath the Cumberland Plateau of Kentucky and Tennessee. The caves of the South were hundreds of millions of years in the making, and the process continues to this day.

Mineral-laden water both excavated these caverns and filled them with dazzling decorations. Around 350 million years ago, a shallow sea covered a vast area of what is today the mid-southern United States. Layers of limestone hundreds of feet thick were deposited on the seabed. When the land rose above sea level, rainwater, converted into a weak carbolic acid solution as it passed through decaying plant matter on the surface, leached through cracks in the limestone below, carving ever-widening passageways. Then the water table fell below the cave passages. Water dripping through the air-filled chambers deposited minerals such as calcite on cavern walls, ceilings, and floors, building cave formations such as stalactites, stalagmites, cascades, nubbly cave popcorn, corkscrew-like helictites, sinuous rimstone dams, and intricate ceiling boxwork.

Scores of the region's caves are open for tours. Electric lights and leveled pathways allow access to the sights within such caves as Arkansas' Blanchard Springs Caverns, Missouri's Meramec Caverns, Tennessee's Cumberland Caverns, and Kentucky's Mammoth Cave, the world's longest known cave system. But for every "show cave," there are hundreds of wild caves that challenge the mettle and expertise of spelunkers from around the world.

The Midwest and Great Lakes

Tilling the Land,
Scraping the Sky

Friendly. Open. Hardworking. Filled with goodwill. These are common perceptions about Midwesterners. They're meant as flattery, though people who live in this enormous and diverse region—in big industrial cities and small rural towns—bristle at such generalizations. Precinct captains from Chicago, they say, have little in common with Rotarians from Wapakoneta, Ohio, which is quite reasonable to assume.

Until they leave. Then, and maybe only then, do they discover something unique about the Heartland: People who live in this part of the country really are interested in their neighbors. They make and keep friends for a lifetime. They have a strong work ethic. They are honest and genuine: What you see is what you get, which Midwesterners are surprised to find doesn't apply everywhere.

It's not hard to conclude that the openness of Midwesterners is closely linked to the region's geography. Covering a great swath of the nation's midsection—from Iowa to western New York, and from the Canadian border south to the Ohio Valley—the Midwest and Great Lakes region has a flat, unremarkable sameness at first glance. It's not the kind of place that breeds proud, provincial attitudes. The wealth of this region comes primarily from the land—fertile prairie soil that stretches from Ohio to Iowa, iron ore out of northern Minnesota and Michigan's Upper Peninsula, coal beneath much of Illinois. These resources underlie a regional character that values, most of all, quiet strength and hard work. Working the

White Iron Lake in northeastern Minnesota (left), ears of feed corn (right). Preceding pages: Wisconsin dairy farm at dawn

land and extracting its riches requires diligence and great effort. It also requires a sense of humility: The caprices of nature—a hailstorm, a flood—can wipe out months or years of backbreaking labor in a matter of minutes.

The region's flatness and fertility are by-products of the glaciers that spread across the land numerous times during the past two million years. As they slowly advanced, these massive walls of ice leveled everything in their paths, gouged out and filled the Great Lakes, and created fine, rich soils by grinding rocks and debris. After they had receded, plants thrived in the fertile earth. The landscape was webbed with wide rivers. What more could civilization ask for?

The merits of the region were apparent to Native Americans, who farmed and hunted the bountiful prairie lands for some seven thousand years before Europeans arrived. The settlement of Cahokia, in present-day Illinois just east of St. Louis, was one of the largest and most powerful pre-Columbian cities in North America. At its apex—around A.D. 1000—its influence as a trading and religious center extended from Wisconsin to Oklahoma. Cahokia waned after some 200 years, but its great temple mounds remain today, rising from the floodplain of the Mississippi River as monuments to a once-flourishing culture.

Europeans were equally quick to sense the wealth of the Midwest and Great Lakes region. In the 1600s, French voyageurs, explorers, and missionaries plied the lakes and rivers by canoe. They were dazzled by the lushness and the wildlife of the region, and they hailed it as "New France." By 1700, forts such as Mackinac and Detroit represented Great Lakes strongholds of the Bourbon king; later, they were sought and captured by forces of the English king.

In the Amish country of northern Indiana, a boy uses mule power to rake hay (right).

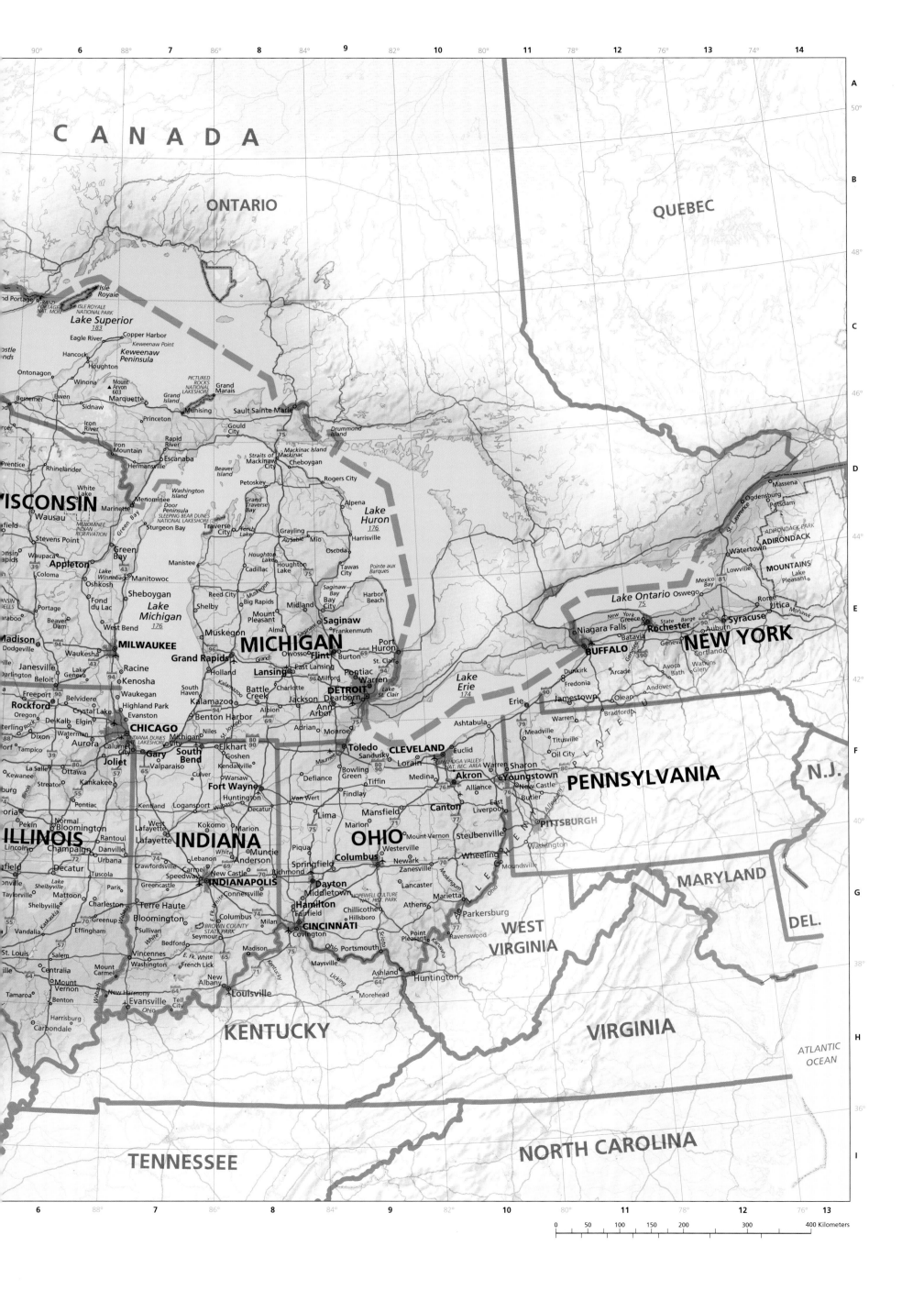

blues and motown

During the Great Migration, which began around 1910, hundreds of thousands of rural African-Americans followed the Mississippi River north to find work in cities such as Chicago and Detroit. And with them, they brought the rich tradition of the blues. But that music, once simple and straightforward, changed rapidly in the urban environment. Plugged in, it was raucous and loud enough to hear above the din of steel mills and El trains.

Muddy Waters, the "Hoochie Coochie Man," solidified the modern Chicago Blues sound with his hard-driving guitar and resonant vocals soon after he arrived in the Windy City in 1943. Playing in blacks-only clubs on the South Side, Waters took over from such early urban bluesmen as Sonny Boy Williamson and Big Bill Broonzy. He soon signed with a fledgling Chess Records and, along with songwriter-producer-arranger Willie Dixon, formed the backbone of the independent label, putting it on the national music agenda in the early 1950s. Other artists—including gravel-voiced giant Howlin' Wolf, blues harp (harmonica) maestro Junior Wells, and slide guitar virtuoso Elmore James—joined the Chicago Blues movement, and it enjoyed a near decade-long heyday. Since then, artists such as B. B. King and Buddy Guy have kept the Chicago sound alive and well. To this day, "Sweet Home Chicago" remains the home of the blues, and every summer

the world convenes on the shore of Lake Michigan for a blues festival like no other.

The '60s was the decade of Motown. At the time, Detroit was possibly the only major U.S. city that didn't have a strong independent record company. Berry Gordy Jr. quickly rectified that situation with his nose for talent and his business acumen. After enjoying modest success with a few songs he penned for Jackie Wilson, Gordy started producing records for local talent, including the Miracles (with Smokey Robinson) and the Holland Brothers, and in 1959 borrowed $800 to start his own record company, which eventually became Motown.

In a span of four years, Motown added the Supremes (with Diana Ross), Marvin Gaye, the Temptations, Martha and the Vandellas, Mary Wells, Stevie Wonder, and the Marvellettes to its stable of vocalists. Backed by seasoned jazz studio musicians known as the Funk Brothers, the label pumped out a brand of smooth, soul-fueled pop that dominated the pop and R&B charts throughout the 1960s.

Motown closed its Detroit offices in June 1972. In the '80s, the company still sold millions of albums, with much help from the Commodores and their front man Lionel Ritchie, but it no longer dominated the charts. In June 1988, Berry Gordy sold Motown to MCA, and surrendered one of the largest black-owned businesses in U.S. history.

After American independence and the Louisiana Purchase, a growing number of settlers from the eastern United States began to arrive; later came great waves of European immigrants. The first wave, which lasted from approximately 1820 to 1860, brought mostly Western Europeans—Irish, Germans, English, and Scandinavians. After the Civil War, patterns of immigration shifted, and most of the newcomers hailed from eastern and southern Europe, especially Italy, Poland, Russia, and the Balkans.

The strong sense of loyalty, trust, and community that characterizes Midwesterners today is a legacy of these immigrant groups, whose cohesiveness allowed them to prosper. Whether they settled in rural areas or in cities, the groups created communities and ethnic enclaves that still exist, such as the Finns of Embarrass, Minnesota; the Poles of Cleveland's Slavic Village neighborhood; the Czechs of "Little Bohemia" in Cedar Rapids, Iowa; and the Swedes of Chicago's Andersonville neighborhood.

The transportation arteries by which most settlers arrived were the Great Lakes and the Ohio River. These waterways, as well as the Mississippi and Missouri Rivers, played a critical role in the region's economic growth and development, providing a fast and efficient way to ship out the products of its farms, factories, and mines: grain, dairy products, lumber, coal, lead, iron ore, steel, automobiles, and a host of other manufactured goods.

Inevitably, the region's greatest cities grew up at strategic points along these lakes and rivers. Buffalo, Cleveland, and Chicago became boomtowns soon after the construction of three canals—the Erie, the Ohio, and the Illinois & Michigan, respectively. Detroit, from its earliest days as a frontier trading post and fort, benefited from its propitious location on the Detroit River between Lakes Erie and Huron. Milwaukee grew up around a swampy natural harbor formed by three rivers as they flow into Lake Michigan. Cincinnati, on the north bank of the Ohio River, ranked as one of the largest and most important cities west of the Alleghenies through much of the 19th century and was nicknamed "Queen City of the West." The Twin Cities of Minneapolis and St. Paul,

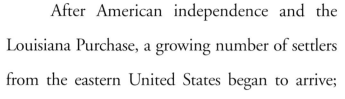

Muddy Waters, the Temptations, and the Supremes (top to bottom left), Miners Castle at Michigan's Pictured Rocks National Lakeshore (top right), freighter on Lake Superior c. 1900 (middle right)

great lakes trade and transport

From the time of birchbark canoes to the modern days of gargantuan cargo ships, the Great Lakes system has been one of North America's most important transportation corridors.

Historians consider Jacques Cartier's 1534 discovery of the St. Lawrence River as the start of Great Lakes exploration by nonnatives. In 1615, Samuel de Champlain reached the lakes via a small river that emptied into Lake Huron's Georgian Bay. Louis Jolliet charted a route across the Great Lakes to the Mississippi in 1673–74, and the explorer La Salle built an enormous ship, filled it with guns, and hauled them in 1679 from Montreal to Green Bay, where he traded them for

furs—the commerce that soon flourished across the region.

Smelling wealth, the French ruled the lakes with an iron fist. They built numerous forts to protect their trade with natives and pushed exploration until 1756, when the British strong-armed them off the lakes. British rule lasted until their 1813 defeat by American commander Oliver Hazard Perry.

Canals built in the following decades spurred settlement of the Midwest and brought a transportation boom on the Great Lakes. The first and most important was the Erie Canal, completed in 1825, which connected the Hudson River to Lake Erie. Two years later, the Ohio Canal linked Lake Erie and the Ohio River, and in 1848 the Illinois & Michigan Canal joined Lake Michigan and the Mississippi River system. Settlers poured into the region via the canals and lakes, and the Midwest's agricultural bounty—especially grain—poured out. Cheap and convenient transportation helped industries such as steel manufacturing

to thrive in Chicago, Detroit, Cleveland, and other cities.

Today, freighters as long as three football fields ply the Great Lakes, carrying as much as 70,000 tons (63,000 metric tons) of iron ore. Despite their seaworthiness and bulk, however, dozens of ships have sunk in the often

treacherous waters, notably the great ore freighter memorialized in Gordon Lightfoot's 1976 ballad "The Wreck of the Edmund Fitzgerald." In the Great Storm of 1913, 35-foot (11-m) waves and 75-mile-per-hour (120-km) winds destroyed 19 ships and killed 248 people.

GREAT LAKES PORTS AND EXPORTS

Michigan's Grand Haven lighthouse (left) presides over a wintry scene along the icebound coast of Lake Michigan.

situated at the northernmost navigable point on the Mississippi River, grew in tandem to become a transportation, commercial, and manufacturing center for a large part of the Upper Midwest. St. Louis, located on the Mississippi just below its confluence with the Missouri, became the principal river port above New Orleans as well as the gateway through which many westward-bound settlers passed.

As the region's economy grew and prospered, so did the commercial ventures of its energetic entrepreneurs. The late 19th and early 20th centuries saw the rise of such looming figures in American business as Marshall Field of the department store, John D. Rockefeller of Standard Oil, Henry Ford of the Ford Motor Company, and Richard Warren Sears of Sears, Roebuck and Company.

Over time, the economics of the country changed, and by the 1970s the soon-to-be "Rust Belt" became identified with closing factories, loss of jobs, troubled inner cities, and so-called "white flight." Detroit, Cleveland, and St. Louis, to name three of the best-known examples, faced increasing poverty and shrinking tax bases.

The economics of farming changed as well. At the beginning of the 20th century, the traditional family farm was still in its heyday: More than half of the region's people lived on farms. By the 1990s the number had dropped to less than 2 percent, a result of competition from large cooperatives and agribusinesses, rising costs of farm machinery, low crop prices, and the lure of high-paying city jobs. As more and more people have left the land, a new problem has arisen: Uncontrolled, residential and commercial sprawl is eating up vast tracts of open land that once surrounded the cities.

the legacy of the glaciers

If glaciers had never plowed across the Midwest and Great Lakes region, the Great Lakes themselves would not exist. The Mississippi, Missouri, and Ohio Rivers would flow along different courses. Minnesota would not have its 10,000 lakes. The terrain would be far more hilly and rugged, the soils thinner and poorer. More than any other part of the country, this region reveals the awesome, land-sculpting power of glaciers.

During the Pleistocene Epoch, which began roughly 1.7 million years ago and ended 10,000 years ago, glaciers advanced over the region at least four times. Reaching thicknesses of more than two miles (3.2 km), these immense sheets of ice devastated everything in their path as they crept southward from their Arctic birthplaces. Like ranks of giant bulldozers, they scraped up and carried trillions of tons of rocks and soil. They ground the rocks into cobbles, gravel, and fine rock flour; later, as they melted and retreated, they deposited this "glacial till" across the region. They transported boulders the size of houses across hundreds of miles. They gouged out deep, broad basins and lined the edges with moraines—tall mounds and ridges of rocks and earth.

By planing hills and filling valleys with debris, the glaciers created the generally flat landscape that characterizes the region today. The thick layer of till they left behind formed the basis of the extraordinarily fertile soils that now yield bounties of corn and soybeans. Enormous glacial basins later filled with water to become the five Great Lakes, while countless smaller depressions became the lakes that draw vacationers to Minnesota and northern Wisconsin. Moraines still snake through many parts of the region, including such popular recreation destinations as Michigan's Sleeping Bear Dunes National Lakeshore and Wisconsin's Kettle Moraine State Forest.

The glaciers also shaped the region's river courses and drainage patterns. Advancing walls of ice blocked the channels of many rivers; changing course, the rivers flowed along the margins of the glaciers. Today, the Ohio and Missouri Rivers closely follow a line marking the southernmost extent of glaciation. As the ice sheets receded, and as ice dams holding back glacial lakes broke open, torrents of meltwater rushed down watercourses, sculpting spectacular gorges like the dells (or "dalles") of the Wisconsin, St. Croix, and Eau Claire Rivers.

GLACIAL ADVANCES

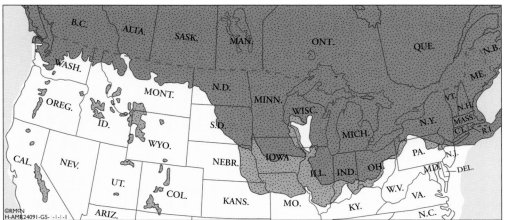

©RMN
H-AM824091-G5- .-l-l-l

■ Greatest extent of Wisconsin glaciation
■ Greatest extent of Illinoisian glaciation

the prairie metropolis

Over the years, Chicago has earned a number of nicknames, some more flattering than others: Paris on the Prairie. City of the Big Shoulders. Hog Butcher to the World. The Windy City. The Second City. Hub of the Nation. The City that Works. There is at least some truth to each of these sobriquets, but even taken together they don't begin to capture the richness and vitality of this, one of the world's great cities.

Chicago's origins trace back to 1779, when French-Caribbean explorer Jean Baptiste Point du Sable built a cabin on the swampy banks of a lazy river the Indians called "Checaugou" after the wild garlic that grew along its banks.

In 1803 the U.S. government, seeking a stronger presence along the country's western frontier, built Fort Dearborn on the south bank of the river, then rebuilt it in 1816 after it was burned down in an attack by Potawatomi Indians. A small town grew up around the fort; at the time of its incorporation in 1833, it held some 340 people.

In 1848, the burgeoning city became the terminus of the first industrial canal built in the Midwest; later, the railroads that helped develop the nation radiated out from the city and its eight major train stations. Soon Chicago was a hub not just for transportation but also for commerce and industry— especially steel making, meat processing, and banking. The tens of thousands of European immigrants who arrived during this period found a city of ambition, chaos, and improbably large buildings over streets so muddy that they were said to swallow horses and children whole.

From the beginning, it seems, Chicagoans never saw problems, they saw solutions. When much of the city burned in the fire of 1871, the citizens rebuilt with it a zeal that saw the invention of the skyscraper. As an increasingly polluted Chicago River sullied Lake Michigan and spawned disease, the city reversed its flow (one of the most significant engineering feats of the 19th century) and the troubles just drained away.

Today Chicago's gritty industrial past is mostly a memory. Financial and business services drive the economic engines. The moneyed center of the city rests in the soaring skyscrapers, tony stores, and lux- urious hotels of the downtown Loop and the glitzy Near North neighborhood. On the lakefront there are 26 miles (42 km) of beautiful parks and beaches. The city is home to world- class cultural institutions such as the Art Institute, the Chicago Symphony, and the Lyric Opera, and such top-ranked universities as Northwestern and the University of Chicago.

The city continues to be a hub of transportation. Its harbor is the busiest on the Great Lakes, and O'Hare International Airport is the busiest in the world: Some 65 million people pass through O'Hare's gates each year.

With a city population of nearly three million, and a metropolitan area population of some eight million, Chicago ranks as the third-largest city in the United States, behind New York and Los Angeles. Its populace comprises people of all races, nationalities and religions. You can travel the world without leaving the city by visiting some of the vibrant ethnic neighborhoods, where sidewalks hum to the sound of many languages, restaurants offer international fare, and stores sell myriad exotic goods.

Navy Pier and the Chicago skyline (top left); *Flamingo* sculpture
by Alexander Calder (middle
left); Wrigley Field (bottom left);
Dutch dancers in Holland,
Michigan (bottom right)

Despite these setbacks, the Midwest and Great Lakes region continues to thrive. Its natural wealth, coupled with the determination and hard work of its people, have ensured its prosperity. Many of the "Rust Belt" cities are flourishing once again, having countered the decline in manufacturing by attracting service industries. For example, Chicago's robust economy is now focused more on financial services than on heavy industry. Manufacturing, of course, is far from dead: The nation's steel still crosses the Great Lakes in enormous vessels, and Detroit remains a major center of automobile manu-facturing. Cleveland's former industrial heart, The Flats, is quickly filling up with upscale shops, trendy restaurants, and popular nightspots. Milwaukee is experiencing a "German Renaissance," preserving its splendid architecture and relishing its old ethnic communities. Minneapolis' commercial strength is being matched in St. Paul by a cultural rebirth, with new museums and a much-polished downtown.

Across the country there is also a newfound appreciation for things Midwestern. It's no coincidence that popular recent novels and movies such as *A Thousand Acres* and *The Bridges of Madison County* were set in Iowa. Heartland homestyle cooking is enjoying a strong revival, with old recipes like corn pudding and chicken pot pie showing up on the menus of fashion-able restaurants. The enormously popular Arts and Crafts style, with its emphasis on superior, "honest" design and craftsmanship, draws directly from styles and companies of this region, including Stickley furniture, Teco pottery, and the architecture of Frank Lloyd Wright. Even the Midwest's most primeval element, the prairie, is making a comeback: Throughout the region conservationists and corporate campuses are restoring tall grasses and flowering plants that were once sacrificed to the settlers' plows.

All these things reflect simple values. Increasingly, they are extolled by politicians, promoted by historians, and embodied by media stars. And as those stars can attest—people ranging from Garrison Keillor to Michael Jordan to Oprah Winfrey—the Midwest may be a calm and peaceful place, but beneath its hardworking surface, it is anything but bland.

FOREIGN-BORN POPULATION IN 1910

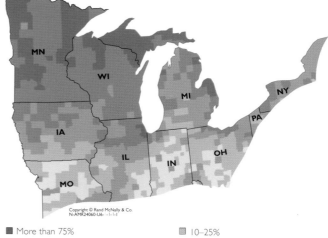

More than 75%
50–75%
25–50%
10–25%
Less than 10%

immigrant influence

Perhaps more than any other part of the United States, the Midwest and Great Lakes region still reflects the broad impact of the European immigrants who poured into the United States in the 19th and early 20th centuries. Their strong presence shaped the character, layout, public institutions—and even the names—of cities and communities across the region.

Immigrants who settled in the eastern United States often faced distrust and discrimination as they moved into well-established communities. But those who headed into the Midwest shared the experience with American-born pioneers who were also lured by the promise of cheap, fertile land, virgin forests, and abundant wildlife. Together, they settled the shores of the Great Lakes, the banks of the Mississippi and Ohio Rivers, and the wide swaths of prairie in between. By contrast, relatively few immigrants settled in the southern United States

because its climate and style of agriculture differed from what they had known in the Old World.

Many of the immigrants were part of organized migrations, such as the Pennsylvania Dutch, who emigrated from Germany and Switzerland to settle in Ohio and Pennsylvania. Most, however, moved independently to join relatives and friends already settled in a particular area. German merchants and tradesmen began arriving in the 1830s, and congregated in urban centers like Milwaukee, Chicago, Cincinnati, and Buffalo. In the 1850s, Swedes and Norwegians settled in Wisconsin, Minnesota, and Iowa, where they worked as lumberjacks and frontier farmers. Other localities gained a strong Polish, Czech, or Finnish character during the 1890s and early 1900s. Immigration rose dramatically during those years, with more than eight million U.S. arrivals between 1900 and 1910. The 1910 census registered the strong immigrant concentration in the Midwest, where many county populations were more than 50 percent foreign-born.

Today many Midwestern towns base tourism around their particular ethnic heritage—for example, Holland, Michigan, has its Dutch WinterFest and Tulip Time Festival; New Glarus, Wisconsin, attracts visitors with its Swiss architecture; and Nappanee, Indiana, is famous for its Amish farms and country markets.

Minnesota
Wild Rice

Upper
Peninsula
Pasties

MI

Mackinac
Island
Fudge

Door County
Fish Boil

Traverse City
Cherry Wine

MI

NY
Buffalo Wings

MN

WI

Wisconsin
Cheese

Racine
Kringle

IA

Milwaukee
Beer

OH

Cincinnati
Chili

IL

Chicago
Pizza

IN

MO

midwestern local dishes

Often referred to as "the Heartland," the Midwest has long been perceived as a bastion of hearty, wholesome food consisting of little more than meat, potatoes, corn, bread, and the occasional casserole—basic fuel for living. While it's true that these staples are the hand-me-downs of pioneers and the early settlers, Midwestern cuisine is much more a melting pot of immigrant tradition, regional bounties, and human ingenuity than it is given credit for.

DOOR COUNTY FISH BOILS

In Door County, on the Wisconsin peninsula that juts into Lake Michigan, an age-old tradition is carried on: fish boils. Scandinavian fishermen and lumberjacks once depended on the abundance of whitefish and potatoes for their meals, and now the fish boil is a cultural mainstay and nearly a theatrical event. Water is boiled in vast kettles, pounds of salt are added, then potatoes and

Chicago-style deep-dish pizza (below); Mississippi River and Fountain City, Wisconsin (right)

chunks of whitefish. Finally, to boil off the fishy-tasting oil, kerosene is thrown onto the open fire with a whoosh! Then the meal is fished out with a basket on a long pole, and served with Swedish limpa bread.

CHICAGO-STYLE PIZZA

Actually, Chicago has two styles of pizza, deep-dish and stuffed. Both were born of Italian restauranteurs attempting to maximize sheer volume of toppings. Deep-dish pizza, created at the famous Pizzeria Uno, features a cornbread crust that supports Chicago mainstays such as sausage and pepperoni. Stuffed pizza resembles a pie, with crust covering all the goodies—spinach and ricotta cheese is the "official" way to stuff it.

MACKINAC ISLAND FUDGE

Locals call tourists "fudgies" because they can't sneak back onto the Michigan mainland without buying several slices of the creamy chocolate treat. The fudge-making itself is a show, which you can watch in any of the candy shops lining Huron Street, the island's primary thoroughfare.

CINCINNATI CHILI In 1949, Greek restauranteur Nicholas Lambrinides introduced chili made of finely ground lamb

and beef, seasoned with native spices and served on spaghetti. Skyline Chili became a citywide hit. It can be enjoyed two-way (chili and spaghetti), three-way (with cheddar cheese), and four- or five-way (with beans and onions layered beneath the cheese). Oyster crackers and hot sauce are put on top.

MILWAUKEE BEER

The Germans who settled in eastern Wisconsin didn't leave behind their thirsts—or their business skills—in their homeland. Bolstered by fertile soil for growing barley and other requisite ingredients for a good beer, Milwaukee became the U.S. brewing capital.

BUFFALO WINGS Like potato chips, this appetizer is a fluke. Teresa Bellissimo, co-owner of the Anchor Bar in Buffalo, concocted a snack for her son by frying up a surplus of chicken wings, slathering them in hot sauce and margarine, and serving them with the house blue cheese dressing for dipping. Somehow word got out, and now the wings can be ordered in all 50 states.

RACINE KRINGLE Danish settlers in Wisconsin continued the art of making kringle, a delicate pastry of light, flaky Wienerbrod dough. Baked and

filled with sweet apples, tart cherries, nuts, and chocolate, the kringle is iced with rich buttercream—making a fattening but fulfilling treat.

UPPER PENINSULA PASTIES

This Cornish meat pie was imported to Michigan by immigrant miners in the 19th century. Pasty cooks carved the initials of the intended eater into the dough, and the eater started at the uninitialed end so that if a meal was interrupted, the pasty could be set down without being taken by another hungry soul. Pasties usually consist of baked flour and lard dough filled with steak, potatoes, turnips, onions, and ground pepper.

Other Midwestern fare simply results from regional geography and climate. In Wisconsin, spectacular cheese is the end product of dairy cattle that graze in the state's lush pasturelands. Orchards bloom along Michigan's Grand Traverse Bay, where 50 percent of the nation's cherries are produced. And in the glacier-carved wetlands of Minnesota, wild rice has been harvested in abundance for hundreds of years by the Chippewa Indians.

The Great Plains

Fields of Gold, Infinite Horizons

A **giant sea** of grasslands and wheat fields rolling down the middle of America, the Great Plains region comes very close to defying description. This is not because the landscape is diverse—though it does offer more variety than most visitors imagine: the flat-topped buttes of the Badlands; the glacial lakes of the eastern Dakotas; the drifting dunes of Nebraska's Sand Hills; the vertical terrain of South Dakota's Black Hills, Oklahoma's Arbuckle Mountains, and Montana's Bears Paw Mountains; and the lush river valleys of the Missouri, Arkansas, and Platte, to name a few. Rather, it's because even the people who live on the Plains can't agree on where the region begins and ends.

North to south is easy enough: The region runs from the Canadian border to the Texas panhandle. The western boundary of the Plains is clear, as well: It's where the horizontal expanses bump into the Rocky Mountains in eastern New Mexico, central Colorado, and west-central Wyoming and Montana. The eastern boundary causes trouble, however. Some residents claim that the eastern borders of the Dakotas, Nebraska, Kansas, and Oklahoma form the boundary. Some claim it's the 98th meridian, which runs through the eastern parts of these Plains states and beyond which settlers found few trees for building houses. Similarly, others claim it's the "20-inch line" of rainfall: East of the line, around the

Oklahoma's Cimarron County (left), black-tailed prairie dog (right). Preceding pages: abandoned church, windmill, and water tower in North Dakota

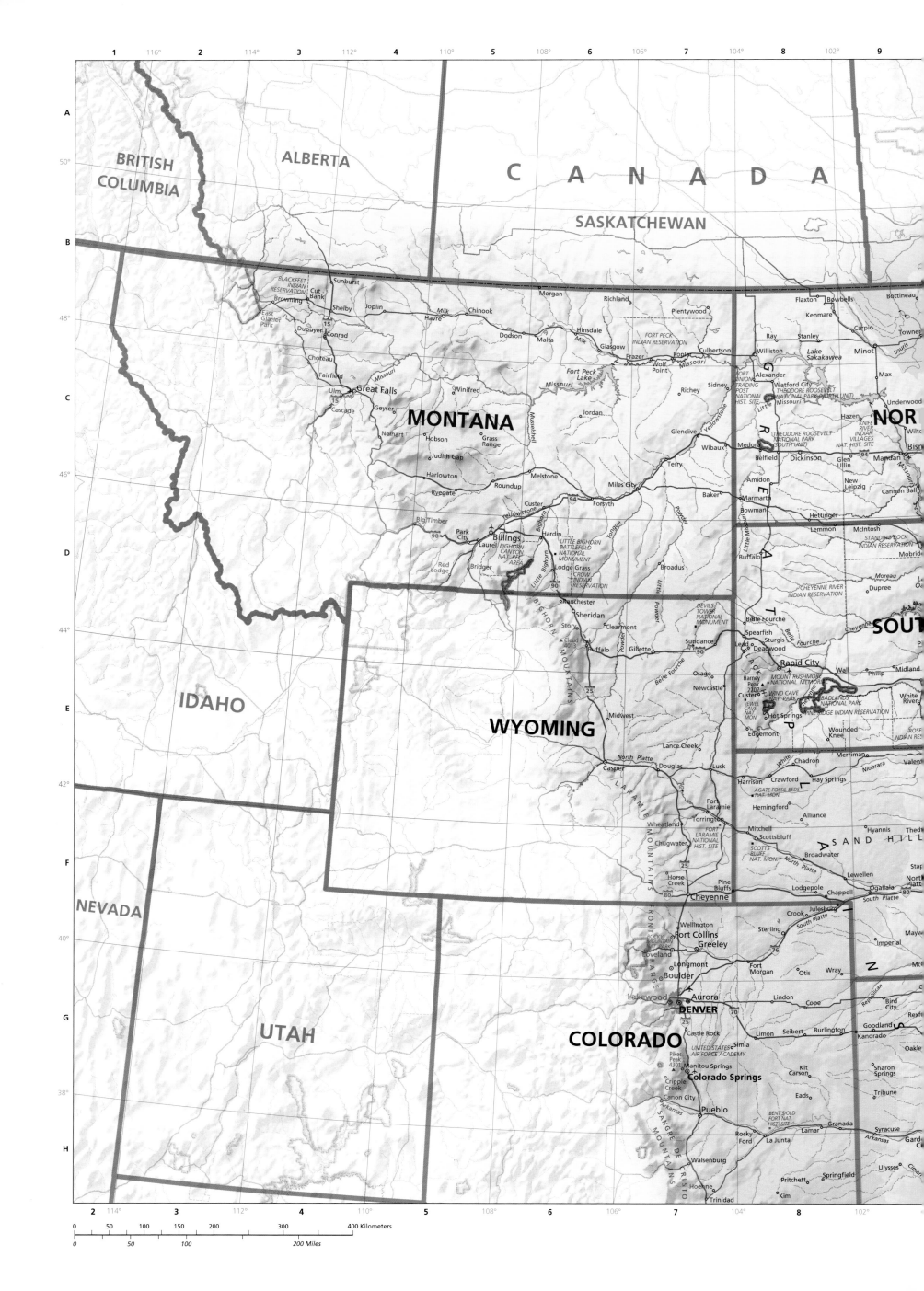

100th meridian, 20 or more inches (50 cm) of rain fall each year and west of the line, significantly less.

Truth be told, the Great Plains may be more a state of mind or an aesthetic sense of place than any determination of weather or longitude. In the big sky country of the Plains, horizons are infinite and the wind has absolute freedom. It seems as though you can see forever, and you almost can. On summer days, fleecy cumulus clouds speckle a brilliant blue sky and it's easy to imagine cruising just below cloud level in a plane, surrounded on all sides by air. The illusion of flying is more pronounced at night, as stars—bigger and brighter than can be seen from any city—appear almost within arm's reach. Lights twinkle on the horizon like some kind of mirage, distorting all perception of distance: You think you're approaching a town, but your map reveals that the town is still 50 miles (80 km) away. On the radio in South Dakota, a disc jockey with a Texas drawl comes in loud and clear from Del Rio on the Mexico border, across half a country of wide open spaces, cattle ranges, and fields of bluestem, sedge, and needlegrass.

The sprawl of the Plains is accentuated by emptiness: In many places not a single tree or building breaks the horizon, and the only markings are austere rectangles of golden wheat and fallow brown soil.

Population density is very low in the region, especially in Wyoming, Montana, and the Dakotas, which average fewer than ten people per square mile (four per sq km). Some counties in the western Dakotas are virtually uninhabited; nearly a third of Nebraska's counties have populations less than 5,000. Where cities in the Great Plains do exist,

The state capitol building in Pierre, South Dakota (right), was built between 1905 and 1910 of fieldstone and Indiana limestone.

Map continues on page 107

only a handful of them have populations exceeding 100,000, with the notable exceptions of Denver in Colorado, Omaha in Nebraska, Wichita in Kansas, Tulsa and Oklahoma City in Oklahoma, and Lubbock and Amarillo in Texas.

The Yellow Mound Area (left) in Badlands National Park features multi-hued mesas and pinnacles eroded by the elements.

Historically, the Plains were never considered a hospitable place for European pioneers to settle, though the Native Americans thrived here, hunting buffalo and growing crops of corn and squash and beans. In the 1840s, hundreds of thousands of white Easterners traveling along the Oregon and Mormon Trails crossed what they called the "Great American Desert"—known for tornadoes, floods, and "hostile Indian" attacks. But few stayed until people realized in the 1850s and '60s that these prairies were nourished by rich soil. The Homestead Act of 1862 helped draw settlers to the Great Plains by guaranteeing that anyone who lived on a plot of land and cultivated it for five years would gain ownership. Thus these early settlers transformed the Great American Desert into one of the world's most important agricultural regions, but only through hard work and ingenuity. In a land with few trees, settlers had to build houses of sod and learn to make fires of dry grass rather than wood. Rain and snow, called "blessed" on the Plains, were also known to freeze stranded cattle to death, or fall or melt too fast and at the wrong time, flooding fields or steaming wheat kernels on the stalk.

badlands and the black hills

In the southwest corner of South Dakota, the Badlands and the Black Hills lie 50 miles (80 km) apart but couldn't differ more dramatically. Badlands National Park is a moonscape of exotic rock pinnacles and spires carved by the erosive force of wind and rain. Black Hills National Forest comprises a range of pineclad mountains laced with lakes and streams, quiet canyons, and meadows of wildflowers.

The Badlands were formed as the Black Hills and the Rockies pushed up, draining away a shallow inland sea covering the northern Great Plains. Layers of sediment were left behind and gradually hardened into multicolored layers of rock, which rivers, wind, and rain sculpted into fantastic shapes. Despite the harsh desert environment and temperature extremes of 116 to minus 42 degrees Fahrenheit (47 to minus 41 C), the 240,000-acre (97,200-ha) park supports more than 50 varieties of grasses and receives 16 inches (40 cm) of rain annually. Birds and reptiles have adapted well, along with badgers, bobcats, mountain lions, porcupines, pronghorns, bighorn sheep, and even a herd of bison.

The inland sea also covered the Black Hills area, but this domed mountain range was formed by long periods of inundation alternating with periods of upheaval and folding of Earth's crust. As the dome of the Black Hills thrust upward and underlying rock layers eroded, a sequence of rock was exposed. The oldest layer dates back two billion years. Named for their dark green forested flanks, which appear black from a distance, the Black Hills stretch 125 miles (200 km) north to south and 65 miles (105 km) east to west. Harney Peak, the tallest summit between the Rockies and the Swiss Alps, rises to 7,242 feet (2,207 m), and an extensive system of roads and trails provides outstanding access to alpine scenery and wildlife.

By the 1930s, when Depression gripped the whole country, times were particularly hard on the Plains. A severe drought, combined with the overfarming and plowing of the semiarid grasslands, created the "Dust Bowl." Millions of tons of topsoil blew away in violent windstorms. During the worst of the dust storms,

Map continues on pages 104–105

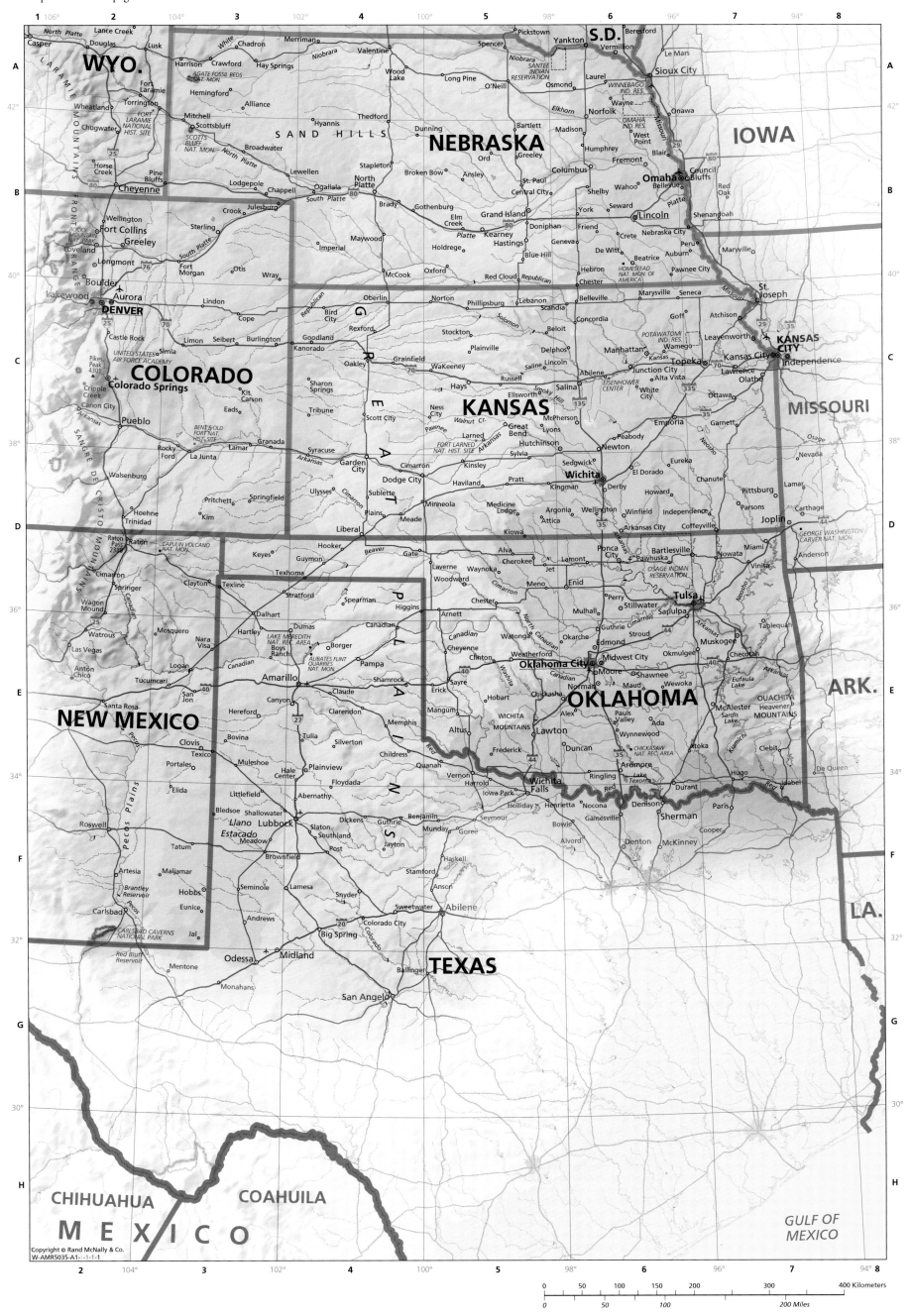

great plains indians

An eerie, kinetic tension gripped the Sioux encampment at Wounded Knee Creek, South Dakota, on the morning of December 29, 1890. High on a bluff surrounding Chief Big Foot and some 350 tribespeople (among the last of the Plains Indians to resist relocation to a reservation) was the U.S. Army's Seventh Cavalry—the same regiment whose members had been massacred by Sioux warriors 14 years earlier at Little Bighorn in Montana. Eventually, a shot was fired, signifying the end of a Great Plains way of life.

For 300 previous years, Native Americans flourished on the Plains. Great tribes such as the Blackfoot, Arapaho, Kiowa, Mandan, Pawnee, Wichita, and Sioux hunted massive herds of bison—as many as 60 million in the 17th century—which provided food, skin for clothing and shelter, bones for tools, and dung for fuel. Some groups, such as the Blackfoot and Comanche, migrated on foot with the herds and hunted year-round, but most tribes lived in permanent riverbank settlements, raising crops of corn, beans, and squash, and hunting bison seasonally, sometimes stampeding the animals off cliffs or into corrals.

Around 1650 the Spanish introduced the horse to the southern Plains; by the mid-18th century horse-trading had spread from the Comanche in Texas to the Blackfoot in North Dakota. The Sarci tribe named the animal "seven dogs" as a measurement of its relative usefulness. The Plains tribes no longer depended on the migratory patterns of the bison; now they could travel with the herds. Many of the farming villages were abandoned, and permanent earthen lodges were replaced by collapsible, bison-hide-covered tepees.

The tradition of the Great Plains Indians was essentially a warrior culture: Young males gained prestige with coups against enemies—stealing a weapon, leading a raid, or taking horses from an enemy camp. In 1806, a group of explorers on the Lewis and Clark expedition is said to have walked back to St. Louis from Montana after Crow warriors stole all their horses.

By the mid-19th century white settlers were flocking to the Plains, competing with the natives for land. Some tribes peacefully ceded territory, but the U.S. government and army routinely negated treaties. New native tribes arrived, too: They came from the Rockies to hunt bison and from the East in advance of the settlers. Intertribal territorial warfare was common, but the most violent engagements were usually provoked by white cattle ranchers and gold prospectors, who often killed bison just for pelts.

Despite the near complete destruction of the bison as a vital resource, the Sioux preserved their land for half a century. But each military triumph, led by Sitting Bull and Crazy Horse, incited brutal reprisals from the U.S. Army. The last major Sioux victory came in 1876 at the Battle of Little Bighorn. In an attempt to secure the Black Hills (sacred to the Sioux) for gold prospectors, Lieutenant Colonel George Custer charged his battalion over a ridge into a village of thousands of Sioux and Cheyenne; all of his troops perished. Fourteen years later, the U.S.-Indian battles culminated in the Wounded Knee Massacre, where the cavalry slaughtered Chief Big Foot and hundreds of his people.

Today those events and others are memorialized at national monuments and historic sites, and the Plains are a center of Native American culture, preserved on reservations, in museums, and in traditional festivals and powwows.

PLAINS INDIANS AT THE TIME OF EUROPEAN CONTACT

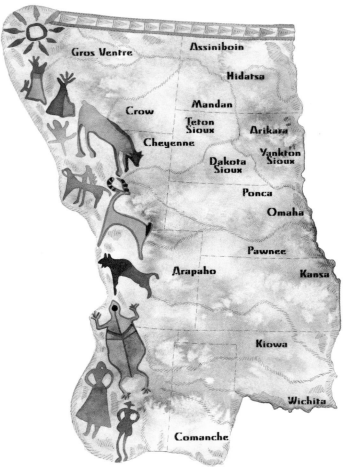

Montana's Little Bighorn Battlefield National Monument (top
left), King-Young Omahaw men
(left), American buffalo (right)

day turned to night, and dust penetrated the lungs of cattle and people, bringing death and disease to both. Crops that did survive the dust were devoured by grasshoppers. Many people abandoned their land and farming altogether, and a large group of "Okies" from Oklahoma migrated west to find work and a better life in California. Remarkably, many remained on the Plains. Either they couldn't afford to leave, or they had faith that things would get better—even on the southern Plains where the drought and dust storms were the worst. Finally, in 1939, the rains came again, and with them renewed hope and new settlement.

Since those days, farmers have implemented soil conservation procedures. Crops are now planted in strips and fields are allowed to lie fallow. Today the Plains region is the major wheat-producing area of the United States; even west of the 20-inch line there is enough rain to grow wheat, hay, oats, rye, barley, alfalfa, sorghum, sugar beets, and several other crops. Ranchers, too, have taken to shortgrass prairie conservation practices with grazing cattle. Other ecologically savvy people have protected the fragile Sand Hills of Nebraska by scattering old tires over the dunes. The Army Corps of Engineers has brought rivers that once overflowed their banks under control with giant dams, such as those built along the Missouri River, which provide hydroelectric power and have created a chain of lakes that stretches from Montana to Nebraska. The waters of the Missouri, so muddy they were once termed "too thick to drink and too thin to plow," now draw fishermen in search of walleye and northern pike, and in some places river water is drawn out and pushed through quarter-mile-long (.4-km) pipes to irrigate fields so farmers can produce corn well to the west of the 20-inch line.

Whether they live on a farm, on a ranch, or in a city or small town, Plains dwellers possess not only an acute awareness of the land, but a healthy respect for it, and for the region's brutal summers and winters. There is an ever-present realization that the forces of nature here can be unforgiving and that plentiful times are not a birthright. Appeals for rain take many forms today, including Native American

american buffalo

Few animals evoke the spirit of the Plains like the bison, or American buffalo. With its enormous bulk, shaggy head, and humped shoulders, the beast is well-suited to the tallgrass and shortgrass prairies and the harsh winters of the Plains. Its thick hide offers protection from bitter winds; its powerful head swings back and forth to clear snow off edible vegetation.

Bison are grass-eating nomads, constantly in search of greener pastures. Mobility is essential: Despite their size—males are often six feet (two m) high at the shoulder and weigh 2,000 pounds (900 kg)—bison are fast runners, with a top speed of 35 miles (56 km) per hour. At slower speeds, bison can cover several miles without stopping, and have been known to swim across a lake rather than walk around it.

In the early 19th century, migrating herds numbering in the hundreds of thousands were common—as late as 1871, a herd 25 miles (40 km) wide and 50 miles (80 km) deep was reported. To the Native Americans, the buffalo provided an inexhaustible source of food and other supplies. They put all parts of the animal to use: flesh for meat; skins for tepees, blankets, and canoes; ribs for sled runners; and hair for rope. But the coming of white hunters and the 1869 completion of the transcontinental railroad led to wholesale slaughter of the animals.

By the time the government took protective steps and made unregulated killing of bison illegal in 1874, the species that had once numbered 60 million had been almost totally exterminated. By 1900, only a few hundred bison remained—22 of them in Yellowstone National Park, where a hunting ban was enacted. Today 2,200 buffalo live in the park, and protected herds numbering more than 200,000 reside in other national parks and wildlife refuges.

rain dances and Christian prayers sent heavenward from thousands of churches—not just in English, but in German, Czech, Scandinavian, and other European tongues of the deeply religious ancestors who came to the Plains in the 19th century. Churchgoing is strong here, perhaps in large measure because the people understand that they cannot control the land, the weather, and their destinies by hard work and perseverance alone.

Although industry is important in the cities, agriculture is dominant everywhere else, and rain or the lack of it can mean a bumper crop or no crop at all. The fate of farmers and ranchers

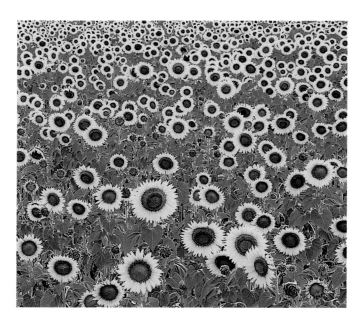

The faces of South Dakota's Mount Rushmore (top), sunflower field (above), tornado ripping across the Plains (right)

is intimately intertwined with that of the townsfolk. If the crops fail or prices are low, the people who run the banks, the hardware stores, the feed stores, and the grain elevators suffer, too. Thus, on the Great Plains people are humble and boasting is rare. Neighbors depend on each other, and a neighbor is not just someone who lives on the adjoining farm or ranch, but one who may live 40 or 50 miles (65 or 80 km) away.

The reverence that Plains people have for their land has inspired a substantial body of literature. Contemporary writers Kathleen Norris (*Dakota: A Spiritual Geography*, 1993), William Least Heat-Moon (*PrairyErth*, 1991), and Ian Frazier (*Great Plains*, 1989) have captured the mystique of the Plains in critically acclaimed books, building on a literary tradition begun much earlier by historians Ole Rölvaag and Walter Prescott Webb, and Plains novelists such as Mari Sandoz, Willa Cather, and Laura Ingalls Wilder. The Center for

Great Plains Studies at the University of Nebraska publishes a scholarly journal and has an encyclopedia in the works. The people of the Great Plains also keep their heritage alive at county fairs, rodeos, round-ups, harvest celebrations, and at dozens of restored military forts and pioneer museums. Dodge City, Kansas, preserves legacies of Wyatt Earp, Bat Masterson, and the magnificent cattle drives, while Deadwood, South Dakota, recalls Wild Bill Hickock and Calamity Jane and the rowdy spirit of the western frontier. Covered wagon excursions re-create the original journeys over the Oregon Trail, and native Plains Indians hold hundreds of powwows and similar events throughout the area. One of the largest is Red Earth Days in Oklahoma City, a four-day celebration held each year in June. The region has dozens of historical Plains Indians sites and monuments, and the state of Oklahoma hosts the headquarters of more than 30 native groups. Its many outstanding Native American museums and cultural centers honor memories of great leaders such as Red Cloud, Sitting Bull, Crazy Horse, and Black Elk.

Life on the Plains is good these days. Despite a national trend toward greater urbanization, a counter trend appears to be especially strong in this region. It's a movement back to the land, to the serenity of the country. True, good jobs may be difficult to come by, but the

tornado alley

Plains dwellers are intimately familiar with the most powerful weather phenomenon in Earth's atmosphere. Since 1900 more than 10,000 people in the United States have been killed by tornadoes, the lion's share of which plow across a swath of the central and southern Plains dubbed Tornado Alley.

Thanks to Plains geology, laws of thermodynamics, and vast temperature variations, Tornado Alley is the most active weather zone in the world, averaging 306 tornadoes per year. Tornado conditions are perfect, as cold air from the Rocky Mountains meets moist Gulf air blocked from expanding westward. Some 30,000 twisters have been tracked here since 1916, the strongest with funnels a mile (1.6 km) wide, winds of 250 miles (400 km) per hour, and speeds up to 110 miles (175 km) per hour.

Tornadoes here, as everywhere, are deadly: In 1947, a twister ripped across the states of Texas, Oklahoma, and Kansas, killing 181 people and injuring 970. But the five deadliest U.S. tornadoes occurred in densely populated Missouri, Illinois, and Mississippi—not in Tornado Alley—largely because there are fewer people, fewer trees, and more visible cloud banks on the Plains. In 1991, for example, one Kansas twister barreled overland for 66 miles (106 km) but destroyed only one farmhouse.

Tornadoes here are also characteristically odd: A 1915 Kansas storm hurled five horses from a barn but set them down unscathed a quarter-mile (.4 km) away, still hitched to their post, while a necktie rack was found 40 miles (64 km) away with all ten ties still intact.

Tornado Alley is to storm chasers what Hawaii's North Shore is to surfers: In May and June, it's not uncommon to see bumper-to-bumper traffic running down a funnel cloud.

plains agriculture and ranching

When explorer Zebulon Pike first saw the dry shortgrass plains of Kansas in 1806, he called the area a desert. In fact, it was neither uninhabitable nor uninhabited: Native Americans had hunted and farmed there for centuries. Yet many European settlers, lured by anomalous periods of reliable rainfall and offers of cheap homesteads, found life unbearably hard. Was there ever a land so beleaguered by drought? By tornadoes? By cataclysmic blizzards, hail storms, and even grasshoppers? By high, hot winds that evaporated rain before it hit the ground?

Nevertheless, many of the immigrants succeeded with dry-farming methods transplanted from their homelands. German-Russian settlers found conditions in the Plains much like those of the steppes they'd left behind. The Mennonites among them were especially adept with a drought-resistant variety of hard red winter wheat called Turkey Red. Here, as in the Midwest, John Deere's 1837 development of the self-scouring steel plow made cultivation of the tough sod possible and changed the landscape forever. Much of what was once soil-enriching prairie in the eastern Great Plains is now cropland.

The World War I years were a boom period for agriculture, but after the war, demand and prices fell. Plains farmers were already in dire straits when the stock market crashed in 1929 and the Great Depression set in. The '30s saw year after year of drought; the lower Plains states formed the heart of the Dust Bowl, with "black blizzards" of windblown topsoil darkening the skies.

Today, efficient farming methods and irrigation of some crops have made the Plains prolific, despite the inhospitable climate. Kansas leads the nation in wheat and sorghum production. North Dakota is the leading producer of barley, sunflower seeds, and flaxseed. In Oklahoma, corn, soybeans, oats, and cotton flourish.

Moving west, wheatfields give way to grazing land as the climate becomes drier, the natural grasses shorter, and the farms and ranches farther from market. In the west, cattle and, in some areas, sheep graze over vast territory on ever more sprawling ranches. In Montana, where three-quarters of all farmland is range, a ranch of 2,500 acres (1,000 ha) is considered average in size. In most of the Plains states, roughly half the annual income comes from crops and half from livestock, with the 100th meridian as a rough dividing line: West of it, annual rainfall of less than 20 inches (50 cm) makes farming a never-ending battle against the odds.

Chimney Rock National Historic Site, Nebraska (left); Kansas feed yard and wheat stalks (bottom left); Carhenge, Salem Sue, and the Mitchell Corn Palace (top to bottom right)

computer revolution and Internet commerce have made it possible for many people to earn city-level incomes while spending most of their time in the country. Others think nothing of lengthy work commutes. In Great Plains states that lost population for decades, modest gains are now the rule, as people move back there to telecommute or to drive 100 miles (160 km) to work in a bigger city. In the 1990s, for example, the populations of South Dakota, Nebraska, Kansas, and Oklahoma all experienced net population increases.

Economies in most of the Plains cities are robust. In the past century, oil and petrochemicals have driven population gains in big cities like Tulsa and Oklahoma City. Omaha and Rapid City have drawn economic strength from military bases, among other industries. Wichita continues to expand its reputation as a builder of aircraft. Omaha has long been a leader in meat-packing and food-processing, and Rapid City's Homestake Mine holds sway as the largest gold-mining operation in the world. High-tech industries have shot up in the area of southeast South Dakota known as Silicon Prairie, and in many other cities on the Plains. Naturally, agribusinesses are everywhere.

The cities and towns of the Great Plains are thriving in other ways, too. Tulsa, Oklahoma City, and Wichita host outstanding symphonies, theater and ballet companies, and art museums. And smaller cities like Sioux Falls, South Dakota, show up on lists of the best places to live in the United States for their hospitable business climate; first-rate schools, parks, hospitals, and housing; good government; clean air; low unemployment and taxes; daily flights to Minneapolis, Denver, and Chicago; and almost no serious crime or poverty. The logical question: "What more could anyone ask for?" Milder winters, maybe.

roadside attractions

To many, the Great Plains is a place you pass through on the way to somewhere else—an amorphous plateau marked only by grain silos and paint-peeled barns. But other markers exist: hundreds of quirky tourist sights and outlandish landmarks. The Plains region has been the epicenter of roadside kitsch ever since Ted Hustead, an enterprising South Dakotan, began doling out free ice water at Wall Drug in 1931. Today additional Plains visionaries offer passersby diversions from tedious driving along endless fields.

NORTH DAKOTA
- World's Tallest Stack of Empty Oil Cans (45 feet/14 m), Casselton
- Geographic Center of North America (marked by a 15-foot-/4.6-m-high obelisk), Rugby
- "Salem Sue," the World's Largest Holstein Cow, New Salem

SOUTH DAKOTA
- Wall Drug, Wall
- Mitchell Corn Palace, Mitchell

NEBRASKA
- Carhenge (an auto-inspired version of Stonehenge), Alliance
- World's Biggest Ball of Stamps (600 pounds/272 kg), West Omaha

KANSAS
- World's Largest Hand-Dug Well (109 feet/33 m deep), Greensburg
- World's Largest Ball of Twine (six million feet/1.8 million m long), Cawker City

OKLAHOMA
- Cow-Chip Throwing Capital of the World (presided over by King Cow Chip, a 15-foot-/4.6-m-tall fiberglass beaver), Beaver

TEXAS PANHANDLE
- Largest Cross in the Western Hemisphere (190 feet/58 m tall), Groom
- Cadillac Ranch (a row of Caddies buried upright), Amarillo

EASTERN NEW MEXICO
- Smokey Bear Museum and Gravesite, Capitan

EASTERN COLORADO
- World's Largest Hercules Beetle, Colorado Springs
- Used Car Dealership Made of Petrified Wood, Lamar

EASTERN WYOMING
- Mother Featherlegs (America's one and only monument to a prostitute), Lusk

The Heart of Texas

Big Country
of Big Heroes

"It's like a whole **other country,**" the saying goes. In fact, the Heart of Texas *was* a whole other country with its own government, army, and flag from 1836 to 1845. The raising of five other flags over Texas (by Spain, France, Mexico, the Confederacy, and the United States) shows how often the region changed hands and how deeply it was coveted for its generous resources, strategic continental position, and gargantuan size.

Size has always mattered to Texans. When Texas joined the Union in 1845 (some Texans prefer to say it was "reduced" to statehood), the United States government suggested that the land be divided into five states of more seemly dimensions. Texans rejected the proposal outright, perhaps because none of the five new states wanted to give up the Alamo. But it's more likely that Texans just liked the notion of bigness, of remaining the jumbo size. Even today people of this region will remind you that the dome of the Texas capitol in Austin was built seven feet (2.1 m) taller than the national capitol in Washington. Or that the King Ranch, an 823,000-acre (333,000-ha) cattle concern on the Gulf coastal plain, is bigger than the state of Rhode Island.

If the people who live in the Heart of Texas are known for boasting and braggadocio, they might be forgiven. The land does offer up incredible riches in oil, natural gas, grazing pastures, and cotton fields, along with wildly diverse terrain. Outsiders imagine the entire region to be a stark, flat, arid plain speckled with cattle. Instead, there are rolling hills,

Goat's-foot daisies on Padre Island (left), nine-banded armadillo (right). Preceding pages: cattle among the oaks of Fayette County

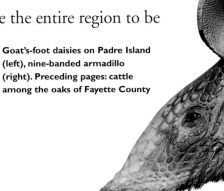

river canyons, swamps, and sandy beaches. Even excluding the Big Bend area (which is part of the Southwest) and the Texas panhandle (part of the Plains), the region's terrain is as varied as any country's.

East Texas is bucolic, with millions of acres of dark piney woods and the Big Thicket Preserve, where abundant rain falls on an impenetrable canopy of dogwoods, magnolias, and azaleas. In the southeast, the balmy Gulf Coast curls from the bougainvillea-scented Louisiana border south to Mexico along expansive stretches of sugar-white beaches, including Padre Island National Seashore, the world's longest barrier island. In the north and central part of the region, a vast, lake-flecked prairie sweeps down from the Red River, then smoothes out in the west to dusty, gray-green plains blanketed with chaparral and prickly pear cactus. And plunked down somewhat incongruously in the middle of the region is a juniper-clad oasis known as the Hill Country—a land of rushing rivers, deep blue lakes, limestone cliffs, and meadows of bluebonnets.

This was the sprawling, diverse land to which Spain laid claim in 1510. Expedition leader Alvar Núñez Cabeza de Vaca first stepped ashore in 1528 after he was shipwrecked and captured by natives near what is now Galveston. Eight years later he escaped to Mexico and circulated tales about gold in the Seven Cities of Cíbola, which attracted treasure-seekers like Francisco Vasquez de Coronado to the region. The French opened

The skyscrapers of Houston, legendary oil giant and the largest city in Texas, loom over green Memorial Park (right).

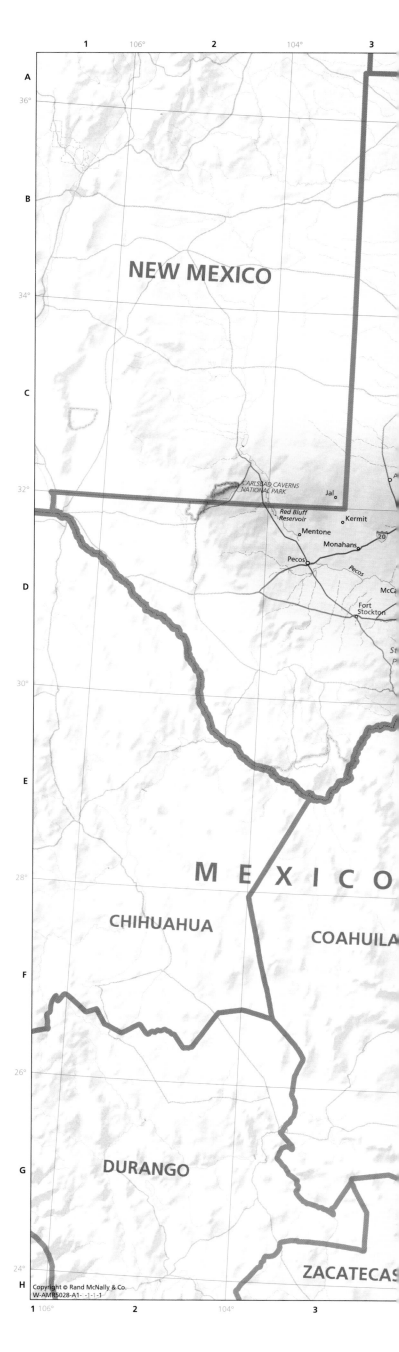

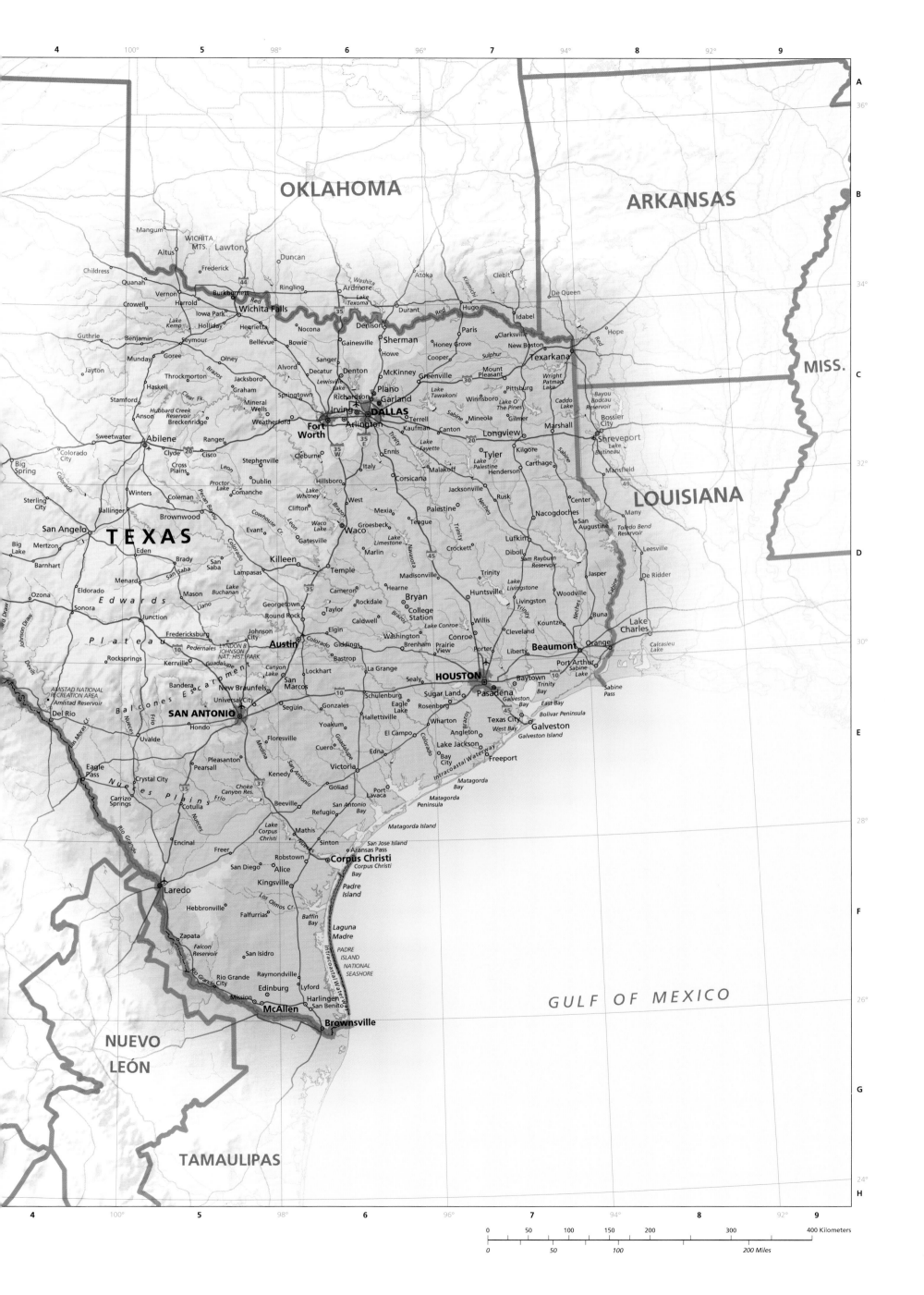

trade with the natives; soon after, Spaniards began to establish missions—36 between 1680 and 1793—to solidify territorial claims, make Christian converts of the Native Americans, and establish the Spanish culture and language, which are still very strong in the region today.

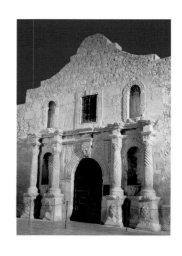

texas oil fields

Until the late 1800s, if you said the word "oil," people thought of Pennsylvania, home of the first U.S. oil well and millions of barrels of black crude. All that changed in 1901 when a gusher named Spindletop was drilled in East Texas.

Because petroleum is made of the compacted remains of plants and animals from ancient seas, finding oil is a matter of finding the right geology. Much of Texas had been underwater in bygone eras; it made sense to assume the land might hold vast oil reserves. Commercial oil wells already existed in Nacogdoches County (1866) and Corsicana (1894) when one-armed brick-plant owner Pattillo Higgins noticed a salt dome—a sign of trapped oil—near Beaumont. He leased the land to Anthony Lucas,

a Louisiana mining engineer, who hit the jackpot on January 10, 1901. Spindletop, a 1,020-foot-deep (311-m) well, gushed oil like a geyser. By the time Lucas's team capped Spindletop ten days later, half a million barrels were wasted, and every house in town needed repainting.

Speculators poured into Beaumont. The lone bank in town was so overloaded with deposits that sacks of money cluttered the lobby. Countless boomtowns followed as "black gold" spurted up all over the state, but the East Texas oil field, discovered in 1930, was the largest site—twice the size of Manhattan. Drills pumped the field relentlessly, pushing the price of oil down to three cents per barrel. Eventually the governor declared martial law, calling out the National Guard to enforce production quotas.

By 1928, Texas was the largest oil-producing state in the country. But the flow peaked in 1972; these days, oil and gas make up only about 10 percent of the gross state product. This is a momentous drop in crude, but still far more oil than burbles out from those mighty gushers of Pennsylvania.

A canopy of green in Big Thicket Preserve in East Texas (right), the legendary Alamo in San Antonio (above), an offshore oil rig (left)

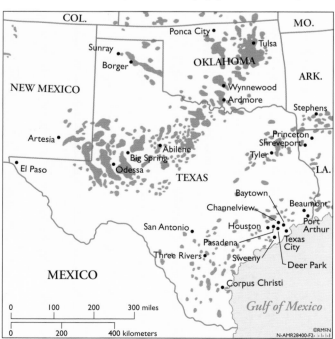

converts of the Native Americans, and establish the Spanish culture and language, which are still very strong in the region today.

The first community of Anglo settlers, 300 families led by Stephen Austin and known as the Old Three Hundred, arrived in East Texas in 1821. Mexico had just won independence—and the Texas region—from Spain, and offered generous land grants to Anglo immigrants who would come and settle in Texas. But in the early 1830s, a charismatic Mexican general named Antonio López de Santa Anna declared himself president and imprisoned Austin. After Texans gathered their own army and defeated the Mexicans at Gonzalez, Santa Anna attacked the Alamo in San Antonio with a vastly superior army of 5,000, killing all defenders and ordering the massacre of 300 prisoners at Goliad. Enraged Texans took up the battle cries "Remember the Alamo!" and the less euphonious "Remember Goliad!" On April 21, 1836, with only 743 raw troops at his command, army commander-in-chief Sam Houston put to rout a seasoned Mexican force of twice that number and captured Santa Anna. Mexico signed the treaty of Velasco, granting Texas independence.

The United States recognized the new country: the independent Republic of Texas. So did several European nations. Countryhood sat well with Texans. They formed a government, sent and received ambassadors, negotiated international treaties, and proudly flew the Lone Star flag. Some people worried about burgeoning Texas hubris; in 1845 Bostonian writer and clergyman Edward Everett Hale published a 16-page pamphlet entitled *How to Conquer Texas Before Texas Conquers Us.* But Texans had every right to be proud. They had fought their own revolution and had won it.

Sam Houston was the archetypal Texan hero of the moment. Early in life he demonstrated a Texan-style independence by leaving home at age

the hill country

The Hill Country of south-central Texas is a surprisingly pastoral oasis of gentle hills, limestone canyons, oak thickets, emerald rivers, and pageants of wildflowers. In the midst of an arid, tumbleweed-littered landscape, the Hill Country boasts clear springs flowing out of rocks, turkey vultures soaring high over sparkling swimming holes, and spectacular autumn foliage displays of maples and oaks.

The Balcones Escarpment marks the eastern and southern edges of the famed Hill Country. Formed millions of years ago by an enormous earthquake, this slope of land rises along a fault that divides the Gulf coastal plain and the semiarid Edwards Plateau. The land south and east of the fault sank, while the earth north and west of it rose to form the Hill Country. The limestone hills were shaped by rivers and streams slicing and smoothing the edges of the plateau.

The Hill Country claims the most rivers and streams in all of the Heart of Texas region. Fed by springs welling up from the limestone, the Nueces, San Saba, Frio, Guadalupe, Sabinal, San Marcos, and Llano Rivers all flow here. The Colorado River also courses through the Hill Country, swelling into lakes and reservoirs behind its numerous dams.

The Comanche Indians once reigned over the Hill Country, defeating the Spanish conquistadors in 1758 at San Saba de la Santa Cruz mission, near what is now the town of Menard. But it is the German, not Comanche or Spanish, heritage that has survived and still thrives in Hill Country towns such as Fredericksburg and New Braunfels. Town founders arrived in the 1840s, attracted to the area by abundant waterways for irrigation and opportunities for trade. The settlers signed a treaty with the Comanches in 1847 and began work as farmers and merchants. Today these settlements retain their German cuisine, architecture, language, and other traditions.

Austin and San Antonio serve as gateways to the Hill Country's narrow curving roadways and its small towns and hamlets. Spectacular state parks showcase the most scenic landscapes, such as Lost Maples State Natural Area, where the Sabinal River is flanked by a stand of bigtooth maples. In Pedernales Falls State Park, the namesake river features high bluffs and prime swimming holes. Guadalupe River State Park boasts legendary fishing for Guadalupe bass, and Hill Country State Natural Area has a network of rocky hiking trails. Enchanted Rock State Natural Area offers a boulder garden with a 425-foot-high (122-m) batholith of pink granite that emits strange moans the Native Americans believed were the whispers of the gods.

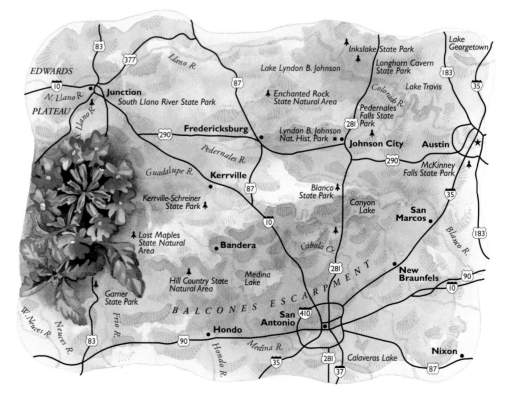

Blanket of Hill Country bluebonnets (above), fishing hole
on the Guadalupe River (left),
taste-bud-paralyzing chili (right)

15 to live with the Cherokee Indians. He was twice elected president of the new republic, and he pushed for statehood, which Texas was granted in 1845. He also served as U.S. Senator and state governor, though he was deposed later for trying to prevent Texas from seceding from the Union.

Other Texan men and women earned hero's reputations, too, merely by surviving in this beautiful but terror-filled land. "If I owned both Hell and Texas," General Philip Sheridan once said, "I'd rent out Texas and live in Hell." Tornadoes and storms called "northers" blasted across the region. Hurricanes wreaked havoc along the Gulf coast. Floods, drought, hostile natives, outlaws, and disease constituted other threats to life and limb. Many early survivors were hardscrabble immigrants—Germans, Czechs, Poles, Greeks, Scandinavians, and Scots—who withstood difficult journeys from Europe and overcame various diseases once they arrived.

Enterprising ranchers and farmers became the next Texas heroes. They returned from Civil War battlefields to find that their scattered cattle had survived nicely and propagated to millions. The ranchers rounded up the cattle, herded them to Abilene, Kansas, on the Chisholm Trail, and shipped them by rail to Eastern cities with a pent-up demand for beef. The cattlemen got rich and yet another hardworking Texas archetype was born—the cowboy. A loner who spent his days and some nights in the saddle, the cowboy became the stuff of legends: brave, rugged, and tough

texas chili

Chili, the official food of the Lone Star State, has inspired more arguments, fistfights, romantic flights, folktales, and recipe variations than any other cuisine in Texas.

Purists say that true chili consists only of beef (chunks or coarsely ground), chile peppers, garlic, cumin, and a few other spices (mostly hot ones). It must not be defiled with beans or anything else—even tomato sauce. One theory holds that chili began as a brown-bag lunch for Texas cowboys in the 1840s. For a hearty meal that would not spoil quickly on the range, cowboys pounded chile peppers and spices into a brick of beef; the spices and peppers preserved the beef until it could be boiled later and eaten as a stew. The raw materials were as abundant then as they are

now—the beef was all around them and the peppers and spices grew wild. Today the region is the number-one producer of beef and the third-leading producer of peppers in the country.

In 1967 humorist H. Allen Smith of Mount Kisco, New York, declared that he could make a better bowl of chili than any Texan, and that he would include beans. Texan chili authority Frank X. Tolbert promptly organized the first chili cook-off, "The Great Chili Confrontation," pitting Smith against a Texan named Wick Fowler and his Two-Alarm Chili. In a scene reminiscent of *High Noon*, Smith and Fowler faced each other down as the clock struck 12 in the ghost town of Terlingua. The judges had to declare the confrontation a draw because the sampling paralyzed their taste buds. The cook-off has taken place every year since; recent crowds number 7,000.

Little controversy surrounds the region's other staple foods: barbecued beef, chicken-fried steak, and Tex-Mex. But be careful how you mess with chili.

as nails—a true Texan. But in the 1880s, as barbed wire began to crisscross the range and the railroad pushed into the region, the cattle drives became unnecessary, and so did cowboys.

Mighty Texas longhorn (below), Gulf shrimp fleet (right), Texas's largest boots, roadrunner, and citizen: Big Tex (bottom right)

The 1900s brought the rise of oil men and women. In 1901 after a gusher named Spindletop spewed black gold into the air for more than a week, East Texas became the country's greatest oil producer. Houston's population soared in the '50s, '60s, and '70s with the oil and natural gas boom. The oil market eventually dropped out; today Houston is known as the home of the National Aeronautics and Space Administration and a thriving business environment for petrochemicals, plastics, biotechnology, and aircraft manufacturing.

Today's Texas heroes include entrepreneurs and risk-takers, many of them the cattle ranchers, oil barons, and others who helped make the region a leading producer of cotton, wheat, peanuts, hay, rice, hogs, eggs, sulfur, electronic manufactures, and petrochemicals. Other Texas entrepreneurs build cities, explore space, and pioneer alternative music. They live in sky-scrapered cities like Dallas, called the New York of the region for wealth in oil, banking, insurance, and the performing arts, and in Fort Worth, known for its folksy western heritage and world-class museums. They live in pretty resort towns on the Gulf like Corpus Christi and Galveston, and in San Antonio, where two thirds of the population is Hispanic and the mission, plazas, and Paseo del Rio (River Walk) evoke the feeling that you're not in the United States at all. They live in border towns that share a heritage with a sister city on the Mexican side: Brownsville with Matamoros, Laredo with Nuevo Laredo, Del Rio with Ciudad Acuña. Or they live in proud, midsize cities like Austin—the state capital, a university town, and the gateway to the computer chip manufacturers of Silicon Gulch.

Clearly, Texans continue to believe they are big enough to do anything. There is a story of a Texas father lecturing his son on decorum: "Son," the father said, "don't ever ask a man where he's from. If he's from Texas, he'll tell you. If he's not, there's no need to embarrass him."

cattle ranching

It used to be more costly to raise a chicken than a Long-horn in the Heart of Texas. A mild climate, few natural predators, and limitless browse made the region a natural grazing ground for cattle. The Spanish provided the essentials for ranching: cattle, brought to Spanish ranches in Texas in the 17th and 18th centuries (they mingled with English farm stock to produce the Texas Longhorn); Arabian horses; and generous land grants for settlers to raise stock.

In 1860, there were six head of cattle per person in Texas. By the end of the Civil War, anybody who could round up wild Longhorns could claim them. Rangeland was not fenced; some men owned thousands of cattle without claiming a single acre of land. But without ready access to markets, a mature steer brought only $2 to $3.

In 1867, an Illinois cattle dealer built pens for the Longhorns and a hotel for the cowboys at the railroad terminus in Abilene, Kansas. For the next 20 years, as soon as the grass came in, cowboys would herd 2,500 to 3,000 Longhorns north to market in Abilene, then Wichita, Dodge City, and Ogallala. Twelve men with five horses apiece could

manage it, and if a lightning storm or a whiff of wolf didn't spook the herd, they could make ten to 15 miles (16 to 24 km) a day.

The railroad reached Texas in 1873, followed in 1874 by barbed wire. Owning land— the more the better—became essential as ranchers fenced in the range. The great cattle drives ended, and a century later there were only 1,500 lean, leggy Longhorns left, replaced by meatier Herefords, Brahmans, and Black Angus. Today Longhorns survive primarily in refuges and on traditional ranches.

Cattle ranching is still big business here, with three head of cattle to every four people in Texas. Chuckwagons still turn out beef, beans, and biscuits for cowhands during the annual roundup, although today the chuckwagon is a pickup truck, cowhands ride helicopters as often as quarterhorses, and ranchers track costs on a computer. These days, livestock sales at the annual Houston Livestock Show and Rodeo, the largest in the world, reach $8 million, and two million people attend events like the World Bar-B-Que Championship. The entry requirement: 60 pounds (27 kg) of barbecued brisket.

big texas

The Heart of Texas region is big—not just in size, but in attitude, pride, and lifestyle. Real Texans will insist that descriptions of their braggadocio are highly exaggerated; they're just "telling it like it is." Not that they don't have plenty to brag about with the immense size of the place and the extremes of landscape: coast and desert, forest and plains, mountains and subtropics.

Still, beyond all that, the citizens of Texas have found ways of perpetuating their own enor-

mous claims to fame and big-ness. Fort Worth boasts the world's largest honky-tonk bar, Billy Bob's Texas, with 100,000 square feet (9,300 sq m) of country music, dancing, arcades, and mechanical bulls for riding. Amarillo, in the Texas panhandle, is home of the Big Texas Steak Ranch, which touts the world's largest steak. The 72-ounce (two-kg) steak dinner is free if you can eat it (with potatoes and greens on the side) in an hour; more than 35,000 people have tried and about 7,000 have succeeded.

Kingsville features one of the world's biggest ranches—in fact, at 823,000 acres (333,000 ha) the King Ranch has more land than Rhode Island. Even the Dallas-Fort Worth International Airport is oversized—bigger than Manhattan.

Then there are the icons: the world's largest jackrabbit in Odessa; the world's largest pecan in Seguin; the world's largest roadrunner in Fort Stockton; and the world's largest mosquito, 25-foot-tall (7.5-m) Willie Manchew, in Clute. At the Dallas State Fair, there's 52-foot-tall (16-m) "Big Tex," and in San Antonio, the world's largest set of cowboy boots graces the North Star Mall.

It's clear that although Texas joined its neighbors in statehood, Texans' sense of

bigness was never shaken from the cultural imagination, especially in Houston, where the first domed stadium, the Astrodome, was originally billed as "the Eighth Wonder of the World," and where breast augmentation surgery was invented in 1962.

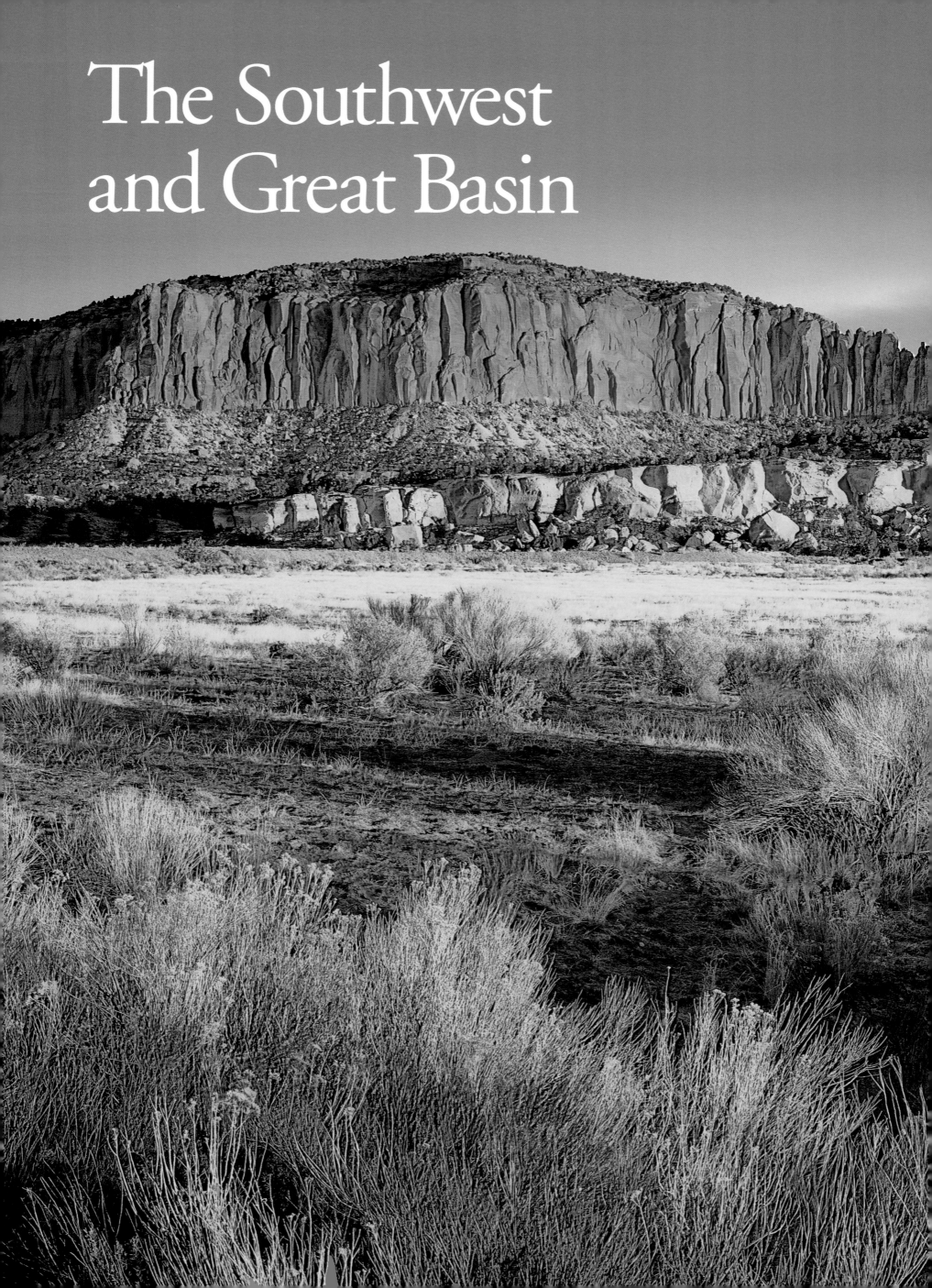

The Southwest
and Great Basin

Desert Panorama of Color and Light

A **majestic** yet terrifying tableau of vast deserts, lofty plateaus and mesas, desolate canyons, and forbidding mountains, the Southwest and Great Basin exudes an otherworldliness that can be shocking. The landscape is utterly unlike any other on Earth. Though isolated cities and towns are sprinkled throughout the region—which includes New Mexico, Arizona, Nevada, most of Utah, southern Idaho, southeastern Oregon, southwestern Texas and Colorado, and eastern California—most of the land is uninhabited, or uninhabitable, by people. The silence and stillness are palpable: To be alone in the desert, in a remote canyon, or on a mountain is to know the true meaning of solitude, loneliness, and not infrequently, fear.

Some of the landforms represent deep wounds in the earth—heaps of boulders and jagged, jumbled shards of rock. They appear to have been created by a violent, cosmic blast. But it didn't happen that way: The raw power of nature has been at work for millions of years here, as volcanoes erupted, simmered, and died; mountains and plateaus pushed up; and ancient seas invaded and receded, leaving marine fossils embedded inside multicolored strata now thousands of feet above sea level.

The great Colorado Plateau comprises a fair amount of the Southwest. Here, eons of wind, rain, and runoff, along with freezing, thawing, and cracking, have sculpted fantastic

Zion's Virgin River Narrows (left), Albuquerque's balloon-fest (below). Preceding pages: Grand Staircase-Escalante National Monument

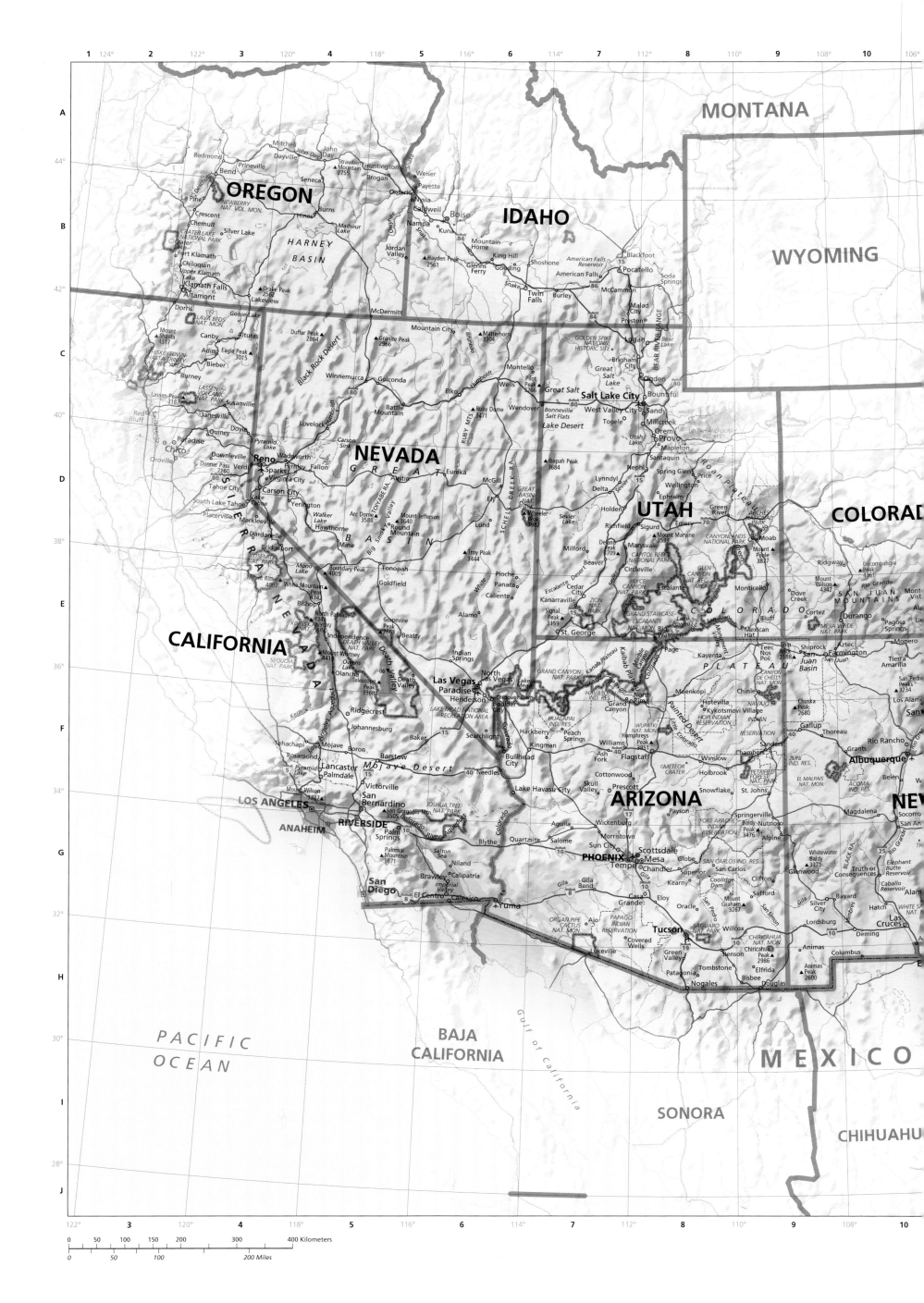

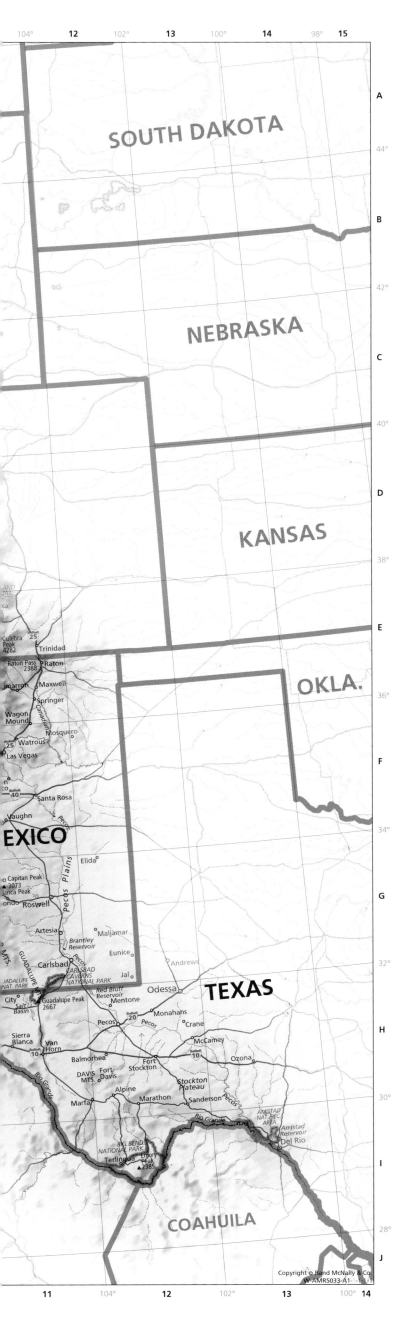

arches, spires, pinnacles, windows, and other exotic formations in national parks such as

A southwestern Texas sunrise in Big Bend National Park, where prickly pear cacti (above) overlook the Rio Grande

Bryce Canyon, Zion, Canyonlands, Arches, Capitol Reef, and Petrified Forest. Inside Grand Canyon National Park, the Colorado River has cut a gash a mile (1.6 km) deep, revealing more than two billion years of geologic history and displaying the oldest rock on Earth: primordial schist. The river has always flowed at about its present level, thus the canyon was formed over the millennia as the Kaibab Plateau slowly rose beneath it, like a cake rising around a knife.

Much of the rest of the region is part of a vast American desert extending from southeastern Oregon south into Mexico. Several distinct deserts exist here, but the most dramatic is the Mojave Desert, in which Death Valley lies. The Mojave receives only two to six inches (five to 15 cm) of rain in an average year; Death Valley, less than two inches. During one two-year period in this century, no rain at all fell in Death Valley. Summer air temperatures exceed 120 degrees Fahrenheit (49 degrees C); the record high was 134 Fahrenheit (57 C) in 1913—only two degrees short of the world record. The ground can sometimes heat up to 190 Fahrenheit (88 C)—more than hot enough to actually fry an egg.

The Mojave abuts the Great Basin, which is characterized by parched valleys of hard-baked sand, gravel, and salt flats broken up by mountains. The term Great Basin is somewhat of a misnomer: In reality,

the colorado river

At its source, some 14,000 feet (4,300 m) high on the western shoulder of Colorado's Rocky Mountains, the Colorado River is little more than a gurgling, high-alpine trickle. Downstream, however, the river is as significant as any ocean. The Colorado is the most dammed, diverted, legislated, and litigated river in the United States—all for the sake of western development. Dubbed "an American Nile," the river is why the West has been able to exist, and why the water table and water rights are contentious issues here.

From the Rockies, the Colorado drops more than 12,000 feet (3,700 m) in elevation—the greatest descent of any North American river—

wending its way south and west for 1,450 miles (2,300 km) until it dries up as a trickle before reaching the Gulf of California. Along the way, the river takes in hundreds of snowmelt-fed tributaries—the Green, San Juan, Gunnison, and Escalante, to name a few—and waters farmland in seven states and two countries. It snakes through dozens of natural treasures, such as Utah's dusty red rock buttes and the arid Grand Canyon. Which is also to say that it is charged with watering the driest spots in the country.

In 1922, Herbert Hoover, then the U.S. Commerce Secretary, mediated the first phase in taming the Colorado. California, with six million people, got the bulk of its water. Colorado, Arizona, Utah, New Mexico, Wyoming, and Nevada begrudgingly accepted their shares. By 1928, the Boulder Canyon Project Act was passed, and plans were drawn for what was then the largest of all modern civil engineering projects: the Hoover Dam. With 66 million tons (60 million metric tons) of concrete standing 726 feet (220 m) high,

the dam, along with its reservoir, Lake Mead, was completed by 1936. In less than a century, the Colorado River spawned hundreds of dams and diversion facilities, keeping the cities of San Diego, Los Angeles, Las Vegas, and Phoenix, among others, from turning into dust. The dams controlled the river's flooding, set up hydroelectric power, irrigated cropland, and provided beautiful gems like Lakes Powell and Mead. But they also destroyed habitat for

native species, and submerged ancient and pristine canyons.

Today the Colorado is home or neighbor to countless national recreational areas. It has inspired the dam-controlling U.S. Bureau of Reclamation and scores of environmental debates, from Clean Water Act issues to Native American water rights. Agriculturally, the Colorado River is responsible for $1.5 billion in revenues, helping produce 15 percent of the country's crops and 13 percent of its livestock.

COLORADO RIVER DRAINAGE BASIN

Glen Canyon's Horseshoe Bend on the Colorado River (top left), whitewater raft on the Colorado (center left), New Mexico's adobe Santa Clara Mission and Taos Pueblo (top to bottom right)

there are dozens of basins, separated by parallel north-south mountain ranges. The water that runs down the mountainsides has nowhere to go—there are no outlets to the sea—and so it collects in shallow pools and washes. From there, most of it evaporates or disappears into the ground.

The landscape, almost lunar in places, appears lifeless. Surprisingly, it isn't. Lots of creatures have survived in this desiccated environment by adapting to it. Lizards, scorpions, rattlesnakes, coyotes, cougars, wild mustangs and burros, and an amazing variety of birds thrive here. The scorpion's thick, laminated shell seals in its body fluids; when it needs water it digs as deep as eight feet (2.4 m) to find it. The kangaroo rat produces water by oxidizing body fat; with no sweat glands, it loses no moisture through perspiration. Plants have adapted in similar fashion. Sagebrush, for example, has two kinds of roots: one shallow and radiating outward to soak up rain before it can evaporate, and the other growing downward to tap into water far below the desert floor. Mesquite can send tap roots as far as 100 feet (30 m), all the way down to the water table.

In many ways, humans have survived by adapting, as well. The Anasazi, ancient ancestors of the Pueblo, Hopi, Zuni, and other Native Americans, lived for hundreds of years all around the Southwest—from the Grand Canyon to the Pecos River, and from the confluence of the Green and Colorado Rivers to a place near Flagstaff. Originally hunters and gatherers, the Anasazi settled into farming: By diverting snowmelt and runoff, they succeeded in growing corn and beans in otherwise sun-baked fields. If the soil wore out or if a drought occurred, they simply moved on and started over. Then, in the 13th century, many of them moved on for good. The reasons remain unclear; theories range from severe drought to attacks by unknown enemies to the lure of a new kachina religion in the Rio Grande Valley.

Descendants of the Anasazi also survived in the desert by adapting. Resourceful Pueblo Indians dealt with the diurnal extremes of desert temperatures by building thick-walled adobe apartments that captured

adobe architecture

Adobe architecture, ubiquitous in New Mexico and popular throughout the Southwest, could hardly be simpler. Its rounded contours resemble natural deposits of clay. Its rooms, doors, and windows appear arranged by necessity, not precedent. It remains stark after a fashion—a fashion that has not just endured in this region but has prevailed.

To Pueblo Indians in prehistoric times, adobe was the most utilitarian of styles, with not just the power to shelter weary bones but the charm to house the human spirit as well. For this reason, the famous Taos Pueblo in New Mexico rises like a natural landform, echoing the shape of sacred mountains in the distance.

Early on, walls were built with handfuls of mud and straw, or constructed of mud bricks cut from streambeds. Little by little, the architecture evolved: For example, in the 1600s, the Spanish conquistadors adapted a Moorish brick-baking technique. But the basic construction, with thick walls for insulation from the heat or the cold and small timbers to frame the flat roof, remains well-suited to the Southwest's high-desert climate.

The modern fashion for adobe began well before most conservation movements in America. In the early 1900s, Santa Feans stopped plans to demolish the ancient Palace of Governors on the town's plaza, and prompted a wave of pride about some of the country's oldest standing structures. Thus came the Spanish-Pueblo Revival style, as represented in the Santa Fe Museum of Fine Arts (1917). Adobe and related building types are now mandatory in the historic district of the city.

Today, adobe houses and hotels have modern superstructures but still feature the traditional simple lines, flowing space, and naturally regulated temperatures. Contemporary houses also retain adobe's neutral-colored surfaces, which make decorating with anything from kachina dolls to oriental rugs a simple pleasure of modern desert living.

las vegas and reno

Legal gambling. Weddings without the wait. High stakes. Cheap meals. Quick divorces. Welcome to Las Vegas, Nevada, the western boomtown that seems to keep booming—with more casinos and hotel rooms than any other city in the world.

Spanish traders discovered its aquifer and artesian wells in the early 1800s, and Mormons had a stronghold by 1855. But Las Vegas wasn't officially founded until 1905, when the San Pedro-Los Angeles-Salt Lake Railroad (which later became the Union Pacific) used the town as an outback pit stop for water. Western-style settlement ensued with hotels, bordellos, gaming houses, and scores of shanty establishments. By 1931, things in Vegas were looking good: A brief ban on gambling had been lifted, the Hoover Dam was under way, and Nellis Air Force Base was soon to be a training ground for WWII machine gunners.

In the 1940s several establishments—the El Rancho hotel (the first "Big One" in Vegas), gangster Bugsy Siegel's Flamingo, and countless other hotel/casino/lounges—engaged in a neon-hued game of one-upmanship and literally paved and lit the way for what is now a $24-billion-dollar-a-year tourism industry. Today, Las Vegas is one of America's fastest-growing metro areas, with 1.2 million residents and 30 million visitors per year.

Before Las Vegas, however, there was Reno, founded in 1859, long before its younger sibling to the south. Like Las Vegas, Reno was an ideal railroad town, thanks to the Truckee River—which drains from California's Sierra Nevada Range—and the Great Basin, across which the Central Pacific steamed en route from the San Francisco Bay to Salt Lake City. Reno grew during the silver-mining boom of the Comstock lode, was incorporated in 1903, and once was known as the Divorce Capital of the World.

These days, the Hoover-Dam-fueled growth of the Southwest draws most tourists and gamblers to Las Vegas, leaving Reno with a population of less than 165,000 and a modest five million visitors per year. Reno is known today as much for weddings as divorces, earns most of its income through gambling, and is a prime recreation destination for skiing, golfing, mountain biking, and beach activities on Lake Tahoe.

desert life

Nevada's Amargosa Desert (left); Las Vegas strip and Reno casinos (bottom left); Death Valley's Mesquite Flat Dunes, saguaro cacti, and sidewinder (top to bottom right)

the heat of the sun during the day, then released it against the cold desert night, warming the interior. In lean times Native Americans of many tribes survived by eating insects and plants, even cacti. A saguaro cactus, for example, was a well-known source of drinkable water. And certain animals adept at finding water unwittingly passed along their know-how. Coyotes smell or sense water below the ground and tunnel downward to reach it, leaving telltale depressions in the sand or clay long after they have slaked their thirst. For the early natives, and later for European explorers who had the misfortune to run out of water in the desert, the ability to recognize a coyote hole made the difference between life and death.

In the 16th century, Spanish missionaries and explorers such as Francisco Coronado were the first Europeans to test their wilderness skills here. Fortunately for them, they had learned survival techniques from their earlier conquests in Mexico. Later came American frontiersmen such as Jim Bridger and Jedediah Smith, tough and resourceful adventurers who also knew how to live off the land. They were followed by waves of American pioneers from the Midwest and the East, who struck out over the Santa Fe Trail in their creaky covered wagons, most with little knowledge of the region's terrain or weather. Many of them perished along the way, victims of their own ignorance. Others died at the hands of Native Americans led by charismatic leaders such as Geronimo and Cochise.

But eventually the pioneers prevailed. Those who stayed, rather than continuing on to California, established ranches and great cattle herds. The railroads took the cattle to market and returned with food, clothing, building materials, household goods, luxury items—and more people. Towns, then cities, sprang up. They grew gradually, then explosively after World War II, when developments such as air conditioning and irrigation for farming transformed the Southwest and Great Basin region into a more hospitable place to live.

The Southwest is commonly viewed as a wasteland of cacti, snakes, scorpions, and little else. But North America's four major deserts—the Great Basin, Sonoran, Chihuahuan, and Mojave—encompass eco-zones ranging from scrubby grasslands to salt flats, from slickrock to alpine tundra, and they teem with hundreds of specially adapted plants and animals.

In the Great Basin, which stretches from the Sierra Nevada to the Rocky Mountains, junipers and 4,000-year-old bristlecone pines dot the rugged mountains. Nicknamed "the Big Empty" due to sparse human population, the Basin has flat dry valleys populated by desert rodents, and shallow temporary lakes and wetlands for migratory birds.

The Mojave Desert's sparse vegetation includes 200 endemic plants, such as the Mojave fishhook cactus and gnarled Joshua Tree. Bighorn sheep, desert tortoises, desert rosy boas, and tarantulas live here at elevations ranging from 282 feet (86 m) below sea level at Death Valley to 11,047 feet (3,368 m) at Telescope Peak.

The Chihuahuan Desert, extending from Mexico into Texas, New Mexico, and Arizona, encompasses White Sands National Monument's gypsum dunes, Carlsbad Caverns, and Lechuguilla Cave. Yuccas, creosote, and ocotillo thrive here, while "sky islands" loom above the lowlands.

The Sonoran Desert is the only place on Earth where the giant saguaro cactus grows; it survives for 200 years by absorbing hundreds of gallons of water from infrequent rains. Other cacti—prickly pear, barrel, organ pipe, and cholla— also grow here, while Sonoran fauna includes sheep, javelina, nocturnal ringtail cats, reptiles, and the spadefoot toad.

The Colorado Plateau, sometimes considered part of the Great Basin, offers colorful, stair-step plateaus. Water and wind have carved the towers of Monument Valley, the fins and rock spans of Arches National Park, the hoodoos of Bryce Canyon, the breathtaking expanse of the Grand Canyon, and the stone mazes of Canyonlands. Wildlife here includes jackrabbits, coyotes, bighorn sheep, bison, and pronghorns.

cowboy poetry

Poetry, Carl Sandburg wrote, is why horses buck for no reason. And cowboy poetry must be why the man bucked off gets up, brushes himself off, and remounts again and again.

For 150 years, cowboys in the Southwest and Great Basin have gathered 'round the campfire and sung ditties or told tall tales. Balladry has been as integral to cowpunching as spurs. But this oral tradition was not formally recognized until 1985, when the National Endowment for the Arts gave seed money for the first Cowboy Poetry Gathering in Elko, Nevada. A smattering of cowboys regaled each other with rhymes about calving, roping, empty skies, desert sunsets, and beans.

Once I fed Rover my beans/his eyes and his nose sprung a leak/he hung out his tongue, took off on a run/and didn't come back for a week! ("Beans" by Anne Slade)

From these very humble beginnings, the cowboy poetry movement gathered speed until, during the 1990s, it became a stampede. Today dozens of cowboy poetry festivals duke it out with one another for audiences. Notable "cowboy culture" events take place in Sierra Vista, Arizona; Glencoe, New Mexico; Lubbock, Texas; Idaho City, Idaho; and the grand-daddy of them all occurs in Elko each January (down-time for working cowpokes).

A cowboy poetry gathering is not a competition. Nobody wins and usually nobody is booed. Instead, poets stand solemnly, twiddling a silver belt buckle or idly twirling a rope before launching into stanzas about "cattle to be pushed, broncos to be rode, and old dogs and horses to live and die with," according to the Cowboy Poets Society. Even the most laconic wordsmith seems loath to leave the stage. And why not? Baxter Black, dean of cowboy poets, once wrote of his fellow bards:

They had come from the ranches and cowtowns, their poetry burstin' their brains/And any poor fool on a corner or stool was subjected to endless refrains.

The growth of the largest cities—El Paso, Las Vegas, Albuquerque, Tucson, and Phoenix—was fueled by the dams and irrigation systems of the Colorado River, the lifeline of the Southwest. Descending from the Rockies, it furnishes water to more than 25 million people in seven U.S. states and in Mexico. But those towns and others are fast outgrowing the capacity of the river, and water tables in the region are already extremely low. The fastest-growing city in the nation, Las Vegas, is experiencing population increases of 4,000 to 6,000 new citizens every month.

In recent years Southwesterners have become more conscious about preserving their precious water. Tens of thousands of homes and hotel rooms have been fitted with showerheads and toilets that cut back on water consumption. Homeowners and businesses have abandoned water-slurping lawns for landscaping with indigenous plants that require little moisture. Golf courses are watered with diluted sewage effluent, and even in profligate Las Vegas, casinos use recycled water in their splashy resort fountains.

Today, with the modern comforts of large cities, interstate highways, easy air travel, and technological amenities, people readily fall in love with the Southwest. Natives and immigrants alike appreciate its sunshine, clear

dry air, mountains, canyons—even its deserts and isolation. Some are drawn to the tri-cultural heritage of the Southwest: Modern Native American pueblos exist next to Anglo mining outposts across from Spanish haciendas, and all three groups preserve traditions and history in rituals and festivals. Retirees flock here as well, settling in sunny, air-conditioned towns like Phoenix and Sun City, Arizona, or St. George, Utah, where the population has grown from 7,000 people in 1970 to 30,000 in the late 1990s. And for golfers, tennis players, mountain climbers, river rafters, amateur archaeologists, and other outdoor enthusiasts, the region is heaven on Earth. On a nice weekend in Moab, Utah, population 4,000, it's not unusual for 10,000 river paddlers and mountain bikers to show up.

Monument Valley Navajo Tribal Park (top), cowboy poet Baxter Black (left), chile ristra and corn on adobe house (below)

A healthy economy has helped to fuel all this population growth. Nevada produces more than half of the gold mined in the United States. Commerce and industry are doing well throughout the region, along with tourism, scientific research, and aerospace and other high-tech activities. Thousands who earn their livings elsewhere are nonetheless determined to live here, traveling to work in Los Angeles via commercial jet.

Today, hardly anyone thinks about the terrors this land once held for those who dared venture into it. Foremost among those attracted to the Southwest for its stunning beauty are the artists. Painter Georgia O'Keeffe, for one, came out from the East and stayed the rest of her life to

anasazi legacy

Tucked inside a sandstone cliff overlooking a juniper-carpeted canyon, the ruins of Cliff Palace in Mesa Verde National Park represent the last refuge of a great American civilization. The Anasazi Indians built this multitiered complex to house 350 people in the early 13th century, having retreated here from their homes to escape some unknown foe. Why the Anasazi settled in cliff dwellings across the Four Corners region—and why they suddenly disappeared from these human aeries and abandoned this land forever—remains a mystery.

Ancestors of the modern Pueblo Indians, the Anasazi—a Navajo word meaning "Ancient Ones"—originated from a nomadic people who hunted and gathered in this region early in the first millennium. Around 700 A.D. they adapted farming methods and settled in small villages, coaxing beans, squash, and corn from the earth while hunting antelope and gathering berries and piñon nuts.

By 900 A.D. this loosely structured agrarian group had developed into a complex society, centered in northwest New Mexico's Chaco Canyon. From 900 to 1050 the Anasazi built dense, apartment-like structures as tall as four stories along canyon floors and mesa tops. These engineering marvels were constructed of sandstone blocks hewn from nearby cliffs; roofs were supported by pine timbers gathered from forests up to 80 miles (130 km) away. Pueblo Bonito in Chaco Canyon was the administrative and cultural hub of Anasazi civilization at the time. Its complex of living and storage rooms surrounding circular ceremonial kivas, along with roads emanating to outlying communities, reflect a society more advanced than any in North America at the time.

By 1050, more than 5,000 people lived here in a region that receives only nine inches (23 cm) of rain a year. Yet the Anasazi thrived, developing an irrigation system of ditches and dams that diverted rainwater runoff to fields and households.

By 1150 people suddenly began abandoning settlements to retreat to remote cliff dwellings, possibly due to warfare with outside tribes, or to a drought that drove the Anasazi to more easily defensible homesteads where they could protect dwindling resources.

By 1300 the Anasazi had moved on, likely merging with neighboring Zuni, Hopi, and Rio Grande people. Anasazi ruins throughout the Four Corners region remain as testament of a resilient people who cultivated their own small empire from a parched land.

ANASAZI SITES IN THE FOUR CORNERS REGION

Mesa Verde's Cliff House (top left), petroglyphs at Wupatki National Monument (center left), Arizona's San Francisco Mountains (below) paint the haunting desert landscapes and flora.

Others—Joseph Henry Sharp, Fremont Ellis, Will Shuster, and Allan Houser, to name only a few—helped turn the old Spanish settlement of Santa Fe, New Mexico, into an art colony known all around the world. And the first artists of the Southwest, the Anasazi, left behind a rich and fascinating artistic legacy in pottery, petroglyphs, and the ruins of their magnificent cave dwellings in Pueblo Bonito, Mesa Verde, and Canyon de Chelly. Contemporary Pueblo artisans and members of other Native American tribes carry on the 2,000-year-old artistic tradition of their Anasazi forebears by creating exquisite pottery today.

For artists, one of the great lures of the region is its spectacular color palette of reds, purples, ochres, pinks, creams, dusty yellows, inky blacks, and marble whites. Ironically, the natural features that made the Southwest and Great Basin life-threatening are the same ones that make it beautiful. John C. VanDyke, a university professor who explored the Southwest in the 1890s, wrote: "It is stern, harsh and at first repellent. But what tongue shall tell of the majesty of it, the eternal strength of it, the poetry of its wide-spread chaos, the sublimity of its lonely desolation! And who shall paint the splendor of its light!"

Ah yes, the light. Without the unique attributes of the light, the Southwest and Great Basin region would be less vivid, less dramatic—and certainly less colorful. You grasp this immediately in places like the Painted Desert and Grand Canyon, where light heightens and changes colors, revealing the fiery burnt orange in ancient rocks and casting sage and cacti in marvelous shadows and silhouettes. The purity and clarity of the air, along with very little industrial pollution and very low humidity, create this dramatic lighting, which rarely goes unnoticed even by those who have lived here a lifetime—ranchers, artists, scientists, technicians, business people, retirees, and people from dozens of walks of life. To ignore the power of the light, and of the landscape, is like trying to ignore the Grand Canyon while standing on the South Rim.

■ National Parks, Monuments, Forests, Recreation Areas, and Wildlife Refuges
■ Military Installations
■ Indian Reservations
■ Bureau of Land Management Holdings
□ Private Lands

Copyright © Rand McNally & Co.

public lands

Come visit the Southwest. You should. You own it. No other U.S. region possesses such an extraordinary concentration of public lands, from national forests to protected monuments to military sites to Bureau of Land Management holdings. And no other region has had to grapple so openly with resulting issues of stewardship and property rights.

Why the Southwest and Great Basin? In part, it's the land's high-desert, high-lonesome ruggedness. Few people have ever lived here: California's Death Valley has never beckoned to optimistic homesteaders; New Mexico's Catron County, site of the Gila National Forest, is both the nation's largest county and its least populous (.4 people per sq mile/.25 per sq km). So when Teddy Roosevelt first proposed the national park system, it was natural to look to the desert Southwest for land. Within decades, huge swaths of Utah, Arizona, Nevada, and New Mexico came under public

control, including such natural wonders as the Grand Canyon, White Sands, and Canyonlands.

Few landholders were displaced by these public acquisitions. But as the region's population grew, some locals questioned whether they shouldn't have greater control over the wild lands in their backyards. In the 1980s and 1990s, battles erupted between environmentalists and ranchers who insisted that they be allowed to graze their cattle on national forest land with little or no oversight. Guns were drawn (although no blood was shed), and many lawyers struck it rich before the Forest Service agreed to allow cattle grazing, but only under strict guidelines.

Today, the Southwest and Great Basin continues to be acquired by, well, you. In 1997, 1.7 million acres (688,500 ha) of Utah's red rock wilderness became the Grand Staircase-Escalante National Monument, the nation's newest federal park.

The Mountain West

The Backbone
of the Continent

Spectacular **snowy peaks** rise abruptly west of the Great Plains, erecting a bulwark of glacier-honed granite that stretches more than 9,000 miles (4,800 km) from the Brooks Range in Alaska to the Sangre de Cristo Mountains of northern New Mexico. Western North America's defining feature, the Rocky Mountains have been a cradle for cowboys and cattle camps, a magnet for prospectors, a barrier to westward migration, and, for centuries prior to European exploration, a home to indigenous peoples.

Within the seemingly endless ranges of the Rockies, evergreen forests and wildflower-strewn plateaus blanket the landscape. The headwaters of the West's greatest rivers—the Snake, the North and South Platte, the Missouri, the Rio Grande, the Colorado—race through canyons, providing drinking water for much of western North America. Along the mountain crest, the Continental Divide forms a spine where a difference of a few feet will determine whether a drop of rainwater ends up in the Pacific Ocean or the Gulf of Mexico. Powerful mountain winds, which once sent pioneer wagons plummeting off precipitous tracks, still overturn semi-trucks on interstate highways. Today the Rockies inspire awe and offer an irresistible lure to those hardy enough to survive the hardships of outdoor mountain living.

Wyoming's Firehole River (left); Salt Lake City, Utah (below). Preceding pages: Colorado's San Juan Mountains

Despite its rugged landscapes and harsh weather, the Mountain West region, which covers western Montana, eastern Utah, and most of Idaho, Wyoming, and Colorado, is experiencing a modern-day population boom. The U.S. Census Bureau has predicted that these states will see a population growth rate two to four times the national average during the next decade. Crowd-weary urban refugees in search of affordable real estate, simpler lives, and solitude—as well as some of the world's best ski slopes—are moving to the mountains in record numbers. Towns long ago born and busted of gold, silver, and copper strikes prosper again as technology attempts to tap potentially vast oil deposits seeped deep in the mountain rock. Abundant property and local efforts to attract business have made present-day boom-towns out of cities such as Butte and Bozeman, Montana, which have thriving telecommunications and service industries; Boise, Idaho, which now produces everything from microbrews to semiconductors; and Cheyenne, Wyoming, which capitalizes on its Wild West heritage with Cheyenne Frontier Days, the world's largest outdoor rodeo. Once-sleepy hamlets like Park City, Utah, and Aspen, Colorado, have become world-renowned full-service resorts attracting winter-sports enthusiasts who come to ski, snowboard, snowshoe, bobsled, snowmobile, drive dogsleds, and partake in aprés-ski activities. When the snow melts, there are ample oppor-

tunities to kayak, raft, bike, hike, camp, fish, and climb. The recreational mother lode of the Rocky Mountains is inexhaustible.

Colorado's Rocky Mountain National Park (left), founded in 1915, attracts three million visitors annually.

But the overwhelming attraction for all is the scenery. Geologic upheaval that began 100 million years ago, as the Farrallon plate slid under the North American plate, created the massive uplift responsible for the wide variety of

Ghost town of St. Elmo, Colorado (below); ski runs above Aspen (right); skiers on slopes at Steamboat Springs (lower right)

old west mining towns

The gold that drew droves of prospectors to places like Cripple Creek, Colorado, and Grasshopper Creek, Montana, first showed up as glittering flakes in stream gravel. Experienced prospectors knew to check the rocks upstream for quartz, but didn't know why.

Geologists do. Superheated water circulating miles deep in magma beneath the Rockies dissolves compounds of gold, copper, tin, lead, silver, and silicon. Pressure forces this metallic solution up into rocky fissures where the metals precipitate out and silicon dioxide hardens into gold-specked quartz. Erosion does the rest by dropping gold particles into sandbars to form what miners call placer deposits, or by concentrating silver in shallow beds called surface bonanzas.

The first wave of prospectors did their mining standing in icy water, sluicing dirt and sand through handheld pans and long wooden troughs. On a good day, a man could wash out $100 in gold dust. On a great day, he could wash out $1,500. Empty gulches grew to camps of thousands in a few months, complete with saloons where miners could gamble away their gold dust. Tents gave way to log cabins, a jail, stores, a theater, and churches. After the placers and bonanzas were exhausted, companies with the equipment to excavate deep veins and smelt ores took over the towns.

Waves of miners came to Butte, Montana, "the Richest Hill on Earth," for gold in the 1860s and silver in the 1870s. In the 1880s, Irish immigrant Marcus Daly discovered a vein of copper that kept the world's largest copper smelter, in nearby Anaconda, busy until the collapse of copper prices in the 1980s.

When the deposits played out, some camps shrank to towns of a few hundred; others disappeared, leaving mounds of tailings behind. Nearby, rows of buildings still stand in ghost towns like Silver City, Idaho, and St. Elmo, Colorado. Other former camps, such as Auraria, Colorado, and Last Chance Gulch, Montana, survived boom and bust to become present-day Denver and Helena.

ranges and rocks that make up the Rockies: spires of granite in Wyoming, peaks hewn from eroded lava in southwestern Colorado, more than 80 distinct mountain ranges in Idaho. Tucked away in the plethora of rocks are waterfall-washed ravines, serene glacial lakes, wildlife refuges, and dinosaur graveyards. From the midst of these snowclad mountain panoramas—some of the Lower 48's most breathtaking and remote— people manage to commute to work, but a small number of corporate pioneers arrange to telecommute via satellite dishes, computers, modems, and other trappings of modern life.

The Mountain West was not always so accessible. As late as the early 1800s, the Rocky Mountains remained little more than the stuff of fantastic rumors: a range of erupting volcanoes, peaks of salt, and the habitat of unicorns, woolly mammoths, and giant beavers. Meriwether Lewis and William Clark, expecting an easy crossing in 1805, were surprised upon reaching the Continental Divide to see range upon range of rugged mountains stretching ever westward. But accounts from surveying parties and adventure seekers only whetted pioneer appetites back East. Their stories lured mountain men like Zebulon Pike, the first to attempt (unsuccessfully) to climb Pikes Peak; John Colter, who raved about the spectacular geysers in what would become Yellowstone National Park; and Jedediah Smith and William Sublette, who opened the Oregon Trail as a passageway to the West.

The great migration of the 1840s through the 1860s brought hundreds of thousands of settlers into the Rocky Mountains, but most continued on to seek land and fortune in Oregon and California. Miners and Mormons were the exceptions. Prospectors came for gold and silver, but copper proved a more valuable resource. Every big strike spawned a

ground zero for winter sports

Alpine, or downhill, skiing—with lifts, instructors, and aprés-ski nightlife—got its start in the Mountain West during the 1930s. Railroad tycoon Averell Harriman wanted to establish a European-style ski resort on an American mountain and built Sun Valley, Idaho, for the rich and glamorous. Its elegant lodge boasted gourmet food and white-glove service; its chairlift—the world's first—began carrying patrons up Bald Mountain in 1936.

After World War II, veterans of the U.S. Army's 10th Mountain Division, which had trained in Colorado for alpine combat, rigged up a salvaged ore tram to a four-wheel-drive Army truck to create a chairlift at Snow King, Wyoming. These days, the tram at Jackson Hole, Wyoming, takes 60 skiers up 4,139 feet (1,262 m) in 12 minutes.

Another 10th Mountain vet started the Vail ski resort in 1962. Prosperous from the beginning, the Vail area now accounts for five million skier days a year.

Today, condo villages are proliferating to accommodate time-share vacationers in ski resorts all through the Rockies. The industry rests on the shape of the mountains, generous snowfall, and on skiers' desire to trace their way through forest trails like Alta's Piney Glade; to carve into steep-sided bowls

like Sun Valley's Lookout or Breckenridge's Contest; to drop down vertical slopes like Telluride's Kant-Mak-Em; or to cruise down open expanses like Big Burn at Snowmass (a broad run on the site of a forest fire set by Ute Indians angry with silver miners).

At some ski resorts, the season starts as early as mid-October and the closing Spring Fling doesn't happen until mid-May. Wyoming's Grand Targhee and Utah's Alta and Snowbird tend to pile up the most snow: 500 inches (1,270 cm) annually. By comparison, Loveland, Colorado, averages 375 inches (950 cm) each season.

These days, skiers also take their sport off the beaten path: Telemarkers free-heel through the backcountry, snowboarders shred ski runs and half-pipes, and heli-skiers copter up high ridges to schuss down unmarked terrain.

SNOWFALL AND MAJOR SKI AREAS OF THE MOUNTAIN WEST

✳ Ski Areas

Snowfall in inches (cm)

◼ Less than 8 (20)	◼ 64–96 (163–244)
◼ 8–16 (20–41)	◼ 96–128 (244–325)
◼ 16–32 (41–81)	◻ 128–256 (325–650)
◼ 32–64 (81–163)	◻ More than 256 (650)

boomtown; every spent vein of ore inspired an exodus to the next big strike. The boomtowns eventually bred ghost towns such as Virginia City, Montana, billed to tourists today as "a living ghost town," and Mineral Point, Colorado, a silver camp abandoned in 1899. But those mineral resources continue to underpin the region's economy: Today, Montana and Utah produce most of the copper mined in the United States. Iron, gold, silver, lead, and zinc are valuable assets, along with molybdenum, beryllium, and uranium. Oil and natural gas deposits also are coming into their own as prime resources—shale laid down in ancient lakebeds may hold more than nine times the hydrocarbons located beneath Saudi Arabia.

Bull-rider competing at Cheyenne Frontier Days (below), sunlight warming Wyoming's Grand Canyon of the Yellowstone (right)

The Mormons who stayed were searching for a different treasure than oil or gold. Driven from Midwestern communities because of their religious beliefs, Mormons led by Brigham Young journeyed west to find a "promised land" where they could practice their faith in peace. Through grit, determination, and hard work—attributes still necessary to brave the mountain backcountry—they made the desert valley bloom. Salt Lake City, Utah's capital, is a thriving beehive of industry and business and the heart of the Mormon religion, the Church of Jesus Christ of Latter-day Saints. Mormons living in Utah, Idaho, Colorado, and Wyoming represent more than ten percent of the Mountain West's present population.

The mountain work ethic held by the Mormons also bred that uniquely western American working-class hero: the cowboy. After the Civil War, cattlemen Charles Goodnight and Oliver Loving drove 2,000 head of cattle north from Texas to Colorado and Wyoming, hoping to profit from railroad workers and miners who craved fresh meat. Hundreds of cowboys and their herds followed on the Chisholm, the Western, and the Goodnight-Loving trails. Rarely the heroic existence portrayed by Hollywood, a cowboy's life was hard and lonely—long months alone on the ranges punctuated by wild binges at trail's end when cattle money

cheyenne frontier days

Believed to be the world's largest outdoor rodeo and western celebration, Cheyenne, Wyoming's Frontier Days enthusiastically revives some of the Old West's most beloved cultural traditions and attracts more than 375,000 visitors during its ten-day run each July.

The Frontier Days celebration, lovingly tagged the "Daddy of 'Em All," began in 1897 with saddle bronc riding, or "bucking and pitching," long before the word "rodeo" was coined. Approximately 50 cowboys came in from nearby ranches, cheered on by Cheyenne townspeople and visitors from Denver who had arrived on excursion trains. More than a century later, the rodeo remains Frontier Days' most popular event. Cowboys kick off the competition by gathering and driving some 500 Mexican steer 12 miles (19 km) from their summer range to Frontier Park. More than 1,200 entrants vie for prized silver and gold championship belt buckles awarded in cowboy, bronc, bull, steer, calf, and barrel racing contests.

After taking in the rodeo competitions, visitors can attend chuckwagon races, a Western art festival and sale, a chili cook-off, free pancake breakfasts, and daily parades. Today's parades are a far cry from their early stagings, when bands of unruly cowboys galloped through town, firing pistols at upper-story windows and lassoing pretty girls. Parades now include antique horse-drawn carriages and automobiles, and feature Native American dancers and marching bands and drill teams from across the United States. Country and western concerts fill the night air with music, while American Indian and square dancing get toes tapping to a lively beat.

More than 2,500 busy volunteers work year-round to organize the celebration and keep alive the magic of the frontier lifestyle in its flamboyance and grit, a tribute to the days when hard-riding, cattle-roping cowboys dominated the mountain landscape.

Logan Pass along the Canadian border in Glacier National Park (above); Teewinot Mountain, Grand Teton National Park (right)

burned holes in his pockets. Out of this cowboy culture rose another icon of the Mountain West: the marshal. Charged with protecting cow towns from drunken cowboys and nefarious cattle rustlers, marshals Wild Bill Hickock, Bat Masterson, and Wyatt Earp became Wild West legends.

Today, most cattle are sold via satellite-dish auctions. Cattle rustling remains a problem, however, and contemporary cowboys are still charged with delivering herds to high-country ranges intact—though they might move their stock with the help of a sport-utility vehicle rather than a horse. And they still might feel lonely in the Mountain West. Despite the recent influx of new residents, the region remains the most sparsely populated in the contiguous United States; in many western counties the population density is less than two people per square mile (3.6 per sq km). This is probably due to the fact that the mountains serve as the country's hot-water heater, air conditioner, and insulation wall, and their uncompromising terrain generates violent weather that even the best human efforts can do little to control. With that weather comes perilous travel, as avalanches can bury mountain roads and isolate small communities, and gusty winds wreak havoc with the flight patterns of small planes.

Still, thousands of eager tourists flock in the summer and fall to the High Rockies' crown jewels: their national parks. The region is home to many of the country's most-visited and best-loved parks, among them Yellowstone, Grand Teton, Rocky Mountain, and Glacier. Yellowstone, the first U.S. national park, was established in 1872, spawning a widespread movement to preserve other large, undisturbed ecosystems. The park, located in Wyoming and Montana, features 10,000 thermal springs and geysers; its icon, Old Faithful, predictably spews water and steam as high as

rocky mountain ranges

The Rockies are not one single line of mountains. They are actually an assemblage of hundreds of individual ranges—each breathtakingly beautiful, each formidably rugged—that form the spine of North America, or the Continental Divide. Among the Rockies' most spectacular ranges are:

THE FRONT RANGE
These Colorado mountains seem to rise from the Great Plains as a jagged, snow-capped wall of granite. The view from the summit of Pikes Peak (14,110 feet/4,301 m) inspired poet Katharine Lee Bates to write "America, the Beautiful."

THE SANGRE DE CRISTO MOUNTAINS Named the "Blood of Christ" because it glows a vivid red in the sunset, this southernmost range of the

Rockies extends south from Colorado into New Mexico. The highest mountain in the range, Blanca Peak (14,345 feet/ 4,372 m), is sacred to the Navajo people.

THE TETONS The sharply honed granite of Wyoming's picture-perfect Tetons is ancient, but the mountains themselves are the youngest of the Rockies, only nine million years old. And they are still rising, approximately one foot (.3 m) every 500 years.

THE WIND RIVER RANGE
Wyoming's largest mountain chain, the Wind River Range is still being shaped by ice; some of the largest glaciers in the 48 contiguous states cling to these mountain crests.

THE BITTERROOT RANGE Lewis and Clark crossed Montana's lofty, jagged Bitterroots, named for an edible herb that may have helped sustain the expedition on its arduous trek.

THE UINTA MOUNTAINS
Trending east-west instead of north-south, these Utah mountains are a puzzle to geologists. Named for the Ute

Indians, the Uintas are rugged and remote mountains whose steep slopes of quartzite and shale often open onto huge, flat-floored basins.

THE SAN JUAN MOUNTAINS A deeply mined treasure trove, the mineral-rich San Juans curve north from New Mexico and then west through southern Colorado. The varied profile of this range's sheer faces, rocky summits, and steep-walled canyons mirrors the intense color shifts of its flanks: slate gray and steely blue to verdigris and vivid crimson.

THE SAWATCH RANGE
The craggy, densely forested Sawatch Mountains have been called the "Roof of Colorado" because they are the state's highest range, topping out at 14,433 feet (4,399 m) on Mount Elbert.

THE LA SAL MOUNTAINS
The majestic, snowcapped, aspen-forested La Sal Mountains loom in the distance over Utah's red rock desert and canyonlands.

The Mile-High City of Denver, Colorado, flanked by the Front Range (below); bison (right) and wolves (bottom right) living in Yellowstone National Park

180 feet (55 m). Other attractions include the Grand Canyon of the Yellowstone River, a fossil forest, and the West's greatest profusion of wildlife: bison, elk, moose, coyotes, pronghorn antelope, and bighorn sheep, to name only a few.

Yellowstone's neighbor to the south, Grand Teton National Park, was established in 1929 to protect this dramatic, glacier-carved mountain range, as well as the mighty Snake River and the fragile sagebrush valley of Jackson Hole. America's largest herd of elk winters along the park border in the 25,000-acre (10,125-ha) National Elk Refuge; Grand Teton is also a sanctuary for bison, moose, mule deer, and trumpeter swans.

Northwest of Denver, the mountain preserve of Rocky Mountain National Park is known for verdant valleys, indigo lakes, pine-juniper forests, and more than 110 peaks that rise higher than 10,000 feet (3,000 m). More than one third of the park's terrain lies above the treeline, carpeted in alpine tundra or laid bare as rock and ice. Within its borders runs Trail Ridge Road, the loftiest paved road in the contiguous United States (it crests at 12,138 feet/3,677 m), and 14,255-foot (4,345-m) Longs Peak, accessible via a 16-mile (25-km) round-trip hike.

Along the Canadian border, Montana's Glacier National Park adjoins British Columbia's Waterton Lakes National Park to form the Waterton-Glacier International Peace Park, the first

such international park in the world. Glacier is named for its 50 glaciers, but also features wildflower meadows, remote backcountry hiking trails, icy alpine lakes, and a healthy population of grizzlies.

Whatever the reason people come to the Rocky Mountains—a scenic vacation; a quest for serenity or instant wealth; the pursuit of the perfect slope or the perfect job; a need to own land, no matter how remote and rugged—they learn to appreciate the Rockies on their own terms. Historically, relatively few people have stayed and settled here. Yet those who do reap the rewards of self-reliance, a sense of community, and a palpable feeling that their home is part of the nation's bedrock, solid as Rocky Mountain granite.

wolves and wildlife

It is for many people the very definition of "wilderness": the high, lonely howl of a wolf ringing through the darkness. But by early this century, the wolf's howl had virtually disappeared from the Rockies, as *Canis lupus* was systematically eradicated by ranchers and others, falling prey to bullets, bounties, and deeprooted human superstitions.

Now the howl is back. Beginning in 1995, the U.S. Forest Service transplanted about 65 male and female wolves from northern Canada to the deepest corners of

Yellowstone National Park and Idaho's Salmon River Wilderness. As hoped, the animals split into packs, breeding, hunting—and howling—much as their forebears had a century before.

Of course, the return of the wolves was not without its opponents. Ranchers near the parks complained bitterly that the predators would decimate livestock. Conservationists worried that the packs were too small to breed effectively. Both groups sued the Forest Service at various times, and one federal court recently declared wolf reintroduction in Yellowstone

illegal—a decision that may well be overturned on appeal.

But neither the ranchers nor the conservationists need have worried. A few cattle did disappear, but the wolves proved far more interested in Yellowstone's massive herds of elk. More than 100 wolves now roam the park's backcountry, along with grizzlies, pronghorn antelope, peregrine falcons, white pelicans, and hundreds of other rare and wild species.

Today, a hike through Yellowstone is as close as we will ever come to seeing the

West as it existed when Lewis and Clark journeyed here. Grizzly bear cubs claw downed branches as two-ton bison galumph through the meadows behind them. Hawks swoop overhead, soaring on mountain updrafts. And somewhere off in the long shadows cast by the Douglas pines comes the wolf's unmistakable howl, the knell of the wilderness.

The Pacific Northwest

Celebrating the Outdoor Lifestyle

 If the country's **magnificent** physical features are a dazzling show of nature, the Pacific Northwest surely represents the grand finale. Snowcapped volcanoes dominate the horizon. Icy streams plunge down coastal fjords and giant redwoods preside over ancient forests. Pacific surf crashes over coastal headlands and bubbles across foggy beaches, giving up creatures from the sea and drift from the Orient. West of the Cascades, mosses hang like bunting and Sitka spruce trees rise more than 250 feet (75 m) in the lush rain forests, where annual precipitation exceeds 140  inches (350 cm). Inland, in the semiarid rainshadow of the Cascades, the sun shines brightly and often on wheat, barley, and potato fields.

Thus the Pacific Northwest—which includes Washington, all of Oregon save its southeast basinland, much of the Idaho panhandle, and California's northern forests and "Lost Coast"—is a region of geographic superlatives. The landscape offers the country's deepest gorge, Hells Canyon on the Oregon-Idaho border, and its loftiest trees, California's 300-foot-high (90-m) redwoods. The tallest of all living things, these giants grew in other locations in North America in another geological age. They survive

Northern California's sequoias (far left), Mount Hood's snowcapped summit above Portland (above), baby Northern Spotted Owl (left). Preceding pages: Washington's Mount Rainier

today only in northern California in the damp, green-velvet moss of the coastal forest, where they can absorb the moist sea air through their burgundy bark and trap flowing creeks in their myriad roots.

Skagit Valley in northwestern Washington is a premier producer of tulip bulbs (above), which grow well in the area's mineral-rich soil.

The region's spectacular volcanoes, part of the Pacific Ring of Fire, are geographic superlatives as well. Washington's 14,410-foot (4,392-m) Mount Rainier has the largest accumulation of glaciers in the continental United States; some 500 feet (150 m) of solid ice plugs its summit crater. Its last major eruption occurred thousands of years ago, but warm springs still bubble from the upper slopes and steam flows through vents near the summit. Another volcanic phenomenon created the deepest lake in the country: Crater Lake. Six miles (ten km) wide and 1,932 feet (590 m) deep, the cobalt-blue lake on the crest of the Oregon Cascades was formed some 7,000 years ago when an ancient stratovolcano 12,000 feet (3,650 m) high blew its top, leaving behind a vast caldera that eventually filled with rain and snowmelt. One of the volcano's three cinder cones, Wizard Island, rises above the lake's surface, and volcanic hot spots still warm the deepest waters.

Other geographic headliners include the most extensive field of coastal sand dunes in the country, the Oregon Dunes, which range three miles (five km) inland, with crests up to a mile (1.6 km) long and 300 feet (90 m) high along the central part of the Oregon coast. Then there is the Olympic rain forest, on Washington's Olympic Peninsula, one of the world's few temperate rain forests and a perpetually damp greenhouse of ferns, mosses, and lichens mixed with towering colonnades of 200-year-old spruce trees and western hemlocks growing out of even older fallen "nurse" logs. The region also boasts the Columbia River Gorge, a 60-mile (95-km) canyon funnelling the flow of the most powerful river on the North American continent into the Pacific. Two centuries ago, pioneers crossed a Columbia roiling with whitecaps; today, hydroelectricity dams

early explorers

Meriwether Lewis and William Clark, two former army officers, led the first American exploring party across the vast expanse of land between the Mississippi River and the Pacific Ocean. Sent forth by President Thomas Jefferson, Lewis and Clark mistakenly believed that only a "short portage" separated the Missouri and Columbia Rivers. Upon leaving St. Louis in May 1804, they expected to be gone for 18 months at most—ample time, they believed, to reach the Pacific, turn around, and return home.

With Sacajawea, their female Shoshone guide and interpreter, they endured a tortuous journey westward across the Rocky Mountains, only to reach the Continental Divide and discover how much of the continent still lay ahead of them. Disheartened and

exhausted, they finally reached the mouth of the Columbia River in November 1805. On their return trip, the two men took different routes: Lewis' group descended the Missouri River, while Clark led the other half of their party down the Yellowstone River. They all received a hero's welcome upon returning to St. Louis in 1806, having traveled almost 8,000 miles (12,800 km) in two years.

Today, the Lewis and Clark Interpretive Center in Washington's Fort Canby State Park offers visitors the reasons for the expedition, a timeline of the entire journey, and diary excerpts of the adventure, as well as mementos and short films. Several expedition campsites are preserved today in Sacajawea State Park and across the state of Washington.

LEWIS AND CLARK EXPEDITION
1804-1806

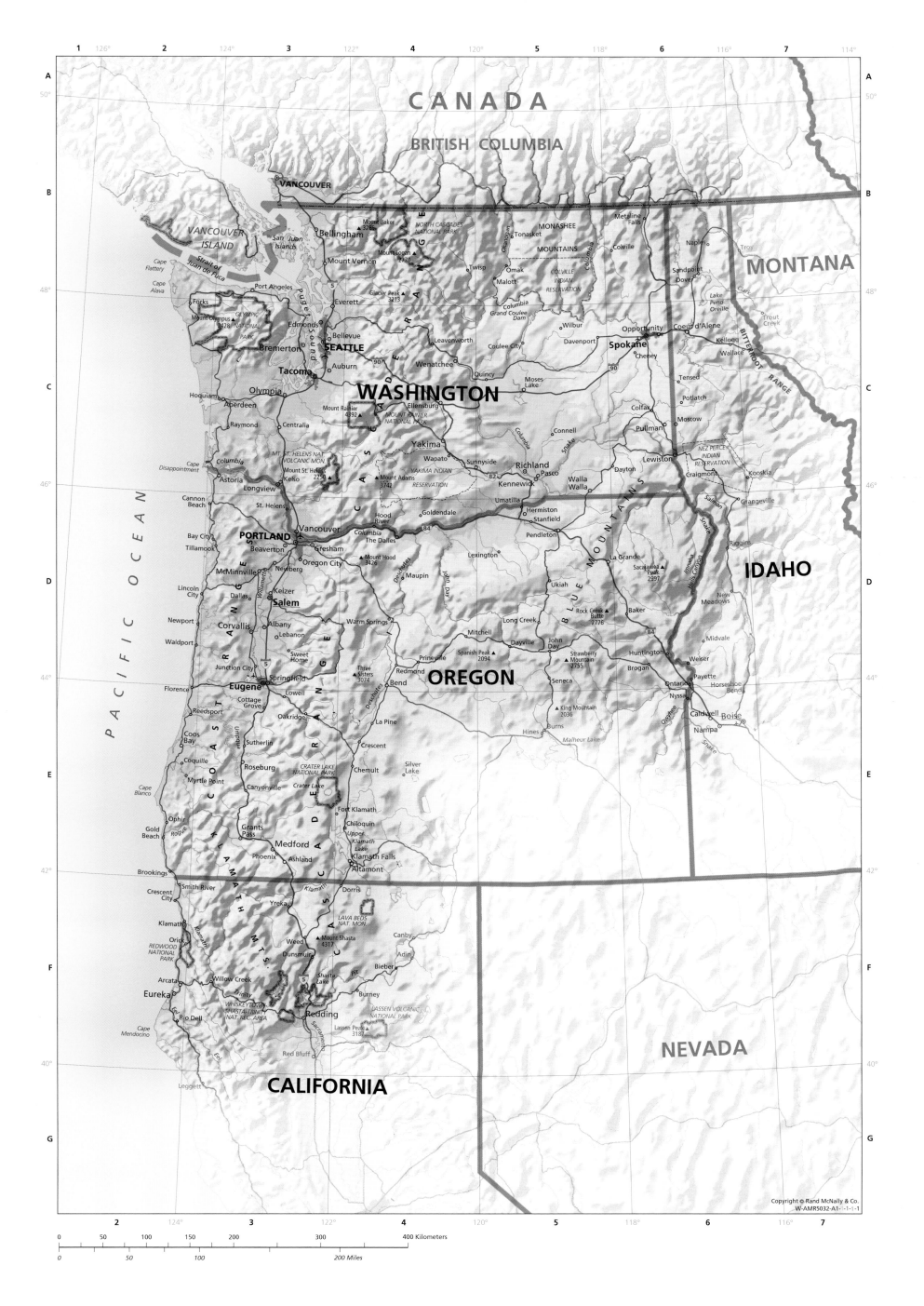

Dramatic sea stacks off the Pacific coast at Otter Point, Oregon (above), Seattle's skyline socked in by rain (bottom right)

have tamed the river's flow. The gorge and most other natural wonders are protected inside beloved national forests, recreation areas, and parks such as Olympic, North Cascades, Mount Rainier, Crater Lake, and Redwood.

Little wonder, then, that the people who inhabit this landscape are known for their ardent appreciation of it. Throughout history, Pacific Northwesterners have revered their mountains and forests and waterways. As early as 1913, for example, prescient Oregonians designated most of their state's spectacular coastline as part of the public domain. And in Washington in the 1990s, when running salmon stalled in the fish ladders on Columbia River dams, concerned environmentalists loaded thousands of fish into trucks and drove them around the dams to deposit them upstream. Pacific Northwesterners respect the physical landscape, but at the same time they have to live off the land's economic bounty of timber, fish, and agricultural crops. Difficult questions have long bedeviled them. What's the most important use for trees: to supply lumber for houses and jobs for loggers, or to remain as untouched natural treasures and a habitat for black bears, Roosevelt elk, and the spotted owl? What are rivers for: to be dammed and diverted for irrigation, electric power,

rain and the cascades **rainshadow**

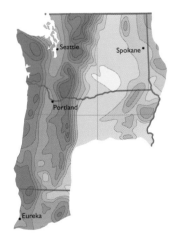

Mean annual precipitation in inches (cm)

☐ Less than 8 (20)
▢ 8 to 16 (20–40)
▢ 16 to 24 (40–60)
▢ 24 to 32 (60–80)
▣ 32 to 48 (80–120)
▣ 48 to 64 (120–160)
▣ 64 to 80 (160–200)
▣ 80 to 96 (200–240)
▣ 96 to 128 (240–320)
▣ More than 128 (320)

Weather patterns in the Pacific Northwest can be schizophrenic at best. West of the Cascade Range, weather is dominated by the wet marine air of the Pacific Ocean, while east of the mountains in the rainshadow of the Cascades the climate is arid, with hot, dry summers and extremely cold winters.

The Cascades halt the flow of moist Pacific air, boxing in gray and damp weather from the mountains west to the coast. Rainfall and snowfall are abundant, especially along the coast and in the Coast Range and Olympic Mountains, where the annual precipitation exceeds 100 inches (254 cm). In the Willamette Valley and Puget Sound area, precipitation is moderate: Portland and Seattle receive fewer than 40 inches (102 cm) of rain a year, on par with Atlanta, Houston, or Baltimore. Marine clouds and fog, however, are prevalent year-round, particularly in the winter and early spring. Winter temperatures in Seattle and Portland range from 30 degrees to about 50 degrees Fahrenheit (-1 to 10 degrees C). Summer highs occasionally reach the 90s (30s C), though pleasant 80-degree days are more the rule. Indian summers can last well into October.

As the Cascades form a barrier to trap moist Pacific air, they also allow a continental weather pattern to prevail in the east. Sunshine is the norm in both winter and summer.

The dry uplands east of the Cascades receive much less rain than the western valleys—from four inches (ten cm) a year in parts of Oregon and Idaho to 20 inches (50 cm) of precipitation, mostly snow, in the mountains. Summer high temperatures can exceed 100 degrees Fahrenheit (37 degrees C), particularly along the Columbia Plateau and the deserts of southern Oregon, but humidity is low and evenings are cool. Spring weather doesn't reach the region until May; fall arrives in September with unpredictable winter weather in tow.

cascades volcanism

With their snow-covered peaks rising serenely into the sky, the Cascades seem to represent stability, immutability, and a kind of permanence. In truth they are a hot zone of dormant volcanoes, part of the Pacific Ocean's "Ring of Fire." While visitors hike trails through Mount Rainier and North Cascades National Parks, creeping geologic plates 60 miles (96 km) beneath them melt rock into pockets of magma, which threaten to explode through the surface.

Extending 700 miles (1,120 km) from the Fraser River in British Columbia to Lassen Peak in California, this range of snowcapped volcanic cones has produced eight eruptions in the past two centuries, including two in the 20th century. Lassen erupted in 1914, but killed no one. But on May 18, 1980, Washington's Mount Saint Helens blew its top, killing 57 people, leveling forests, and showering ash as far east as North Dakota.

That eruption was relatively insignificant by Cascades standards, though. Roughly 7,000 years ago, a peak scientists now call Mount Mazama exploded violently, creating the great caldera in which Crater Lake later formed, and spewing 100 times more ash than the 1980 eruption.

Three volcanoes present the greatest threat today: Mount Saint Helens, currently in a state of "restless sleep"; Mount Adams, dormant for thousands of years but dangerous still; and Mount Rainier, classified as potentially the most lethal due to its proximity to densely populated areas. Today the Cascades are a center of geologic study, where experts track daily activity and predict mudflow paths to warn residents of potential danger.

MOUNTAINS OF FIRE
Most recent major eruptions

- Mt. Baker (1880)
- Glacier Peak (c. 1700)
- Seattle WASHINGTON
- Mt. Rainier (c. 1825)
- Mt. St. Helens (1980)
- Mt. Adams (c. 7535 B.C.)
- Portland Mt. Hood OREGON (1866)
- Mt. Jefferson (c. 950)
- Three Sisters (c. 350)
- Crater Lake Mt. Mazama (c. 4895 B.C.)
- Medicine Lake (c. 1075) Mt. Shasta (1786)
- Eureka CALIFORNIA
- Lassen Peak (1914)

and flood control, or to run free so salmon can swim upstream to spawn?

Mount Saint Helens blowing its top (left), sailboards in Columbia River Gorge (right), nordic skier on Hurricane Ridge (bottom right)

The earliest environmentalists were the Native Americans who populated the area long before the Spanish explorers and English surveyors arrived. Among them were the ancestors of present-day Nez Perce, Spokane, Chinook, Yakima, Clallam, Paiute, Shoshone, Coeur d'Alene, and Hupa Indians. These natives fished from dugout canoes and hunted abundant game in the forests and mountains.

Sir Francis Drake, Captain James Cook, and Captain George Vancouver all surveyed the coast or searched for the fabled Northwest Passage between 1579 and 1792, but they founded no colonies in the region. The first white man to come ashore was Captain Robert Gray, an American fur trader who sailed into Tillamook Bay in 1792 to trade with the natives. Soon after, in 1805, Meriwether Lewis and William Clark and the Corps of Discovery journeyed here and spent a peaceful winter at Fort Clatsop near a Native American settlement on the Columbia River, the means by which they reached the Pacific Ocean. The natives could easily have slaughtered the weary explorers, but instead provided the men with everything from food and fresh horses to guide services. And so Lewis and Clark penned glorious reports of the place to President Thomas Jefferson, who had sent them forth to explore the lands of the Louisiana Purchase.

Next came mountain men like Jedediah Smith, the Bible-toting adventurer who became the first white man to trek overland from southern California to the Northwest. The mountain men were trappers who sold beaver pelts that later became fashionable hats for dandies in the East. But they also helped open the way west for pioneers like Elijah White, who in 1842 led the first wagon train from Independence, Missouri, over the 2,000-mile-long (3,200-km) Oregon Trail to the fertile Willamette Valley. The journey west across endless prairies, swollen rivers, stark deserts, high mountain passes, and hostile Indian lands generally took six months. Throughout the 1840s, some 12,000 settlers lit out on the Oregon Trail to a rugged territory with very little cultivable land, attracted by tales of wild

recreation
in the northwest

Steady drizzle and stubborn cloud cover do little to hamper outdoor recreation in the Pacific Northwest, where love of playing outside is part of the regional psyche.

Here the outdoor landscape is integrated into people's everyday lives at work and play. Sports outings are not confined to a summer vacation or a weekend family trip: Seattle

businesspeople mountain-bike park trails during lunch hour. Oregonians take their evening jogs in the Cascade foothills or on coastal beaches. Northern Californians walk their dogs up Siskiyou mountain trails bathed in evening alpenglow.

In the Pacific Northwest athletes hardly have to travel beyond the outskirts of town to find world-class venues for hiking, biking, paddling, windsurfing, skiing, and climbing. A sampler of the region's favorite sporting destinations includes the following.

NORTHERN CALIFORNIA
In Redwood National Park, standing among 200-foot-tall (60-m) cathedrals of bark makes hikers feel magnificently puny. Along the Pacific, the best beachcombing starts where

development ends: along the wild, fog-shrouded Lost Coast, which begins where Highway 1 juts inland to meet U.S. 101. Also inland, some of California's most rollicking whitewater—the Klamath, Scott, and Salmon Rivers—flows between the Cascades and the Coast Ranges.

WASHINGTON
Hiking national park trails in Washington reaps great rewards, such as Kodak-moment views of glacier-topped peaks in North Cascades National Park or of emerald curtains of moss in Olympic National Park's Hoh Rainforest. The summit ascent up 14,410-foot (4,392-m) Mount Rainier is not for the faint of heart or quadriceps, but its reward is an eagle-eye perspective on the

snowcapped volcanoes of the Cascades. East of the Cascades, mountain bikers benefit from sunny dry weather and a plethora of logging roads outside the eastern Washington towns of Leavenworth and Winthrop. And in Puget Sound, sea kayakers can bump into interesting neighbors: dolphins, sea lions, and orcas.

OREGON
The highest mountain in the state, 11,240-foot (3,426-m) Mount Hood, hosts the continent's longest ski season—November through October. Farther south in the Cascades, mountaineers ascend the Three Sisters peaks as hikers traverse a moonscape of obsidian lava flows below. At the Oregon Dunes along the central Pacific coast, beachcombers climb billowing mounds of sand, while in the

south part of Oregon, on the wild and scenic Rogue River, paddlers maneuver through billowing waves of whitewater. At the Columbia River Gorge, screaming winds propel windsurfers through Hood River's monstrous whitecaps.

IDAHO PANHANDLE
At Silver Mountain, in Lewis and Clark territory outside Kellogg, the world's longest single-stage gondola carries skiers 3,400 vertical feet over 3.1 miles (1,030 m over five km). To the north, 43-mile-long (69-km) Lake Pend Oreille is Idaho's most legendary fishing hole, home of 30-pound (14-kg) Dolly Varden trout. Also in the Idaho panhandle, the roaring whitewater of the scenic Lochsa River tumbles through verdant canyons and thick evergreen forests (Idaho boasts more whitewater river miles than any state in the Lower 48).

mountains and fertile valleys. In 1883, the railroads arrived, the Pacific Northwest's abundant wheat and apples began to be shipped to the East, and Seattle became a bustling rail terminal for both goods and passengers.

Sea beasts: orca, sea star, and otters (top to bottom left); field of golden barley in eastern Washington (right); logs in Astoria awaiting shipment and Northern Spotted Owl (bottom right)

sea creatures

Off the Pacific Northwest's fog-cloaked beaches lurk strange sea beasts. Sleek Dall porpoises and Pacific white-sided dolphins, clownish seals and sea lions, and omnipotent orcas with black stiletto fins slicing arcs through the waves are typical members of the Pacific Ocean's cold-water cornucopia. Oddball denizens of the deep include the transparent candy-stripe shrimp, the camouflaged Red Irish Lord reef fish, the saw-toothed wolf eel, and North America's largest clam, the geoduck (weighing up to 35 pounds or 16 kg).

Even the smiling sea otter with its meticulous grooming habits leads a harsh existence as an aggressive predator. It consumes 25 percent of its body weight in food each day to survive. Otters devour invertebrates and steal food from each other; males have

even grabbed pups away from their mothers to ransom them for meals.

The sea star is another Pacific Coast oddity: Four or five symmetric arms radiate from a toothless mouth on the underside of a central body. One species, the sunflower star, grows up to 24 arms and 15,000 tube feet. These carnivores evert their stomachs to digest prey and can regenerate lost arms or even grow a new body and arms from a single severed limb.

Undisputed kingpin of the marine monsters is the giant Pacific octopus, the world's largest. Mature giant octopi weigh between 25 and 35 pounds (11 and 16 kg) although one overgrown cephalopod weighed in at 600 pounds (270 kg) with an armspan of 31 feet (9.3 m)—dimensions Jules Verne could scarcely have fathomed.

The region is still attracting settlers today, who arrive not by covered wagon and Pacific steamship but by 727s and sport-utility vehicles.

Not surprisingly, the Pacific Northwest has managed to retain much of the natural splendor that Lewis and Clark recorded in their journals nearly two centuries ago. And those natural attributes have given rise to an outside-oriented lifestyle today: Participants draw vigor from the great outdoors by hiking, biking, backpacking, skiing, mountain climbing, swimming, sailing, kayaking, beachcombing, and whale watching. At the same time, Pacific Northwesterners have historically integrated these same outdoor resources—mountains, forests, rivers, ocean, fertile fields—into their vibrant economy in commercial fishing, timber, and agriculture. They have, in other words, discovered the secret of living both in and off this land they love so much.

This lifestyle balanced by work and play is a big reason people move here from California, other parts of the country, and from Asia. The Pacific Northwest has seen double-digit population increases in the past decade—not only because there's so much to do in the outdoors, but because natural splendor is readily accessible, even from major cities like Seattle, Portland, and Vancouver, Canada. Some residents of Hood River, Oregon, have been known to ski Mount Hood on summer mornings until the trails turn slushy, then ride their bicycles downhill to the Columbia River for an afternoon of boardsailing in the Gorge. In Seattle, businessmen and women can kayak Puget Sound over lunch hour, work in the office all afternoon, and still set up camp in the Olympic Mountains by sunset. Great outdoor venues are practically in the backyards of smaller communities, such as Eureka, California; Bend, Coos Bay, Eugene, Astoria, and Salem, Oregon; Coeur d'Alene, Lewiston, and Pocatello, Idaho; and Bellingham, Olympia, Yakima, and Spokane, Washington.

protecting the
environment

The tiny Northern Spotted Owl seems too unassuming to have started an environmental revolution. But the fluffy nocturnal bird, all 22 scrawny ounces (624 g) of it, became a symbol in the late 1980s of the fight for conservation in the Pacific Northwest, a region until then best known for lusty resource extraction. Logging, fishing, and mining provided the lion's share of the employment and profits in a region blessed with abundant natural beauty and wealth.

Then came a series of court cases pitting the rights of the endangered owl, which can nest only in old-growth forests, against those of loggers, who at the time were receiving upwards of $200,000 for a single 300-foot-high (92-m) redwood tree. "Save an owl. Ban logging," read one common bumper sticker. "Save a logger. Eat an owl," retorted another.

But rather than becoming lunch, the owl, backed by the powerful Endangered Species Act, prevailed in decision after decision, effectively halting logging in large stretches of Washington, Oregon, and California. Hundreds of thousands of jobs were lost—

all of which produced, paradoxically, a stronger economy. As lumbering fell off in much of the Pacific Northwest, high-tech industries moved in. Today, most counties in the region have experienced a net increase in jobs.

Just as importantly, the forests have been flourishing. Where once the centuries-old redwoods echoed to the sounds of saws and trucks, they now sit quiet, dark, and cool. Lumber companies that cleared live trees now collect primarily dead and fallen wood. Tourists have replaced lumber trucks. The Northern Spotted Owl population is recovering, as are those of the equally endangered marbled murrelet seabirds and the coho salmon that need shade

from tall redwoods to spawn. In the process, the experience of the Pacific Northwest has become a kind of environmental benchmark for conservationists everywhere—proof that saving one species need not mean savaging another.

Seattle, Washington, is known to tourists and locals alike for its landmark Space Needle (left), its famous cappuccino bean juice (right), and its world-class bookstores and bike paths.

Postcard views and the environmental ethic are not the only attractions, however. Cosmopolitan Portland and Seattle boast first-rate music, theater, and art, gourmet restaurants serving locally produced truffles and pinot noir, congenial coffeehouses, well-stocked bookstores, and artsy bed-and-breakfasts. Business and industry are booming, with timber, commercial fishing, tourism, software, wheat, and apples playing important economic roles. These wheat and apple crops, along with the pears, potatoes, and vineyards, orchards, and dairy farms of the wet Willamette Valley, make this region one of the world's most productive agricultural areas. In the Seattle area, where Boeing and Weyerhauser used to be the only big-name employers and where shipbuilding is still a major industry, Starbucks, REI, and Microsoft have made their mark. In fact, the computer software industry has fueled the area's population growth. As the gateway cities to southwestern Canada and the countries of the Pacific Rim, Portland and Seattle also benefit from international commerce and are home to an ethnically diverse population that includes Asian immigrants and Native Americans from Canada and Alaska.

Still, despite its considerable urban pleasures and economic successes, the Pacific Northwest best captures the imagination with its raw natural beauty. Its attraction was perhaps most clearly illustrated by John Muir, the pioneer naturalist and conservationist who explored the Cascades and the Columbia Gorge around 1899, and who was largely responsible for the creation of two national parks in the region: Mount Rainier and Crater Lake. Muir advised, "Thousands of tired, nerve-shaken, over-civilized people are beginning to find out that going to the mountains is going home; that wildness is a necessity; and that mountain parks and reservations are useful not only as fountains of timber and irrigating rivers, but as fountains of life."

seattle's coffee culture

Seattle's reign as the undisputed birthplace and the capital of America's coffee culture started in 1970 when Seattle's Best Coffee—originally an ice cream and coffee shop called The Wet Whisker—began serving freshly ground coffee. Starbucks was founded next, in 1971 in the Pike Place Market, by three former English majors from the University of Washington who named their company after the coffee-swilling first mate in Herman Melville's *Moby Dick*.

In 1983, a Starbucks executive traveling in Italy was impressed by the popularity of the espresso bars he saw there—1,500 in Milan alone. The following year he opened the company's first Italian-style coffee bar. Business boomed and by the end of the decade, coffee shops or espresso carts were on every Seattle street corner. The same thing happened in most American cities.

No one can say with authority why the specialty-coffee roasting and drinking phenomenon took off first in Seattle. Some believe that the long, gray, wet winters encourage the sipping of hot drinks. Others point to Seattle's reputation as a breeding ground for successful entrepreneurs like William Boeing and Bill Gates.

Today there are more than 200 licensed espresso carts and more than 50 espresso bars or cafes in Seattle. Freshly brewed espresso and its numerous variants show up in many other kinds of locations, too: car washes, laundromats, bookstores, restaurants, and even dental clinics.

Residents of the city may be their own best customers for the aromatic brew; they consume nearly one million cups every day.

Coastal California
to the Sierras

Promised Land in the Golden West

 A **mythic** landscape of valleys, mountains, and surf, central and coastal California has always beckoned people seeking better prospects in life. Stretching from the Pacific Ocean to the Sierra Nevadas, and from the northern "Lost Coast" to the Baja Peninsula, the region is blessed with the kinds of natural resources—oil, metals, fertile land, a near-perfect climate—that symbolize promise for resourceful men and women. New World explorers, Gold Rush Forty-Niners, Dust Bowl Okies, and scores of immigrants from Mexico and the Pacific Rim have historically come in search of the California Dream, an idyllic existence where the good life reigns and all enterprise is possible.

The grandeur of the land is dreamlike itself. When people back East and abroad first heard of the West's lofty peaks, turbulent shores, extravagant wildlife, and mammoth trees, many didn't believe the tales. Others wouldn't be content until they saw for themselves craggy cliffs towering nearly a thousand feet (300 m) above the Pacific and the Sierra Nevada Mountains flaunting their glacier-streaked flanks, including Mount Whitney, the highest peak (at 14,494 feet or 4,418 m) in the Lower 48 states. They wanted to experience the great Yosemite Valley, where more than half of the country's highest waterfalls cascade over granite cliffs, and

Lake Tahoe (left), Chinese-American children in New Year's Parade in San Francisco (below). Preceding pages: Big Sur coast

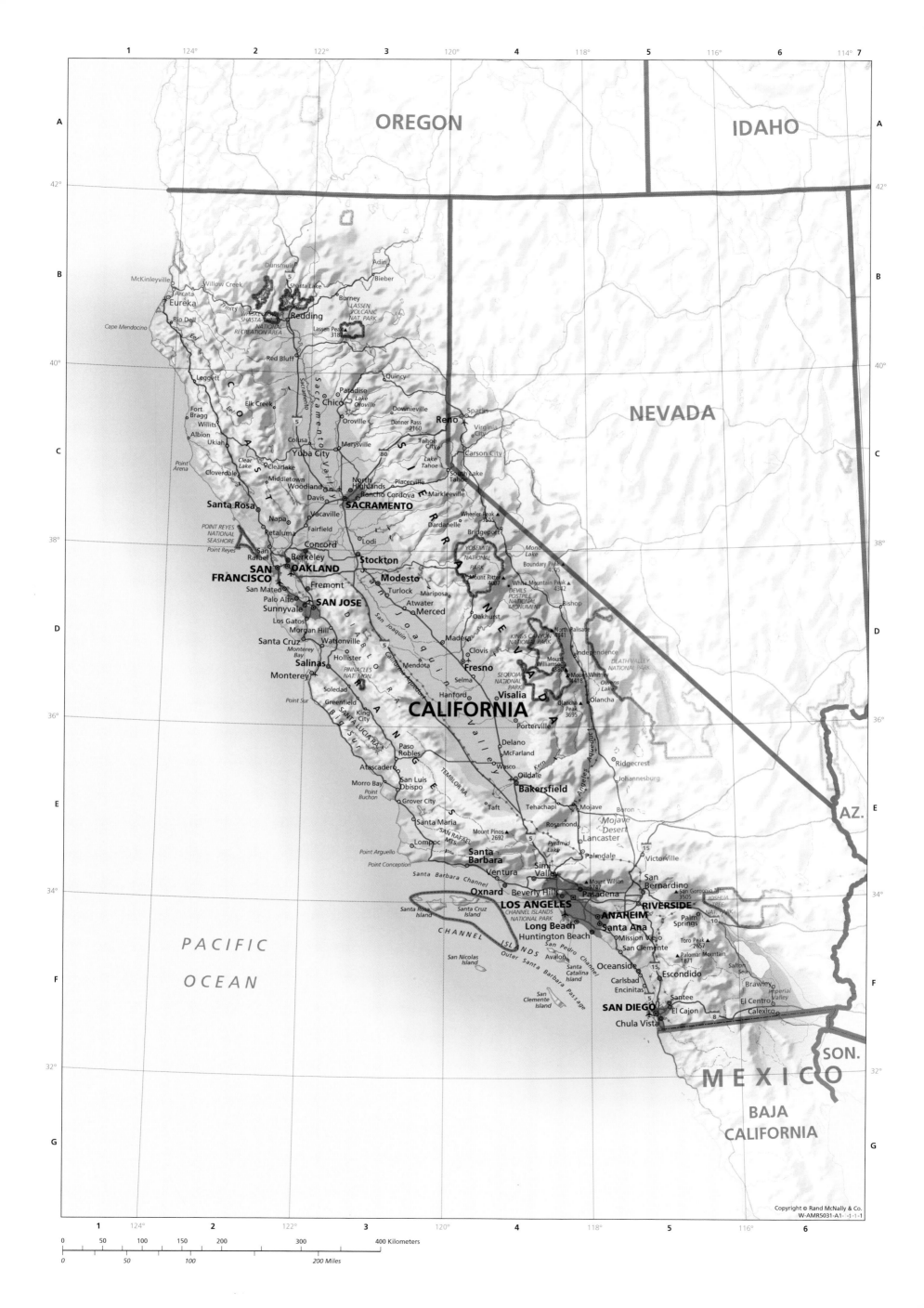

to view majestic redwoods and sequoias—the world's tallest and largest trees—in groves that have existed more than 2,000 years. They came to see golden eagles and the California condor (the largest bird in North America) sweep the skies, Roosevelt elk and cougars prowl the forests, and whales and sea lions roam the ocean.

The first people to lay eyes on this richly endowed land were the descendants of prehistoric hunters who crossed the Bering land bridge in search of big game. They were the ancestors of the Native Americans, 300,000 of whom were living here when Spaniard Juan Rodriguez Cabrillo first sailed into San Diego Bay in September 1542. In 1579 Sir Francis Drake dropped anchor off the coast of northern California just long enough to claim the region for England, but 200 years passed before any European country made a serious effort to colonize. The Spanish finally got around to it in 1769 when Gaspar de Portola stepped ashore where Cabrillo had anchored 227 years earlier. A Franciscan missionary on that expedition, Junipero Serra, established Mission San Diego de Alcala that year, the first in a chain of 21 missions that would stretch far beyond San Francisco Bay and give rise to such important cities as San Francisco, Santa Barbara, Santa Cruz, and San Jose.

The California territory became part of Mexico in 1822, shortly after Mexico won its independence from Spain. But the region didn't remain in Mexican hands for long. The urge to "wester" was stirring among Americans in the East. Frontiersman Jedediah Smith was the first white man to lead people west over the Sierra Nevada Mountains into central California in 1827, and the first organized expedition of American settlers successfully traveled overland to California in 1841. The better-known Donner party was not so fortunate, trudging across endless plains, fording raging rivers, and crossing a broad desert only to be trapped in October 1846 by heavy snows atop the high Sierra pass that now bears their name. They ate tree bark and finally their own dead before rescuers reached them. Their tragedy came to symbolize both the dangers of the new western territories and the incredible tenacity of the pioneers hell-bent to get there.

quakes and faults

A conundrum in California goes like this: If the San Andreas fault continues shifting at its present rate, and Los Angeles ends up next to San Francisco in a far-off era, which city will be the suburb of the other? The answer obviously depends on which city you come from, but the geological prediction is widely accepted.

California from the coast to the Sierras is highly prone to earthquakes because it sits over the boundary between the shifting Pacific and North American plates. Here, the San Andreas fault system, a rupturing fracture in Earth's crust, extends more than 800 miles (1,280 km) from Mexico north past San Francisco. The plates of the San Andreas slip horizontally, creeping about two inches (five cm) a year, but tend to "lock up" around San Francisco and Los Angeles, where major earthquakes are felt as the lock breaks. The infamous 1906 San Francisco earthquake displaced the land west of the fault as much as 21 feet (6.5 m).

The 1906 temblor and a 1857 earthquake at Fort Tejon, near Los Angeles, are the most powerful California earthquakes on record; both occurred on the San Andreas proper. The Hayward Fault that runs directly through Oakland and Berkeley has also produced devastating quakes exceeding magnitude 7. Other ancillary faults and blind faults, such as the one that caused the 1994 Northridge earthquake, or the newly discovered Puente Hills fault under Los Angeles, pose as great a risk as the San Andreas itself.

Earthquake preparedness industries thrive in the region. Earthquake insurance must be offered to every California homeowner. Several firms supply survival kits—food, water purification, first aid—designed to get people through a week without gas or electricity. Some contractors specialize in retrofitting buildings; other companies sell valves to shut off the gas at a certain magnitude of shaking. And schools and businesses hold "duck and cover" earthquake drills, especially during Earthquake Preparedness Month in April.

FAULT COUNTRY

©RMcN
N-AMR24500-B5- -|-|-|

Most damaging earthquakes since 1900, measured on the Mercalli Intensity Scale

❶ San Francisco, 1906 (11)
❷ Central California, 1952 (11)
❸ San Fernando, 1971 (11)
❹ Southeast of El Centro, 1940 (10)
❺ Long Beach, 1933 (9)
❻ Loma Prieta, 1989 (9)
❼ Landers, Yucca Valley, 1992 (9)
❽ Northridge, 1994 (9)
❾ Central California, Coalinga, 1983 (8)
❿ Whittier, 1987 (8)
⓫ Humboldt County: Ferndale, Petroli, 1992 (8)
⓬ Big Bear Lake, Big Bear City, 1992 (8)

Two events in 1848 sealed the future of the region and the entrepreneurial character of its residents. That year Mexico ceded California to the United States and James Wilson Marshall

gold rush!

On January 24, 1848, while he was inspecting the tailrace of a sawmill in the western foothills of the Sierra Nevadas, James Wilson Marshall spotted several shiny metallic chips in the water. He thought the metal was pyrite, or "Fool's Gold," but after hammering the chips and finding them malleable, he realized he had discovered true gold.

Within weeks, thousands of Californians raced to the foothills. The following spring, in 1849, tens of thousands of "Forty-Niners" from across the country and around the world set out for the California gold fields.

Hundreds of gold camps sprang up overnight, with colorful names like You Bet, Rough and Ready, and Hangtown. Gold nuggets and flakes were abundant in quartz outcroppings and in

"placers"—the auriferous gravel of flowing and ancient "fossil" rivers. With only a pick and a pan, a miner could yield upwards of $50 in gold per day; a lucky few struck it rich with claims worth hundreds of thousands of dollars.

By the end of 1855 most surface deposits had been exhausted, and miners turned to hydraulic methods: Using ditches, flumes, and hoses, they blasted gravel-bearing hills with powerful water jets, then removed the gold as the gravel washed down sluices. Hydraulic mining was effective but environmentally devastating, washing away entire hills and creating rocky wastelands. An 1887 U.S. Circuit Court ruling finally put a stop to the practice.

The impact of the Gold Rush was far-reaching. It prompted the construction of the first transcontinental railroad. Gold wealth boosted the American economy, and some historians speculate that the outcome of the Civil War was decided by California gold that enriched Union coffers.

discovered gold in the Sierras east of Sacramento. Hundreds of thousands raced to the gold country: Some creaked across the prairies in wagons; some walked; others came by sea, sailing all the way around Cape Horn or cutting overland across Panama to sail up the Pacific (the Panama Canal was not yet built). In 1847, San Francisco was a hamlet of 450 people. By the end of 1849 it was swarming with 25,000 treasure-seekers from the East and from abroad. Immigrants from China, Mexico, France, Spain, Germany, Great Britain, Chile, and Peru came for the gold and for subsequent work on the transcontinental railroad, creating in San Francisco a cosmopolitan culture. The Forty-Niners may have looked like a ragtag bunch, but in fact many were well-educated, with the financial means to travel and buy necessary wagons, draft animals, and supplies. These men were already successful but came to make it big, or at least better, in the Golden West of California—much like the "techies" who arrive in Silicon Valley today.

Surfers on a Southern California beach (above), Forty-Niners panning for gold (left), grapes on the vine in Napa (right)

napa valley
wine country

NAPA WINERIES

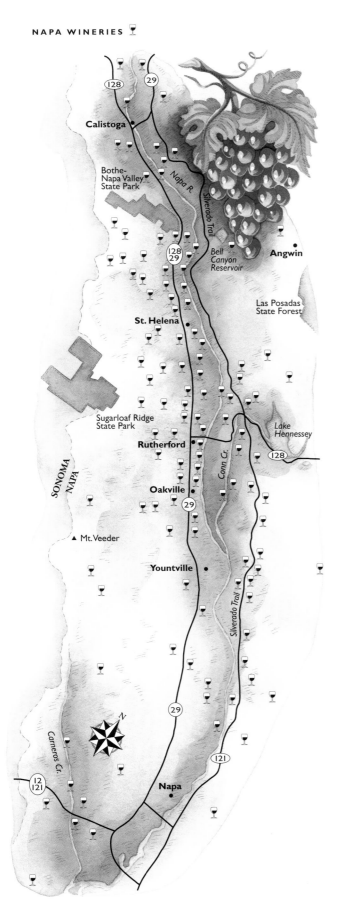

Viticulture has had a dreamlike effect on the Napa Valley wine country, with its graceful chateau wineries and European ambience. Along with the Sonoma and several other valleys, this fertile region of northern California produces four-fifths of all the wine in the United States and is a premier romantic getaway.

European settlers arrived in the Napa and Sonoma Valleys 200 years ago, attracted to dramatic hills and delightful weather, a day's ride northeast from San Francisco at that time. They quickly discovered that fruit would tolerate the area's intermittent droughts better than wheat and corn. The climate was ideal for growing grapes: hot sun moderated by cool sea breezes and fogs, along with summer mists considered excellent for white grapes like chardonnay. In addition, Napa Valley's soils—volcanic, rocky, and well-drained—were perfect for the fussy roots of most grapes, especially reds like cabernet sauvignon.

The earliest vintners were Germans Charles Krug and Jacob Schram—names still on Napa Valley wine labels—who settled here in the 1870s and set about to develop grapes suitable to the soil and climate. Their enduring contribution was zinfandel, now considered the native grape of the area. Italians also came, founding Italian Swiss Colony along the Russian River in Sonoma, growing sangiovese, nebbiola, and other grapes familiar to them.

Vineyards quickly bolstered the area's economy, but France's vintners did not have to worry much about competition at first.

Most early California wine went into barrels or tanks, was sold to shippers, and bottled elsewhere, with little concern for purity, much less subtlety of bouquet and finish. Prohibition soon put a hold on most everything, but it did not change the natural conditions of the wine country. By 1950, a farm called Stony Hill Vineyard in northern Napa County started growing what are now legendary chardonnays. Around the same time the Hanzell winery undertook a strict wine-making regime adopted from Burgundy.

While makers of jug wine were still growing grapes in volume and calling them "chablis" or "chianti" based mostly on color, there was continued improvement in wine quality. Viticulturists noted that complex wines could be coaxed from the geologic mélange beneath the surface. Today some say they can detect hints of the serpentine stone ground into the soil, or rhyolite lava, chert, gabbro, and other varied constituents of the earth.

In 1976 a Paris-based wine competition pitted California against France. In a result that has been borne out in the years since then, two Napa vineyards, Chateau Montelena and Stag's Leap, were preferred to French counterparts. California grapes, nurtured in perfect soil with a long growing season, and California wines, with their higher alcohol content, were suddenly noted and taken seriously.

Today, although almost every type of wine is made here, Napa's signature grapes are cabernet sauvignon, which first became dominant 100 years ago, and zinfandel, a California original.

Napa Valley adapted nicely to its fame, opening up to tourists its wineries and small towns such as St. Helena and Calistoga and Yountville. Writer John McPhee extolled the picturesque wineries—some 60 of which exist along Highway 29 between Napa and Calistoga and on the Silverado Trail to the east—as a kind of "agricultural Disneyland."

The enterprising nature of the region's early residents also was evident in canny entrepreneurs and merchants who catered to the miners' needs and wants, supplying them with food, clothing, implements, whiskey, and anything else that would turn a profit. With their boundless optimism, self-confidence, and gamblers' instinct, many of these miner-merchants took their goldfield earnings to San Francisco and built great fortunes. In assessing the impact of the Gold Rush, historian John Caughey described California as the only place where "a rush for gold was made to serve as the base for an ever-widening superstructure of attainment."

Sierra high peaks over Owens Valley (above), surf-pounded Point Reyes coast (below), San Francisco (center right), Los Angeles (bottom right)

Another example of enterprise by irrepressible Californians was the creation of the 450-mile-long (725-km) Central Valley agricultural plot known as the "Salad Bowl." The Central Valley's vast irrigation system harnesses rivers flowing from the north and east and distributes water throughout the valley, transforming this normally arid lowland into the world's largest producer of fruits and vegetables (while at the same time alleviating Los Angeles' water shortage). Nearly every variety of fruit and vegetable that grows in the United States now thrives in the Central (made up of the Sacramento and San Joaquin Valleys) and other valleys of the region, adding up to $20 billion in annual agricultural production.

As if the spectacular beauty and bounty of the land weren't enough, the region also ranks number one in industrial employment. Electronic equipment—chiefly computers developed in the San

a tale of two cities

Lured by gold, sunshine, and dreams of success, people from every corner of the world have flocked to find the good life in the Golden West. California's two most important population centers, Los Angeles and San Francisco, have become larger-than-life addresses, attracting visionaries, innovators, and star-struck hopefuls. But the cities couldn't be more different: San Francisco, a northern, cosmopolitan, romantic city of rolling fogs, hilly streets, and diverse arts and culture; and Los Angeles, a southern, glamorous, sun-drenched desert metropolis.

SAN FRANCISCO

San Francisco is a city of contrasts, with cool fogs and glorious sunshine, horizontal expanses of water and vertical hills, and residents of every race, religion, and lifestyle, including the first large population of Chinese and one of the largest gay communities in the country. San Franciscans thrive on these diversities, proud of their reputation as civic-minded nonconformists.

The city's population of 750,000-plus is the heart of the nine-county Bay Area, with more than 6.2 million residents. First established as a Spanish presidio and mission in 1776, San Francisco welcomed the Gold Rush throngs, as treasure seekers arrived from all over the world—and stayed. The 1869 completion of the railroad introduced another population boom, and World War II stimulated shipbuilding, military bases, and embarkation centers.

Today, the economy is based largely on tourism, banking, and the high-tech industries of Silicon Valley. Earthquakes and mudslides have done very little to dampen San Francisco's status as California's cosmopolitan and cultural sweetheart.

LOS ANGELES

America's second-largest city, with more than 3.5 million residents (14 million in the metropolitan area), is a model of urban sprawl and casual glamor. Centered between the Santa Monica Mountains and the Pacific Ocean, Los Angeles spreads south along an industrial corridor and north into the San Fernando Valley, crisscrossed by the world's largest urban highway network.

First established in 1781 as El Pueblo de Nuestra Señora La Reina de Los Angeles de Porciuncula, the city was incorporated in 1850. Soon after, the Central Pacific and Santa Fe Railroads arrived, along with an influx of sun-seekers from the

East. Flourishing orange groves and the discovery of oil in 1891 spurred Los Angeles' initial population boom from 12,000 in 1880 to 320,000 in 1910. But it was the silver screen film studios, which emerged in Hollywood around 1910, that transformed the City of Angels into a dazzling destination. Today the film industry is a major part of L.A.'s financial core and at the heart of its sun-and-fun, anything-is-possible image.

Despite suburban sprawl and inner-city poverty, Los Angeles remains a point of light as the country's largest center for immigrants, primarily from the Pacific Rim and Latin America.

Jose-Palo Alto area, or Silicon Valley—is the leading industry, followed by tourism, construction, aerospace engineering, telecommunications, and the motion picture and television industry, the biggest in the world. Altogether, the region's goods and services amount to more than 10 percent of the U.S. gross national product. Small wonder, then, that the economic abundance of this region has spurred multiple population booms: the Gold Rush, Dust Bowl farmers during the Depression, soldiers and immigrants after World War II, and, more recently, entrepreneurs from the Pacific Rim, entertainment industrialists, high-tech professionals, and immigrants from Latin America. Today California is the most populous state in the union, with 30 million residents—slightly more than half of them ethnic minorities, including the largest populations of Mexicans, Japanese, and Native Americans in the country.

Yosemite's sheer-faced El Capitan (right), cauliflower in the Central Valley (left), California's famed oranges (bottom left)

There is little uniformity, much less conformity, among those residents, especially in the Los Angeles area, which has an extremely diverse population of Hispanics, whites, Asians, and African Americans, and a reputation for celebrating unconventional behavior and dress. San Franciscans strive for a more sophisticated image, but also celebrate the unconventional: The hippie culture flowered here in the Haight-Asbury neighborhood, topless dancing got its start in North Beach, and the free speech movement first hit the headlines on the campus of U.C.-Berkeley. Juxtapositions do abound: Beverly Hills, the epitome of glamor and the good life, lies just a few miles from troubled neighborhoods plagued by gangs and violence. And while the region is sometimes called a haven for kooks and cultists, it also boasts one of the country's finest university systems and the most Nobel Laureates. Even periodic floods, brush fires, mudslides, earthquakes, Santa Ana winds, and El Niño storms tend to be shrugged off as a small price to pay for the chance to live the California Dream. "Californians have seemed capable of almost anything," wrote San Diegan Neil Morgan in his book, *California Syndrome.* "These unusual people in this extraordinary place come equipped with vitality and with dreams... California is ranging out ahead of America."

agriculture
in the central valley

The Great Central Valley, stretching from Redding in the north to the Tehachapi Mountains in the south, is the farming heartland of a region that leads the nation in agriculture. Central California grows the most spinach, lettuce, lima beans, carrots, celery, broccoli, and cauliflower in the country and leads in total production of vegetables, grapes, lemons, apricots, plums, prunes, raisins, strawberries, peaches, avocados, cantaloupes, and honeydew melons. And it produces nearly all of the dates, figs, almonds, nectarines, walnuts, and olives grown here. It ranks a respectable second in the production of oranges, grapefruit, tangerines, pears, sweet corn, tomatoes, asparagus, rice, and, though you wouldn't want to eat them, commercial roses, flower seeds, and cotton.

This vast flatland between the Sierra Nevada mountain range and the coastal ranges is on average 50 miles (80 km) wide. There is no plain like it west of the Rockies. The loamy soil, coupled with the flatness of the land, make for optimal growing conditions. But the valley, drained by the San Joaquin River in the south and the Sacramento River in the north, is also naturally arid. So over the past century and a half, national and state governments have drained nearby lakes and marshes and redirected the rivers to make sure that the valley is adequately irrigated for farming. Today, a vast and complicated system of more than 20 dams and 500 miles (800 km) of canals, created by the Central Valley Project, provides the water necessary to grow abundant crops.

Although draining the wetlands for irrigation destroyed migrating birds' wintering grounds and dammed access to freshwater habitats for various fish, local officials are working to remedy the situation. The Central Valley Improvement Act of 1992 has established wildlife refuges to eventually provide a balance between agricultural and environmental needs.

yosemite national park

John Muir, founder of the Sierra Club and early champion of Yosemite preservation, listed this mountain park's attractions as "the most songful streams in the world, ...the noblest forests, the loftiest granite domes, the deepest ice-sculptured canyons, and snowy mountains soaring into the sky." A century later, Yosemite National Park still offers every kind of natural beauty imaginable: glacier-carved mountain peaks, mighty granite domes, giant sequoia groves, spectacular waterfalls, two wide glistening rivers, flower-strewn meadows, pine and aspen forests, and an astounding variety of wildlife large and small.

Yosemite's 1,170 square miles (3,030 sq km), midway down the length of the Sierras,

encompass some of the most beloved and beautiful geological formations in the country—many of them within the seven-mile-long (11-km) Yosemite Valley. Here, Yosemite Falls plummets 2,425 feet (740 m) in three magnificent cascades, while across the valley Bridalveil Falls floats down 60 feet (18 m) in wispy sheets of mist. The stalwart granite monolith of El Capitan, 3,593 feet (1,096 m) from base to summit, is twice as big as the Rock of Gibraltar and is the largest single exposed granite face in the world. Sentinel Rock and Cathedral Spires are other superb granite carvings, along with Half Dome, which soars 5,000 feet (1,525 m) above the valley floor. Outside the valley lie the Mariposa, Tuolumne, and Merced Groves of giant sequoias that rise to 300 feet (90 m).

The oldest tree, Grizzly Giant, is estimated to be 2,700 years old.

Yosemite didn't always look like this. Five hundred million years ago it was sediment covered by a sea; magma rose and cooled as huge blocks of granite below the surface. As the sea receded and the Sierras started to rise and tilt, the Merced River cut its canyon. The scouring ice of glaciers and weathering of the bare uplifted granite carved the valley and its fantastic domes, monoliths, and waterfalls, sculpting Yosemite into one of the country's crown jewels of geology.

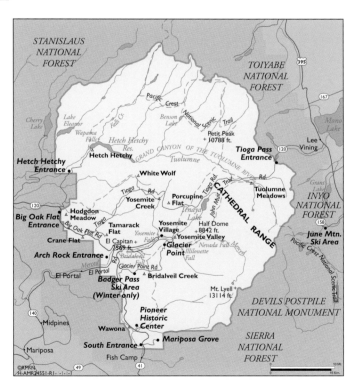

Hawaii

Pacific Islands Born of Fire

The oldest and **most isolated** archipelago in the world, Hawaii is a paradise born of fire. Here, smoking volcanoes loom over lush tropical rain forests, and sun-drenched fields roll into volcanic ash beaches. Separated from the U.S. mainland by more than 2,000 miles (3,200 km) of ocean, Hawaii is American in name but strongly Polynesian in character, retaining the culture brought by successive waves of Pacific and East Asian immigrants. Their legendary hospitality—the spirit of *aloha*—has long welcomed throngs of seasonal tourists and transplanted U.S. mainlanders. Hawaii has withstood the onslaughts of new arrivals by absorbing each group into its island culture, and today fosters an artfully blended multiethnic society.

Palm trees near Kona (left), Kauai's majestic Na Pali Coast (above). Preceding pages: Kalaupapa National Historical Park, Molokai

Arcing southeast to northwest across the Pacific, the Hawaiian Islands beckon invitingly to outsiders, and six of the eight major islands—Oahu, Hawaii, Kauai, Maui, Molokai, and Lanai—receive hordes of visitors. Most travelers first experience the islands' charm in the state capital of Honolulu on Oahu. Oahu's dense population—more than three out of four Hawaiians live there—and intensive development for tourism give it a distinctly urban character. Yet beyond the bustle of world-famous Waikiki Beach, Oahu has its share of rugged mountains, picture-perfect sands, and remote rain forests.

Evidence of its fiery origins bubbles at the surface of Hawaii, the largest island. Formed by five volcanoes, the "Big Island" continues to grow from the two that remain active: Mauna Loa and Kilauea, Earth's most active volcano, whose molten lava smolders, crackles, and is transformed by Pacific waves into fresh deposits of black sand in Hawaii Volcanoes National Park. Mauna Kea (13,796 feet/4,205 m) towers nearby, dormant for nearly 4,000 years but as formidable as its rumbling neighbor.

Kauai's untouched landscapes typify popular images of the Hawaiian Islands. Majestic fluted columns of volcanic rock, chiseled by wind and rain, rise above the famed Na Pali Coast. Rock crumbled to sand forms miles of golden strands, and high, lacy waterfalls pour onto deserted beaches accessible only by boat, air, or a strenuous hike. Inland, Kauai's gaping Waimea Canyon drops 3,657 feet (1,108 m), and Mount Waïalële (5,148 feet/1,569 m) is known as the wettest place on Earth, averaging 460 inches (1,170 cm) of rain annually.

Maui, the Valley Isle, is Hawaii's second most popular destination, after Honolulu. Framed by white sand coves and crystal blue waters, it boasts the breathtaking Haleakala Crater, where hikers can descend past burnt red cinder cones and ebony lava flows. East of the park, Oheo Gulch, or Kipahulu, presents a dazzling series of cataracts and waterfall pools that cascade into the ocean. In the west, rain-drenched Puu Kukui in the Iao Valley is one of Hawaii's few remaining stretches of virgin rain forest.

Calm isolation accentuates Lanai's dramatic beauty. In Hulopoe Bay, snorkelers can cavort with spinner dolphins, surrounded by a golden-sand beach. Hilly and intermittently blanketed by pine forests, "The Pineapple Isle" was owned by the Dole Company for many years, and was the world's largest pineapple producer for much of the 20th century.

surf capital of the world

Surfing has been Hawaii's signature sport since the arrival of the earliest Polynesians, who elevated wave-riding to an art form. As a testament to their love of surfing, their languages are peppered with numerous words to describe different characteristics of breaking waves.

An unusual combination of natural conditions makes Hawaii a premier surfing destination. Isolated in the Pacific, the islands are fully exposed to far-reaching swells from every direction. With no continental shelf to slow or shrink them, these monstrous coils of raw energy barrel in from deep water, hitting Hawaii's shallow offshore coral reefs and unleashing their power in huge, explosive waves. Oahu's North Shore lies in the direct path of the strongest waves, generated more than 2,000 miles (3,200 km) to the north by Arctic storms; some waves crest at more than 30 feet (nine m).

From November to March, barefoot surfers in colorful gear descend upon Waimea Bay and several other North Shore beaches to pit themselves against the unforgiving breaks. Their sleek boards of foam and fiberglass, often weighing less than five pounds (2.2 kg), are a far cry from the 100-pound (45-kg) planks of *wiliwili*, *ulu*, or *koa* wood carved by their ancient predecessors.

Surfing was unknown to much of the world until Hawaii's Olympic swimmer Duke Kahanamoku became its unofficial ambassador in the early 1900s, bringing the sport to Australia, Europe, and the west coast of the United States. Other famous surfers include Hawaiians George Freeth, who popularized surfing in California, and Eddie Aikau, who legitimized the first staging of the International Professional Surfers tour in 1976. Mark Foo, a Hawaiian champion who died in a 1994 surfing accident, cultivated the sport's high-profile image with his masterful, publicity-seeking performances in the 1980s and early 1990s.

Thanks to Foo's efforts, surfing has become a lucrative profession. Many surfers, hoping for fame and endorsements, compete in Hawaii's annual contests. Best known is the Triple Crown of Surfing—consisting of both men's and women's events—with a grand prize of one million dollars.

Copyright © Rand McNally & Co.
W-AMR6542-A1- - -1-1-1

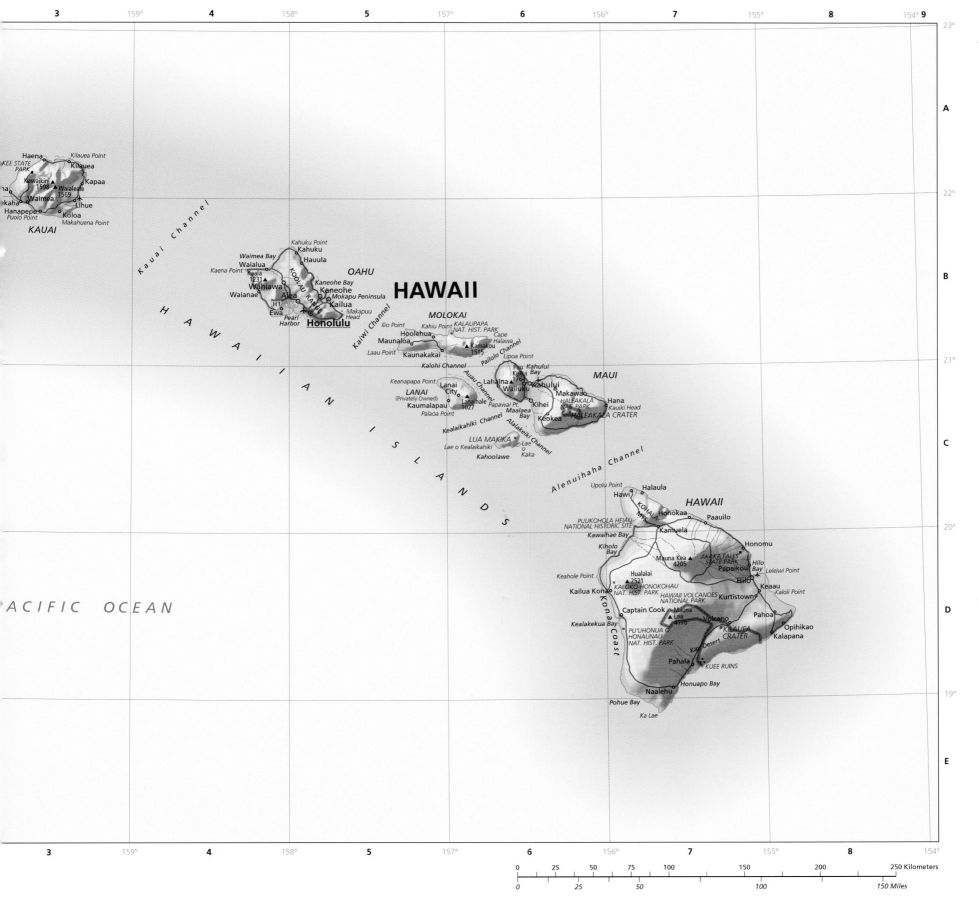

Haena
KEE STATE PARK
Kilauea Point
Kilauea
Kawaikini 1598
Waialeale
Kapaa
Waialeale 1569
Lihue
Waimea
Hanapepe
Koloa
Puolo Point
Makahuena Point

KAUAI

Kauai Channel

HAWAIIAN ISLANDS

Kahuku Point
Waimea Bay
Kahuku
Waialua
Hauula
Kaena Point
OAHU
Kaala
1231
Waipahu
Kaneohe Bay
Wahiawa
Kaneohe
Waianae
Mokapu Peninsula
Aiea
Kailua
H1
Makapuu Head
Pearl Harbor
Ewa
Honolulu

HAWAII

KOOLAU RANGE

Kaiwi Channel

Ilio Point
MOLOKAI
KALAUPAPA NAT. HIST. PARK
Hoolehua
Cape Halawa
Maunaloa
Kamakou 1515
Lipoa Point
Laau Point
Kaunakakai
Pailolo Channel

Kalohi Channel

Puu Kahului
Kukui Bay
Kahului
Keanapapa Point
Lahaina 1767
Wailuku
MAUI
LANAI
Lanai City
Kahoolawe
Hana
(Privately Owned)
Lanaihale 1027
Papawai Pt.
Makawao
Kauiki Head
Kaumalapau
Maalaea Bay
HALEAKALA PARK
Palaoa Point
Kihei
HALEAKALA CRATER
Keokea

Kealaikahiki Channel
Alalakeiki Channel
LUA MAKIKA
Lae o Kealaikahiki
Auau Channel
Lae
Kahoolawe
Kaka

Alenuihaha Channel

Upolu Point
Halaula
Hawi
KOHALA MTS.
Honokaa
HAWAII
PUUKOHOLA HEIAU NATIONAL HISTORIC SITE
Kamuela
Paauilo
Kawaihae Bay
Honomu
Kiholo Bay
Mauna Kea 4205
AKAKA FALLS STATE PARK
Hilo Bay
Hilo
Keahole Point
Hualalai
Papaikou
Leleiwi Point
Kailua Kona
2521
KALOKO-HONOKOHAU NAT. HIST. PARK
Keaau
Kaloli Point
Captain Cook
Mauna Loa 4170
HAWAII VOLCANOES NATIONAL PARK
Kurtistown
Kealakekua Bay
Volcano
Pahoa
Opihikao
PU'UHONUA O HONAUNAU NAT. HIST. PARK
KILAUEA CRATER
Kalapana
Kau Desert
Pahala
KUEE RUINS
Naalehu
Honuapo Bay
Pohue Bay
Ka Lae

Kona Coast

PACIFIC OCEAN

0   25   50   75   100   150   200   250 Kilometers
0   25   50   100   150 Miles

Above Molokai's secluded white beaches tower the world's tallest sea cliffs, some more than 2,000 feet (600 m) high. Since 1873 Molokai's Kalaupapa Peninsula has been home to a protected colony of Hansen's disease (leprosy) sufferers. After the disease was brought under control in the 1940s, colony residents were allowed to travel or relocate; today a small population—fewer than 100—has chosen to remain on the peninsula.

The remaining islands, Niihau and Kahoolawe, are not tourist destinations. Niihau is privately owned by the Robinson family—cattle ranchers who attempt to preserve native Hawaiian culture there by discouraging visitors. Uninhabited Kahoolawe was once used by the U.S. government for military target practice, but is being restored as a cultural site for future visitors.

Surfers riding a big break in Oahu's Waimea Bay (left), the coral reef-dwelling stripebelly pufferfish (below)

island agriculture

Thanks to 25 million years of volcanic eruptions, Hawaii's soil is an agricultural gold mine of mineral-rich lava ash and soft, sandy stone. Add to that the islands' mild, sunny climate, cooling breezes, and generous annual rainfall of more than 100 inches (250 cm), and the result is a farmer's dream-come-true.

Agriculture actually shaped the state's history. In the 1800s, when Americans saw how well local crops sustained the Hawaiian population, they realized that large-scale island agriculture could become a lucrative industry. Sugarcane thrived in Hawaii's rainy climate, and it became the crop of choice. From the mid-19th to the mid-20th century, the islands were filled with large sugar plantations controlled by powerful American corporations. To avoid sugar and fruit tariffs levied by the U.S. government on imports, the corporations toppled the Hawaiian monarchy in 1898 and replaced it with a republic headed by Sanford Dole, the future pineapple king.

Escalating costs and foreign competition ended the golden days of sugar and pineapple soon after Hawaii became a state in 1959. Since then, Hawaiian agriculture has diversified to include cattle ranches, coffee farms, and fields of taro, yams, bananas, flowers, ginger, papayas, watermelon, and a variety of vegetables and exotic fruits. Hawaii is the only U.S. state that produces coffee and ginger, and it ranks fourth nationally in the wholesale value of potted plants and cut flowers. In addition, it is the world's top producer of macadamia nuts, grown in orchards around the islands.

These eight major islands, as well as more than 125 smaller islets and atolls, emerged from a bubbling fissure in Earth's crust during countless millennia of intense geologic activity. Ongoing volcanism is avidly monitored by scientists and tourists from crater-view observation areas, while islanders periodically leave offerings to Pele, goddess of fire, on the steep slopes. Originally barren lava promontories, the islands acquired all their flora and fauna from elsewhere. Wind and ocean currents brought seeds and spores that took hold in volcanic soil. Today, as a result of their isolation, more than 90 percent of Hawaii's flowering plants do not grow naturally anywhere else on the planet. Only two animal species braved the 2,500-mile-long (4,000-km) sea journey from the nearest continent on their own initiative: the Hawaiian monk seal and the Hawaiian hoary bat.

Humans braved the same journey. Polynesian islanders settled the Hawaiian archipelago in two waves: The first are thought to have journeyed from the Marquesas Islands as early as 400 A.D. Tahitians arrived 1,000 years later. This second group included accomplished seafarers and farmers who lived by *kapu*, a rigid polytheistic religious and social system. It was these Pacific islanders who perfected the sport of *hele nalu*, or wave-sliding. We know it as surfing, and Hawaii, which boasts some of the world's best surfing spots, is its undisputed center.

The lives of the islanders changed forever on January 20, 1778, when English Captain James Cook happened upon the Hawaiian Islands while searching for the fabled Northwest Passage. Cook stopped at Waimea on Kauai and named the archipelago the Sandwich Islands to honor the Earl of Sandwich, the head of the British Admiralty, who had sponsored the expedition. Although Cook was killed by natives the following year on his return voyage, his arrival heralded the era of European influence. In the early 1800s, King Kamehameha used European weapons to conquer and unify all but one of the islands, Kauai (which entered the Kingdom of Hawaii through negotiation). In 1819 Hawaiian religion dissolved under Kamehameha's

Taro field (top), Mokulua Islands off Oahu (below), lava meeting the ocean at Hawaii Volcanoes National Park (top right), Kilauea (right)

hawaiian hot spot

On the night of January 3, 1983, plumes of glowing lava began spraying from Pu'u' O'o, a vent along the east rift zone of Kilauea on the Big Island of Hawaii. Streams of molten rock surged seaward to an explosive encounter with the ocean, and flows of viscous lava crept down the mountain's flanks through forests, fields, and villages. Today the volcano is still erupting, having already added more than 550 acres (220 ha) to the island. This eruption is the longest in Hawaii's recorded history, but it is merely a brief episode in the life of the Hawaiian Islands, the latest chapter in a geologic chronicle that extends back at least 70 million years and more than 3,000 miles (4,860 km) northward to Russia's Kamchatka Peninsula.

Every island in the chain—all the way to Midway and Kure Atoll, the farthest flung—owes its existence to a hot spot, a place where molten rock from Earth's mantle rises to the surface and pierces through the crust as lava. Hot spots remain stationary as Earth's tectonic plates move slowly over them. The hot spot beneath Hawaii lies in the middle of the Pacific plate, fueling smoking craters and red-hot rims above the surface. You can follow the plate's progress by tracing the arc of the Hawaiian Islands, the Midway Islands, and, farther to the northwest, the line of the submerged Emperor Seamounts, all created by the hot spot.

From the Big Island of Hawaii, which broke through the Pacific waves around 700,000 years ago, to Kauai, the five-million-year-old island matriarch, the major Hawaiian Islands are composed of at least 17 separate volcanoes. The Big Island alone boasts five: Others besides Kilauea include still-active Mauna Loa, dormant Hualalai, and extinct Mauna Kea and Kohala. The chain continues past Kure Atoll, but erosion has worn these islands down so that they no longer break the ocean's

surface. West of Kure Atoll, the line of seamounts takes a dogleg turn and heads almost due north, evidence that the plate changed direction about 40 million years ago. The oldest seamount, 70- to 80-million-year-old Meiji Seamount, is slowly sliding into the Aleutian Trench.

Another volcano is rising today just 17 miles (27.5 km) southeast of the Big Island. Lo'ihi Seamount's activity was heralded by a series of earthquakes in

1970 and confirmed in 1996 by a submersible expedition that verified the collapse of its summit, a common stage in a volcano's formation. Lo'ihi—which probably began forming thousands of years ago—already rises more than 2.8 miles (4.5 km) from the ocean floor; its peak is just over a half-mile (0.8 km) below the surface. In a few tens of thousands of years, Lo'ihi may emerge as Hawaii's newest island.

TRAIL OF THE HAWAIIAN HOT SPOT

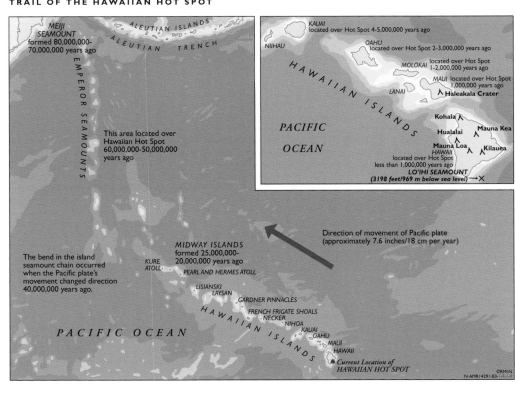

polynesian migration

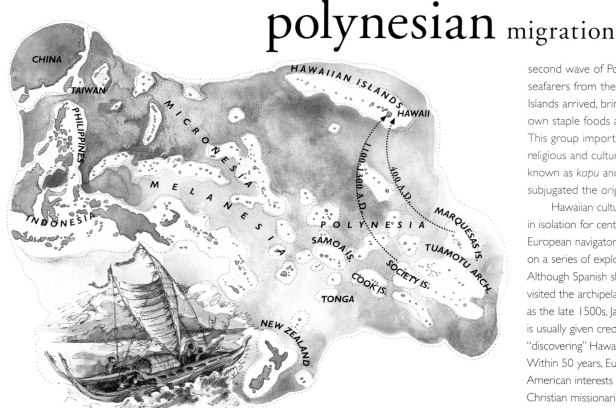

Hawaii is America's true melting pot, where people from all parts of the Pacific Rim have settled, intermarried, and contributed to the island culture.

The first Hawaiians were part of a great Polynesian migration that began between 3,000 and 4,000 years ago. From Southeast Asia (recent DNA studies have traced islanders back to present-day Taiwan), consummate seafarers island-hopped for centuries in large, double-hulled canoes to Melanesia, Micronesia, and Polynesia before setting out for the islands we know as New Zealand, Easter Island, and Hawaii.

Various theories attempt to explain why Polynesians undertook such lengthy ocean voyages. The islanders may have observed and followed avian migration patterns. Fishermen might have discovered the islands by chance. Or these master navigators may have hoped to discover new islands. Whatever inspired their wanderings, they succeeded because of their expertise at celestial navigation and their intimate knowledge of ocean currents.

Marquesas Islanders, who arrived on Kauai as early as 400 A.D., were Hawaii's first settlers. They brought their staple food plants of taro, breadfruit, yams, bananas, coconuts, wild ginger, and sugarcane—none of which is native to the Hawaiian Islands—and domestic animals such as dogs, pigs, and chickens. Between 1100 and 1300, a second wave of Polynesian seafarers from the Society Islands arrived, bringing their own staple foods and animals. This group imported the strict religious and cultural system known as *kapu* and quickly subjugated the original settlers.

Hawaiian culture developed in isolation for centuries until European navigators embarked on a series of explorations. Although Spanish ships may have visited the archipelago as early as the late 1500s, James Cook is usually given credit for "discovering" Hawaii in 1778. Within 50 years, European and American interests had sent Christian missionaries who strove to abolish *kapu* and other ancient religious practices. Influential land barons—intent on exploiting the rich volcanic soil—established sugarcane and pineapple plantations that became magnets for Asian laborers—Chinese, Japanese, Filipinos, and Koreans—who have since added their rich cultures to Hawaii. The latest immigrants to leave their mark on the islands are also Pacific Islanders—Samoans who began to arrive after World War II.

Each wave of immigrants brings something to the islands. Tolerance is Hawaii's watchword, and here you'll find a host of individual languages, cuisines, and religious observances. Chinese New Year, the Japanese Cherry Blossom Festival, the Kona Stampede (a rollicking Hawaiian rodeo), Fiesta Filipina (a month-long celebration of Filipino culture), and Samoan Flag Raising Day are all on Hawaii's official roster of annual events.

No matter when they came to Hawaii—whether they are *Kanaka Maoli* (descendants of the original Hawaiians), *kama'aina* (those who have lived long in the islands), or *malihini* (newcomers)—Hawaiians of all cultures are devoted to maintaining their multiethnic society.

luau

Honolulu's famous Waikiki Beach (above), native totem poles (bottom left), luau food display (right), orchids (bottom right) successor, Queen Kaahumanu, and a year later missionaries brought Christianity and literacy from New England—along with measles, tuberculosis, and venereal diseases. Estimated at 300,000 when Europeans arrived, the Hawaiian population dwindled to 70,000 by 1853.

During the 1800s, the islands became increasingly important to U.S. trade and security, and by 1900 Hawaii had become a U.S. territory. Its strategic importance was clearly demonstrated when Japan bombed the American fleet at Pearl Harbor on December 7, 1941. Today Hawaii remains a key military outpost and an important port: Honolulu handles more than eight million tons (7.2 million metric tons) of cargo annually. Fueled by Hawaii's mild climate, agriculture (sugarcane, pineapple, taro, macadamia nuts, and other crops) and tourism are the economic mainstays. Seven million visitors—undeterred by high prices stemming from the necessity to import fuel and food from the mainland—arrive annually to tour, sunbathe, swim, surf, scuba dive, and relax in this Pacific paradise.

Despite the influx of travelers, Hawaii's culture remains distinct from that of the rest of the United States. Islanders, no matter what their ethnicity, unite to celebrate luaus, surfing contests, outrigger canoe races, and festivals such as the Merrie Monarch, which features the islands' premier hula competition. The spirit of *aloha* and cordial relationships between native, Asian, European, and American cultures vie with Hawaii's beauty as the primary draw for visitors and new residents alike.

Mention traditional Hawaiian culture to most Americans, and they'll think immediately of a *luau*. Luaus originated as semi-religious events where early Polynesians gave thanks to the gods for their good fortune in reaching Hawaii safely. Later, the feast celebrated any happy event, such as a wedding or birthday. Today, many Hawaiians enjoy luaus as casually as other Americans enjoy backyard cookouts.

In this sumptuous barbecue, the main course is steamed pig. Known locally as a *kalua*, the pig is seasoned, wrapped in *ti* leaves, and placed in an *imu*, an underground oven lined with red-hot rocks. Once the pig is in the imu, it's covered with earth and left to steam in the ti leaves and its own juices for about 12 hours. It is then uncovered and unwrapped, usually with some fanfare, and eaten—always with great gusto. Guests sit at outdoor tables, often in a grove of palm trees or on a white sand beach bathed in the light of a Pacific sunset.

The word luau originally referred to the leaves of the taro plant. Later it referred to the food prepared from taro leaves, and finally to the feast itself. Taro remains important to the luau; its roots are ground into a purple paste known as *poi*. Other foods typically served at a luau include appetizers known as *pupus*, yams, rice, noodles, teriyaki beef, salmon, and mahi mahi, a flavorful local fish that tastes something like lobster. Guests are encouraged to eat with their fingers, a practice that probably becomes easier after imbibing a couple of rum-laced tropical drinks.

Entertainment at commercial luaus consists chiefly of Hawaiian dancing. The dances often tell the story of how early Hawaiians braved the swells and storms of the Pacific on their long ocean journey from Polynesia. Other dances may express Maori and Samoan themes. The hula dance is a staple of many Hawaiian luaus, complete with grass skirts, *leis*, and free lessons for everyone.

Alaska

W9-BNV-645

Name | Map Ref. | Page

Raleigh, NC C5 65
Ramapo, r., US A2 28
Ramapo Mountains, US A2 28
Rampart, AK B8 194
Ramsey, NJ A2 28
Ranchester, WY C9 144
Rancho Cordova, CA C3 172
Randolph, VT E5 14
Rangeley, ME C7 14
Range Ponds State Park, ME D7 14
Ranger, TX C5 118
Rantoul, IL F6 90
Rapidan, r., VA E2 41
Rapid City, SD D8 104
Rapid River, MI C7 90
Rappahannock, r., VA F4 41
Raritan Bay, US C2 28
Rathbun Lake, IA F4 90
Rat Island, AK e2 194a
Rat Islands, AK e2 194a
Raton, NM E11 130
Raton Pass, NM G10 144
Ravena, NY F4 14
Ravenswood, WV D6 52
Rawlins, WY E9 144
Ray, ND B8 104
Raymond, WA C3 165
Raymondville, TX F6 118
Reading, PA C9 52
Readstown, WI E5 90
Red, r., NA B2 90
Red, r., US E9 8
Red, r., KY C9 76
Red Bank, NJ C2 28
Red Bluff, CA B2 172
Red Bluff Reservoir, US D3 118
Red Cloud, NE F10 104
Red Devil, AK C7 194
Redding, CA B2 172
Redfield, SD D10 104
Red Hook, NY F4 14
Red Lion, PA D4 41
Red Lodge, MT C8 144
Redmond, OR D4 165
Red Oak, IA F3 90
Redoubt Volcano, AK C8 194
Red Wing, MN D4 90
Redwood Falls, MN D3 90
Redwood National Park, CA F2 165
Reed City, MI E8 90
Reedsport, OR E2 165
Refugio, TX E6 118
Rehoboth Beach, DE E5 41
Reidsville, NC B5 65
Reisterstown, MD D4 41
Remington, VA E3 41
Reno, NV D4 130
Republican, r., US C4 107
Revillagigedo Island, AK D12 194
Rexburg, ID D7 144
Rexford, KS C3 107
Reyes, Point, CA D2 172
Rhinelander, WI D6 90
Rhode Island, state, US C13 8
Rhode Island Sound, US G6 14
Richardson, TX C6 118
Richey, MT C7 144
Richfield, UT D7 130
Richford, VT D5 14
Richland, MT B6 104
Richland, WA C5 165
Richmond, IN G8 90
Richmond, KY C8 76
Richmond, ME D8 14
Richmond, VT D4 14
Richmond, VA B6 65
Ridgecrest, CA F5 130
Ridgefield, CT A4 28
Ridgewood, NJ B2 28
Ridgway, CO F9 144
Ridgway, PA C7 52
Riggins, ID C4 144
Ringling, OK E6 107
Ringwood, NJ A2 28
Ringwood State Park, NJ A2 28
Rio Dell, CA F2 165
Rio Grande, r., NA F8 8
Rio Grande see Grande, Rio, r., NA F5 118
Rio Grande City, TX F5 118
Rio Rancho, NM F10 130
Ripley, TN D6 76
Rising Sun, MD D4 41
Rison, AR E4 76
Ritter, Mount, CA D4 172
Rivanna, r., VA F2 41
Riverhead, NY B5 28
Riverside, CA F5 172
Riviera Beach, FL G4 65
Roanoke, VA E7 52
Roanoke, r., US B6 65
Roanoke Rapids, NC B6 65
Roan Plateau, US F8 144
Robert Moses State Park, NY B4 28
Roberts, ID D6 144
Robertsville, NJ C2 28
Robins Island, NY B6 28
Robstown, TX F6 118
Rochester, MN E4 90
Rochester, NH E6 14
Rochester, NY E12 90
Rock, r., US F6 90
Rockaway, NJ B1 28
Rockaway Point, NY B3 28
Rock Creek Butte, OR D5 165
Rockdale, TX D6 118
Rockford, IL E6 90
Rock Hall, MD D4 41
Rock Hill, SC C4 65
Rockingham, NC C5 65
Rock Island, IL F5 90
Rockland, ME D8 14
Rockland, MA F7 14
Rockport, MA F7 14
Rock River, WY E10 144
Rocksprings, TX D4 118
Rock Springs, WY E8 144
Rockville, MD D3 41
Rockwell City, IA E3 90
Rockwood, ME C8 14
Rockwood Lake, CT A3 28
Rocky Ford, CO D3 107
Rocky Mount, NC C6 65
Rocky Mountain National Park, CO E9 144
Rocky Mountains, NA E9 144
Rocky Point, NY B5 28
Rocky Point, NY A6 28
Rocky Point, NY A7 28
Rodney, Cape, AK C5 194
Rogers, Mount, VA E6 52
Rogers City, MI D9 90
Rogue, r., OR E2 165
Rolla, MO G5 90
Rolla, ND B10 104
Romano, Cape, FL H4 65
Romanzof, Cape, AK C5 194
Romanzof Mountains, AK B10 194
Rome, GA F4 52
Rome, NY E13 90
Roosevelt, UT E7 144
Rosamond, CA F4 130
Rosebud Indian Reservation, SD E9 104
Roseburg, OR E3 165
Roselle, NJ B2 28
Rosenberg, TX E7 118
Rosholt, SD D11 104
Ross R. Barnett Reservoir, MS E6 76
Roswell, NM G11 130
Rotterdam, NY F3 14
Rough, r., KY C7 76
Round Mountain, NV D5 130
Round Rock, TX D6 118
Roundup, MT C5 104
Rouses Point, NY C4 14
Royale, Isle, MI B6 90
Royal Gorge, CO F10 144
Ruby, AK C7 194
Ruby Dome, NV C6 130
Ruby Mountains, NV C6 130
Rugby, ND B10 104
Rumford, ME D7 14
Rump Mountain, ME C6 14
Rushville, IL F5 90
Rusk, TX D7 118
Russell, KS C5 107
Russell Cave National Monument, AL F3 52
Russellville, AR D4 76
Ruston, LA E4 76
Rutherford, NJ B2 28
Rutland, VT E5 14
Rye, NY B3 28
Ryegate, MT C5 104
Rye Lake, NY A3 28

S

Sabine, r., US D8 118
Sabine Lake, US G4 76
Sabine Pass, US G4 76
Sable, Cape, FL H4 65
Sac, r., MO C4 76
Sacajawea Peak, OR D6 165
Sac City, IA E3 90
Saco, ME E7 14
Saco Bay, ME E7 14
Sacramento, CA C3 172
Sacramento, r., CA C2 172
Sacramento Mountains, NM G11 130
Sacramento Valley, CA C3 172
Safford, AZ G9 130
Sagamore Hill National Historic Site, NY B4 28
Sagavanirktok, r., AK B9 194
Sag Harbor, NY B6 28
Saginaw, MI E9 90
Saginaw, r., MI E8 90
Saginaw Bay, MI E9 90
Saguaro National Park, AZ G8 130
Saint Albans, VT D4 14
Saint Anthony, ID C7 144
Saint Augustine, FL F4 65
Saint Charles, MO G5 90
Saint Clair, MI E9 90
Saint Clair, Lake, NA E9 90
Saint Cloud, MN D3 90
Saint Croix, r., NA C10 14
Saint Croix Island National Monument, ME C10 14
Saint Croix National Scenic Riverway, US D4 90
Saint Elias, Cape, AK D10 194
Saint Elias, Mount, NA C10 194
Saint Elias Mountains, NA C10 194
Saint Francis, r., NA A8 14
Saint Francois Mountains, MO C5 76
Saint George, SC D4 65
Saint George, UT E7 130
Saint George, Cape, FL G8 76
Saint George Island, AK D5 194
Saint George Island, FL G8 76
Saint Helens, OR D3 165
Saint Helens, Mount, WA C3 165
Saint James, NY B4 28
Saint John, r., NA A9 14
Saint Johns, AZ F9 130
Saint Johns, r., FL F4 65
Saint Johnsbury, VT D5 14
Saint Joseph, MO G3 90
Saint Joseph, r., US F8 90
Saint Lawrence, r., NA D13 90
Saint Lawrence Island, AK C4 194
Saint Louis, MO G5 90
Saint Marys, AK C6 194
Saint Marys City, MD E4 41
Saint Matthew Island, AK C4 194
Saint Michael, AK C6 194
Saint Michaels, MD E4 41
Saint Paul, MN D4 90
Saint Paul, NE F10 104
Saint Paul Island, AK D5 194
Saint Petersburg, FL G3 65
Saint Regis, r., NA D3 14
Saint Regis, West Branch, r., NY D3 14
Saint Regis Falls, NY D3 14
Saint Regis Indian Reservation, NY D3 14
Saint Vincent, MN B2 90
Sakakawea, Lake, ND B8 104
Salem, IL G6 90
Salem, MA F7 14
Salem, NH F6 14
Salem, NJ D5 41
Salem, NY E4 14
Salem, OR D3 165
Salem, VA E6 52
Salida, CO F10 144
Salina, KS C6 107
Salinas, CA D3 172
Saline, r., AR E4 76
Saline, r., KS C5 107
Salisbury, MD E5 41
Salisbury, NC C4 65
Salmon, ID C5 144
Salmon, r., ID B4 144
Salmon Mountain, NA C6 14
Salmon River Mountains, ID C5 144
Salome, AZ G7 130
Salt, South Fork, r., MO G5 90
Salt Basin, TX H11 130
Salt Lake City, UT E7 144
Salton Sea, CA G6 130
Saluda, VA F4 41
Salvador, Lake, LA G5 76
Samalga Pass, AK e4 194a
Samp Mortar Reservoir, CT A4 28
Sam Rayburn Reservoir, TX D7 118
Sanak Islands, AK E6 194
San Angelo, TX D4 118
San Antonio, NM G10 130
San Antonio, TX E5 118
San Antonio, r., TX E6 118
San Antonio Bay, TX E6 118
Sanatorium, MS F6 76
San Augustine, TX D7 118
San Benito, TX F6 118
San Bernardino, CA E5 172
San Blas, Cape, FL G8 76
San Buenaventura see Ventura, CA E4 172
San Carlos, AZ G8 130
San Carlos Indian Reservation, AZ G8 130
San Clemente, CA F5 172
San Clemente Island, CA F4 172
Sanders, AZ F9 130
Sanderson, TX H12 130
Sandersville, GA D3 65
Sand Hills, NE F8 104
San Diego, CA F5 172
San Diego, TX F5 118
Sand Point, AK D6 194
Sandpoint, ID A4 144
Sands Point, NY B3 28
Sandusky, OH F9 90
Sandy, UT E7 144
Sandy, r., ME D7 14
Sandy Bay Mountain, ME C7 14
Sandy Hook, NJ C3 28
Sandy Hook Bay, NJ C2 28
Sanford, FL F4 65
Sanford, ME E7 14
Sanford, NC C5 65
Sanford, Mount, AK C10 194
San Francisco, CA D2 172
Sanger, TX C6 118
San Gorgonio Mountain, CA F5 130
Sangre de Cristo Mountains, US G10 144
Sanibel Island, FL G3 65
San Isidro, TX F5 118
San Joaquin, r., CA D3 172
San Joaquin Valley, CA D3 172
San Jon, NM E3 107
San Jose, CA D3 172
San Jose Island, TX F6 118
San Juan, r., US E8 130
San Juan Basin, NM E9 130
San Juan Islands, WA B3 165
San Juan Mountains, CO G9 144
San Luis Obispo, CA E3 172
San Luis Valley, CO G10 144
San Marcos, TX E6 118
San Mateo, CA D2 172
San Nicolas Island, CA F4 172
San Pedro, r., NA G8 130
San Pedro Channel, CA F4 172
San Pedro Peaks, NM E10 130
San Rafael, CA D2 172
San Rafael Mountains, CA E4 172
San Saba, TX D5 118
San Saba, r., TX D5 118
San Simon, r., AZ G9 130
Santa Ana, CA F5 172
Santa Barbara, CA E4 172
Santa Barbara Channel, CA E3 172
Santa Catalina Island, CA F4 172
Santa Cruz, CA D2 172
Santa Cruz Island, CA F4 172
Santa Fe, NM F10 130
Santa Fe Baldy, NM F11 130
Santa Lucia Range, CA E3 172
Santa Maria, CA E3 172
Santaquin, UT D8 130
Santa Rosa, CA C2 172
Santa Rosa, NM F11 130
Santa Rosa Island, CA F3 172
Santa Rosa Island, FL F7 76
Santee, CA F5 172
Santee, r., SC D5 65
Santee Indian Reservation, NE E10 104
Sapulpa, OK D6 107
Saranac, r., NY D4 14
Saranac Lake, NY D3 14
Sarasota, FL G3 65
Saratoga, WY E9 144
Saratoga National Historical Park, NY F4 14
Saratoga Springs, NY E4 14
Sardis Lake, MS D6 76
Sardis Lake, OK E7 107
Satilla, r., GA E3 65
Saugatuck, r., CT A4 28
Saugatuck Reservoir, CT A4 28
Saugerties, NY F3 14
Sauk Centre, MN D3 90
Sault Sainte Marie, MI C8 90
Savannah, GA D4 65
Savannah, r., US D4 65
Sawatch Range, CO F9 144
Saxis, VA F5 41
Sayre, OK E5 107
Sayreville, NJ C2 28
Sayre Woods South, NJ C2 28
Sayville, NY B4 28
Scammon Bay, AK C5 194
Scandia, KS C6 107
Scapegoat Mountain, MT B6 144
Scarsdale, NY B3 28
Schell Creek Range, NV D6 130
Schenectady, NY B9 52
Schoharie, NY F3 14
Schroon, r., NY E4 14
Schroon Lake, NY E4 14
Schulenburg, TX E6 118
Schuyler, VA F2 41
Schuylkill, r., PA C5 41
Schwatka Mountains, AK B7 194
Scioto, r., OH G9 90
Scotch Plains, NJ B2 28
Scotlandville, LA F5 76
Scott City, KS C4 107
Scottsbluff, NE F8 104
Scotts Bluff National Monument, NE F8 104
Scottsdale, AZ G8 130
Scranton, PA C9 52
Sea Cliff, NY B3 28
Seaford, DE E5 41
Sea Islands, US E4 65
Sea Isle City, NJ D6 41
Sealy, TX E6 118
Searchlight, NV F6 130
Searcy, AR D5 76
Seaside Park, NJ D6 41
Seattle, WA C3 165
Sebago Lake, ME E7 14
Sebec Lake, ME C8 14
Secaucus, NJ B2 28
Sedalia, MO G4 90
Sedgwick, KS D6 107
Seguam Island, AK e4 194a
Seguin, TX E6 118
Seibert, CO C3 107
Selawik, AK B7 194
Selawik Lake, AK B6 194
Selby, SD D10 104
Selbyville, DE E5 41
Seldovia, AK D8 194
Selma, AL E7 76
Selma, CA E4 172
Seminole, OK E6 107
Seminole, TX C4 118
Seminole, Lake, US F8 76
Seneca, KS C6 107
Seneca, OR D5 165
Sequoia National Park, CA D4 172
Severna Park, MD D4 41
Sevier, r., UT E7 130
Sevier Lake, UT D7 130
Seward, AK C9 194
Seward, NE F11 104
Seward Peninsula, AK B6 194
Seymour, IN G7 90
Seymour, TX C5 118
Shageluk, AK C7 194
Shagwong Point, NY A7 28
Shaktoolik, AK C6 194
Shallowater, TX F3 107
Shamrock, FL F3 65
Shamrock, TX E4 107
Sharon, PA F10 90
Sharon Springs, KS C4 107
Shasta, Mount, CA F3 165
Shasta Lake, CA F3 165
Shawnee, OK E6 107
Shawneetown, IL C6 76
Sheboygan, WI E7 90
Sheenjek, r., AK B10 194
Sheffield, AL D7 76
Sheffield Island, CT A4 28
Shelburne Falls, MA F5 14
Shelby, MI E7 90
Shelby, MT B4 104
Shelby, NE F11 104
Shelbyville, IL G6 90
Shelbyville, TN D7 76
Shelbyville, Lake, IL G6 90
Sheldon, IA E2 90
Sheldon Point, AK C5 194
Shelikof Strait, AK D8 194
Shelter Island, NY A6 28
Shelter Island, NY A6 28
Shelton, CT G4 14
Shenandoah, IA F3 90
Shenandoah, r., US E2 41
Shenandoah National Park, VA D7 52
Sheridan, WY C9 144
Sherman, TX C6 118
Sherman Mills, ME C9 14
Sherwood Island State Park, CT A4 28
Sherwood Point, CT A4 28
Sheyenne, ND C10 104
Sheyenne, r., ND C11 104
Shiloh National Military Park, TN D6 76
Shinnecock Bay, r., NY B5 28
Shinnecock Hills, NY B6 28
Shippan Point, CT A3 28
Shiprock, NM E9 130
Ship Rock, NM E9 130
Shirley, NY B5 28
Shishaldin Volcano, AK E6 194
Shishmaref, AK B5 194
Shoshone, ID D5 144
Shoshone Basin, WY D8 144
Shreveport, LA E4 76
Shumagin Islands, AK E6 194
Shungnak, AK B7 194
Shuyak Island, AK D8 194
Siasconset, MA G8 14
Sidnaw, MI C6 90
Sidney, MT C7 104
Sidney Lanier, Lake, GA F5 52
Sierra Blanca, TX H11 130
Sierra Blanca Peak, NM G11 130
Sierra Nevada see Nevada, Sierra, CA D4 172
Signal Peak, UT E7 130
Sigurd, UT D8 130
Sikeston, MO C6 76
Silver Bay, MN C5 90
Silver City, NM G9 130
Silver Lake, OR B3 130
Silvermine, r., US A4 28
Silver Sands State Park, CT A4 28
Silver Spring, MD D3 41
Silverton, TX E4 107
Simi Valley, CA E4 172
Simla, CO C2 107
Sinclair, WY E9 144
Sinton, TX F6 118
Sioux City, IA E2 90
Sioux Falls, SD E11 104
Sipsey, r., AL E7 76
Sitka, AK D11 194
Sitkalidak Island, AK D8 194
Skagway, AK D11 194
Skilak Lake, AK C8 194
Skowhegan, ME D8 14
Skull Valley, AZ F7 130
Skunk, r., IA F5 90
Skwentna, AK C8 194
Slaton, TX F4 107
Sleeping Bear Dunes National Lakeshore, MI D7 90
Sleepy Eye, MN D3 90
Sleepy Hollow, NY A3 28
Slidell, LA F6 76
Sloatsburg, NY A2 28
Smith Bay, AK A8 194
Smith Mountain Lake, VA E7 52
Smith River, CA F2 165
Smithtown, NY B4 28
Smithtown Bay, NY B4 28
Smoky Hill, r., US C6 107
Smyrna, DE D5 41
Snake, r., US B4 8
Snowflake, AZ F8 130
Snow Hill, MD E5 41
Snowmass Mountain, CO F9 144
Snowy Mountain, NY E3 14
Snyder, TX F4 107
Socorro, NM F10 130
Soda Springs, ID D7 144
Soldotna, AK C8 194
Soledad, CA D3 172
Solomon, r., KS C5 107
Solon, ME D8 14
Solon Springs, WI C5 90
Somerset, KY C8 76
Somerset, NJ C2 28
Somerset, PA C7 52
Somerset, NJ C2 28
Somers Point, NJ D6 41
Somersworth, NH E6 14
Somerville, NJ B1 28
Somerville, NJ C6 41
Sonora, TX D4 118
Souderton, PA C5 41
Souhegan, r., NH F6 14
Souris, r., NA B9 104
Sourland Mountain, NJ C6 41
South Amboy, NJ C2 28
Southampton, NY B6 28
South Anna, r., VA F3 41
Southaven, MS D5 76
South Beach, NY B5 28
South Bend, IN F7 90
South Boston, VA B5 65
Southbridge, MA F5 14
South Burlington, VT D4 14
South Carolina, state, US E11 8
South Dakota, state, US C7 8
South Fork, CO G9 144
South Haven, MI E7 90
South Hero, VT D4 14
Southington, CT G5 14
South Lake Tahoe, CA C4 172
Southland, TX F4 107
Southold, NY A6 28
South Oyster Bay, NY B4 28
South Paris, ME D7 14
South Plainfield, NJ B2 28
South Platte, r., US C7 8
South Portland, ME E7 14
South River, NJ C2 28
South Skunk, r., IA F4 90
Southwest Harbor, ME D9 14
Spanish Peak, OR D5 165
Sparks, NV D4 130
Sparrows Point, MD D4 41
Sparta, NJ B6 41
Sparta, TN F4 52
Sparta, WI E5 90
Spartanburg, SC C4 65
Spearfish, SD D8 104
Spearman, TX D4 107
Speedway, IN G7 90
Spencer, IA E3 90
Spencer, NE E10 104
Sperryville, VA E2 41
Spirit Lake, IA E3 90
Splitrock Pond, NJ B2 28
Spokane, WA C6 165
Spotsylvania, VA E3 41
Spring, r., AR C5 76
Springer, NM E11 130
Springerville, AZ F9 130
Springfield, CO D3 107
Springfield, IL G6 90
Springfield, MA F5 14
Springfield, MO C4 76
Springfield, OH F9 90
Springfield, OR D3 165
Springfield, TN C7 76
Springfield, VT E5 14
Spring Glen, UT F7 144
Spring Grove, MN E5 90
Spring Lake Heights, NJ C2 28
Springtown, TX C6 118
Spring Valley, NY A2 28
Spruce Knob, WV D7 52
Spruce Knob-Seneca Rocks National Recreation Area, WV D7 52
Squam Lake, NH E6 14
Square Lake, ME B9 14
Stafford, VA E3 41
Stafford Springs, CT G5 14
Staked Plain see Estacado, Llano, US F3 107
Stamford, CT A3 28
Stamford, TX C5 118
Stanardsville, VA E2 41
Standing Rock Indian Reservation, US D9 104
Stanfield, OR D5 165
Stanley, ND B8 104
Stapleton, NE F9 104
Starke, FL F3 65
Starkville, MS E6 76
State College, PA C8 52
Staten Island, NY B2 28
State Road, NC E6 52
Statesboro, GA D4 65
Statesville, NC C4 65
Statue of Liberty National Monument, NJ B2 28
Staunton, VA D7 52
Staunton see Roanoke, r., US B6 65
Steamboat Mountain, WY E8 144
Steamboat Springs, CO E9 144
Stephenville, TX C5 118
Sterling, CO F8 104
Sterling, IL F6 90
Sterling City, TX D4 118
Steubenville, OH C6 52
Stevenson Entrance, AK D8 194
Stevens Point, WI D6 90
Stewartstown, PA D4 41
Stewartville, MN E4 90
Stickney, SD E10 104
Stillwater, MN D4 90
Stillwater, OK D6 107
Stockholm, NJ A1 28
Stockton, CA D3 172
Stockton, KS C5 107
Stockton Plateau, TX H12 130
Stockton Springs, ME D9 14
Stone Harbor, NJ D6 41
Stone Mountain, VT D6 14
Stones River National Battlefield, TN D7 76
Stonington, ME D9 14
Stony, r., AK C7 194
Stony Brook, NY B4 28
Stony Point, NY A3 28
Stony River, AK C7 194
Storm Lake, IA E3 90
Story, WY C9 144
Story City, IA E4 90
Stowe, VT D5 14
Strasburg, PA D4 41
Stratford, CT A4 28
Stratford, TX D3 107
Stratford Point, CT A4 28
Stratton, ME C7 14
Stratton Mountain, VT E5 14
Strawberry Mountain, OR D5 165
Strawberry Point, IA E5 90
Streator, IL F6 90
Stroud, OK E6 107
Stryker, MT A5 144
Stuart, FL G4 65
Stuart Island, AK C6 194
Sturgeon Bay, WI D7 90
Sturgis, SD D8 104
Stuttgart, AR D5 76
Sublette, KS D4 107
Suffern, NY A2 28
Suffolk, VA B6 65
Sugar, r., NH E5 14
Sugar Land, TX E7 118
Sugarloaf Mountain, ME C7 14
Sullivan, IN G7 90
Sullivan, MO G5 90
Sulphur, LA F4 76
Sulphur, r., US C7 118
Summit, NJ B2 28
Summit, SD D11 104
Sumter, SC D4 65
Sunburst, MT B4 104
Sunbury, PA C8 52
Sun City, AZ G7 130
Suncook, r., NH E6 14
Sundance, WY D7 104
Sunken Meadow State Park, NY B4 28
Sunnyside, WA C4 165
Sunnyvale, CA D2 172
Sun Valley, ID D5 144
Superior, AZ G8 130
Superior, WI C4 90
Superior, WY E8 144
Superior, Lake, NA C6 90
Sur, Point, CA D2 172
Surf City, NJ D6 41
Susanville, CA C3 130
Susitna, r., AK C8 194
Susquehanna, r., US D4 41
Sutherlin, OR E3 165
Sutton, AK C9 194
Sutton, WV D6 52
Sutwik Island, AK D7 194
Suwannee, r., US F3 65
Suwanee see Suwannee, r., US F3 65
Swans Island, ME D9 14
Swanton, VT D4 14
Sweet Home, OR D3 165
Sweetwater, TX F4 107
Sylacauga, AL E7 76
Sylvania, GA D4 65
Sylvia, KS C5 107
Syosset, NY B4 28
Syracuse, KS C4 107
Syracuse, NY B8 52

T

Tacoma, WA C3 165
Taconic Range, US F4 14
Taft, CA E4 172
Tahlequah, OK D3 76
Tahoe, Lake, US C3 172
Tahoe City, CA C3 172
Talkeetna, AK C8 194
Talkeetna Mountains, AK C9 194
Talladega, AL E7 76
Tallahassee, FL F8 76
Tallapoosa, r., US E8 76
Tallulah, LA E5 76
Tamaroa, IL G6 90
Tamiami Canal, FL H4 65
Tampa, FL G3 65
Tampa Bay, FL G3 65
Tampico, IL F6 90
Tanacross, AK C10 194
Tanaga Island, AK e3 194a
Tanana, AK B8 194
Tanana, r., AK C9 194
Tangier, VA F5 41
Tangipahoa, r., US F5 76
Taos, NM E11 130
Taos Pueblo, NM G10 144
Tappahannock, VA F4 41
Tappan, NY A3 28
Tappan, Lake, US A3 28
Tar, r., NC C6 65
Tarpon Springs, FL F3 65
Tarrytown, NY A3 28
Tatum, NM F3 107
Taum Sauk Mountain, MO C5 76
Taunton, MA G6 14
Tawakoni, Lake, TX C7 118
Tawas City, MI D9 90
Taylor, TX D6 118
Taylorville, IL G6 90
Teague, TX D6 118
Teaneck, NJ B2 28
Teec Nos Pos, AZ E9 130
Tehachapi, CA E4 172
Telescope Peak, CA E5 130
Tell City, IN B7 76
Teller, AK B5 194
Temblor Range, CA E4 172
Tempe, AZ G7 130
Temple, TX D6 118
Tennessee, state, US D10 8
Tennessee, r., US D6 76
Tensas, r., LA F5 76
Tensed, ID C6 165
Ten Thousand Islands, FL H4 65
Terlingua, TX I12 130
Terre Haute, IN G7 90
Terrell, TX C6 118
Terry, MT C7 104
Terryville, NY B4 28
Teshekpuk Lake, AK A8 194
Teton Range, WY D7 144
Texarkana, TX C7 118
Texas, state, US E8 8
Texas City, TX E7 118
Texhoma, OK D4 107
Texico, NM E3 107
Texline, TX D3 107
Texoma, Lake, US E6 107
Thayer, MO C5 76
The Dalles, OR D4 165
Thedford, NE F9 104
Theodore Roosevelt National Park (North Unit), ND C8 104
Theodore Roosevelt National Park (South Unit), ND C8 104
Thermopolis, WY D8 144
Thibodaux, LA G5 76
Thief River Falls, MN B2 90
Thomaston, GA D2 65
Thomaston, ME D8 14
Thomasville, GA E3 65
Thompson, r., US F4 90
Thoreau, NM F9 130
Three Forks, MT C7 144
Three Sisters, OR D4 165
Throckmorton, TX C5 118
Ticonderoga, NY E4 14
Tierra Amarilla, NM E10 130
Tiffin, OH F9 90
Tifton, GA E3 65
Tigalda Island, AK E6 194
Tillamook, OR D3 165
Tinton Falls, NJ C2 28
Titusville, FL F4 65
Titusville, PA F11 90
Toano, VA F4 41
Togiak, AK D6 194
Toiyabe Range, NV D5 130
Tok, AK C10 194
Toledo, OH F9 90
Toledo Bend Reservoir, US D8 118
Tomah, WI D5 90
Tombigbee, r., US F6 76
Tombstone, AZ H8 130
Toms River, NJ D6 41
Tonasket, WA B5 165
Tongue, r., US D6 104
Tonopah, NV D5 130
Tooele, UT C7 130
Topeka, KS C7 107
Torbert, Mount, AK C8 194
Torch Lake, MI D8 90
Toro Peak, CA F5 172
Torrington, CT G4 14
Torrington, WY E7 104
Towanda, PA C8 52
Towner, ND B9 104
Townsend, MT B7 144
Towson, MD D4 41
Trail Ridge, US E3 65
Trap Falls Reservoir, CT A4 28